FRENCH
EAGLES
SOVIET HEROES

FRENCH EAGLES
SOVIET HEROES

The 'Normandie-Niemen' Squadrons on the Eastern Front

JOHN D. CLARKE

FOREWORD BY GÉNÉRAL JOSEPH M. RISSO

SUTTON PUBLISHING

First published in the United Kingdom in 2005 by
Sutton Publishing Limited · Phoenix Mill
Thrupp · Stroud · Gloucestershire · GL5 2BU

British Library Cataloguing in Publication Data
A catalogue record for this book is available from the British Library.

ISBN 0-7509-4074-3

Typeset in 10.5/15pt Photine.
Typesetting and origination by
Sutton Publishing Limited.
Printed and bound in England by
J.H. Haynes & Co. Ltd, Sparkford.

CONTENTS

Appendices

ACKNOWLEDGEMENTS

Without the help of my good friend Rémi Theys, the task of telling the story of this unique French Fighter Air Squadron would have proved almost impossible. His detailed knowledge of the Normandie-Niemen Regiment was quite astounding. His kindness in allowing me access to the Eichenbaum documents (of which he is the custodian) was exceptionally helpful. His ability to obtain information and photographs relating to this French Fighter Squadron was amazing. Most of all, his contact with the veterans has proved invaluable.

My unreserved gratitude to Général Joseph Risso, ace of the Normandie-Niemen Regiment, for his generosity of spirit in providing first-hand accounts, original documents and photographs of that illustrious fighter squadron. Not least is my gratitude for his time spent reading the manuscript and making comments and corrections for this book. It was a great privilege meeting Général Risso and to learn first hand of his personal experiences serving Free France, first in the RAF and later during the momentous years flying combat missions on the Eastern Front with the Soviet Air Force.

My appreciation also to Captain Dr Marcello Ralli of Rome, the leading aeronautical artist, for providing such excellent detailed drawings of Soviet fighter aircraft.

It is not possible to thank personally veterans like Igor Eichenbaum and Jean de Pange or others who kept the Normandie-Niemen Service Journal, which forms the day-by-day basis of this account of the Regiment, for these illustrious scribes have long since joined the band of immortals.

My thanks to my brother A.A. Clarke, whose knowledge of all things aeronautical has proved essential, especially the technical details of Russian aircraft of the Second World War, and to Ross Eden for translating the wartime Normandie-Niemen Service Journal.

FOREWORD

My very warm congratulations as well as my best thanks to John D. Clarke for all his immense work, which goes beyond the saga of the Free French Fighter Squadron No. 3, 'Normandie', later to be known as the 'Normandie-Niemen Regiment'.

Reflecting on those days of action has reminded me of the earlier so exalting two years spent with the Royal Air Force, especially the time I served in the night fight initiation known as 'Turbin-Light'.

It has been a rare privilege to be a member of 253 Squadron RAF, where we were all united around a common goal. The squadron comprised of both British and Dominion pilots as well as two Norwegians, two Americans and the four French pilots who, besides myself, included such good comrades as Béguin, Massart and Mahé.

As softly autumn mist settles and slowly the horizon dims in the far, it is good to join and recall the faithful companions so never their remembrance leaves us.

With all my gratitude,
Joseph M. Risso

Général de Brigade Aérienne
Grand Croix de l'Order de la Légion d'Honneur
Compagnon de la Libération

INTRODUCTION

Fighting for one's country is every patriot's duty. When this duty entails the hazards of escaping to serve in foreign lands, having to accept different military disciplines and customs, perhaps even wearing another country's uniform, it requires a special dedication to the cause of freedom. It may also involve the knowledge that if captured by the enemy one would probably be executed and one's family sent to a concentration camp. So we can be sure that the men who volunteered for service with the Free French Groupe de Chasse 3 on the Eastern Front would have been of an extraordinarily formidable and tenacious character. Such were the pilots serving in the escadrilles of Normandie, later to be known as the Normandie-Niemen Regiment.

Some years ago my curiosity was kindled after learning that the prosecuting papers filed against Field Marshal Keitel at Nuremberg revealed that Keitel's name had appeared on a document dated May 1943, issuing orders that 'Aviators of the Squadron Normandie shall be handed over for execution on capture'. I wanted to know why these French aviators were so special, and so feared by the Nazis that they had to be treated like the British commandos who from November 1942, on the direct orders of Hitler, were to be executed on capture.

Normandie-Niemen was no ordinary fighter unit. By any standards it was unique; its accomplishments were quite staggering. Its pilots became the most highly decorated French fighter group of all time. They flew 5,240 combat sorties on the Eastern Front. Their abilities to engage and beat the Luftwaffe in aerial combat became legendary. The number of enemy aircraft they destroyed on the Eastern Front was confirmed to be 273, with a further 37 probable. In the last few months of the war in the skies over East Prussia they fought many duels with and beat the pilots of the formidable German Moulders Group. The Normandie-Niemen Regiment became the second-

highest scoring fighter regiment serving in the Soviet Air Force. Four of the
French pilots became Heroes of the Soviet Union and recipients of the Order
of Lenin; others were decorated with the highest French and Soviet awards.
All this came at a heavy price: forty-two Normandie pilots were killed during
service in the Soviet Union. And the men of the Normandie-Niemen
Regiment became the first of the Western allies to set foot upon and capture
German territory.

It had always been my intention one day to set out a comprehensive
history of the Regiment. Then quite by chance I had a phone call from Paris
telling me that a batch of original Normandie-Niemen research documents
from the desk of the late Igor Eichenbaum, Secretary-General of the
Normandie veterans' association, had surfaced in Paris. Reading these unique
papers, I found the story so fascinating that I was determined to set down the
facts. Naturally, in France the exceptional story of the 'Groupe Normandie-
Niemen' is well known and honoured, but, apart from brief details appearing
in international technical journals catering for aeronautical buffs and
aviation specialists, very little of this epic story has ever appeared in the
English language.

Details have been taken directly from Normandie veterans, from the
recently discovered Eichenbaum papers, and from the wartime Normandie-
Niemen Service Journal. This journal sets out events from the time the
Groupe de Chasse 3 was formed in Rayak on 1 September 1942 right
through to the time Normandie-Niemen returned from the Soviet Union on
20 June 1945. The Service Journal, or Squadron Diary, was kept by dedicated
officers, who entered the daily missions and combat victories of each
escadrille, including the official duties and social happenings of the Regiment.
The diary, often written by the light of petrol lamps after the officers had
completed their arduous service duties, frequently after a period of extreme
fatigue, records glorious achievements and great sadness.

Capitaine François de Labouchere, RAF, 613 Squadron
Killed in action, 5 September 1942.
Asked why he decided to leave France in 1940 for England,
Labouchere replied,

Because I felt it was my duty.
It was seeing where one's duty lay,
not doing it,
that had become so difficult.

PART ONE

PART ONE

ONE

GÉNÉRAL DE GAULLE: CUSTODIAN OF FRANCE'S HONOUR

Germany invaded the Low Countries on 10 May 1940, reaching and crossing the Albert Canal in Belgium the following day. With all bridges left intact by the defenders, the enemy's advance never faltered. On 13 May 1940 German troops crossed the River Meuse at Huy and advanced into France, driving a wedge into the thinly held front of the French Ninth Army, overpowering the 55th and 71st Divisions.

In the 1930s Charles de Gaulle had set out and published the case for the use of mobile forces spearheaded by heavy armour. It was at this time of national emergency that de Gaulle was called upon to command the 4th Reserve Armoured Division, a division in the process of being brought together and at that time completely inexperienced. Général Joseph Georges, the Commander-in-Chief of the north-east front, had long been an opponent of using armoured corps, but, with desperate tidings reaching him hourly, he knew positive and immediate action needed to be taken. He sent for de Gaulle and received him with the words, 'Come, de Gaulle, here's the chance to act.'

Even at this late stage de Gaulle planned and launched on 17 May an attack towards Montcornet in an effort to stop Guderian's advance on Laon and the Somme; however, the French tanks were greatly outnumbered by the advancing panzers. Undaunted, de Gaulle renewed his attack on 19 May, and this time a number of his French tanks, with great élan, got within a mile of the German headquarters. Guderian's staff, now under threat, had to ask for the intervention of the Luftwaffe. The resulting aerial bombardment forced de Gaulle to call off this brave counter-attack, but he consolidated the division ready for its next assignment. His handling of this aggressive action was to be the defining moment that linked his future with that of France.

In recognition of his successful handling of the 4th Reserve Armoured Division, Général de Gaulle was appointed Under-Secretary of War, and it was in this capacity that he attended the last desperate cabinet meetings of the French government.

On 17 June Marshal Petain announced over the radio that he had asked the Germans for an armistice. Enraged at this defeatist move, de Gaulle left for England immediately. In a broadcast from London on the following day, he called on all Frenchmen to join him in continuing the fight. 'France is not alone. She has an immense Empire behind her. . . . Whatever happens, the flame of French resistance must not be extinguished. France has lost a battle but France has not lost the war.' He then declared the existence of the 'Free France' organisation with himself at its head.

When it was known in London that the French front was fast disintegrating, the British Expeditionary Force was ordered to withdraw towards Dunkirk. It was at Dunkirk, starting on 26 May 1940, that the Royal Navy together with hundreds of small requisitioned boats, many with civilian crews, evacuated the troops from the sand dunes and beaches. This epic action averted a potentially worse disaster as the surrounded British rearguard was forced to make a fighting retreat to the sea. The evacuation was completed by 4 June. Some 224,585 British troops together with 112,546 French and Belgian troops were taken off the beaches to England. The French troops that had been evacuated from Dunkirk were to form the nucleus of the Free French forces in Britain.

Général de Gaulle's vision of establishing a power base outside mainland France drove him to annex and raise the Free French tricolour in the overseas colonies, although he had referred in his 18 June broadcast not to colonies but to France's 'immense empire'. Some distant territories like Chandernagor, New Hebrides, Polynesia and New Caledonia immediately answered his rallying call. Then French Equatorial Africa moved to support de Gaulle, starting with Chad and then Cameroon. It was in Cameroon that the people remembered the previous German administration, suspended in 1918; now, by a display of popular patriotic fervour, they persuaded the local administration to support Free France. Then the politically important Brazzaville, capital of the French Congo, moved to support Free France. Brazzaville was to receive de Gaulle's man Colonel de Larminat as Governor General in the name of Free France. Algeria, Dakar and Syria were among those French territories whose political officials and generals were reluctant at that time to go over to de Gaulle and Free France.

But many individuals in these same reluctant colonies did not hesitate to answer de Gaulle's call from London, and joined the French units that were now forming in Britain. Ships, soldiers and airmen from the colonies and mainland France, all determined to carry on the fight, travelled by every available means to join the Free French forces in Britain, eager to serve under the leadership of Général de Gaulle.

In mainland France it was not long before the puppet Vichy government headed by Marshal Petain, who had assumed the presidency, and his appointed Prime Minister Pierre Laval began to collaborate openly with the Germans. This more than anything else made the French people realise they had to look to Général de Gaulle for their leadership. Under the armistice arrangements signed by Petain, the Germans had allowed Petain's government to retain a small air force in the south of France for 'defence against external aggression'. This air force soon became even smaller as patriotic pilots made the short flight to England to serve the cause of freedom.

FREE FRENCH PERSONNEL SERVING IN THE RAF

To fight the enemy is one's duty, but it is not easy to carry on the fight from a land where a foreign language and customs have to be faced and mastered. The French pilots did that and much more. The French pilots who joined Général de Gaulle's forces before the liberation of North Africa in November 1942, and who served with the RAF squadrons, showed a dedicated excellence.

One arrival was Marcel Boisot, who had flown to freedom from Morocco. He recounted his story to his RAF commanding officer: 'My landing at Gibraltar on 28 June 1940, after escaping from jail in Meknes, Morocco, in a little trainer, having only amassed a total of twenty-five flying hours, felt great. Having landed on a race-track and later learned there was a certain French general in London whose name was de Gaulle, and who was ready to fight on, I decided that this was for me.' He later completed his training and flew combat missions over his beloved France and eventually flew a Spitfire in support of the D-Day landings.

Another sixteen pilots from l'École de Chasse 3 slipped aboard a Swedish ship from Bayonne sailing for Casablanca. When they arrived in North Africa they met up with a large number of Poles trying to make their way to Britain to carry on the fight. The pilots managed to mingle among the Poles and boarded a British ship that was about to sail to Gibraltar. They eventually reached England and immediately joined the first two Free French squadrons, 340 'Ile de France' and 341 'Alsace' Squadrons (the Free French Wing), which had been formed by the early French personnel who had followed Général de Gaulle to England in 1940. Eight of these original sixteen pilots were posted to 340 Squadron, but sadly only two survived the war. One survivor, Oliver Massart, was shot down in March 1945 and taken prisoner, but liberated by Canadian troops only a few weeks later. Another one of the 'sixteen' was Raymond van Wymeersch, who had been posted to 174 Squadron RAF. Flying a Hawker Hurricane, he took part in the Dieppe raid of 19 August 1942 but was shot down during the operation and became a prisoner of war. No. 174 Squadron had lost five pilots in the Dieppe raid, including their Free French commanding officer, Commandant Fayolle.

Wing Commander R.W.F. Sampson, OBE, DFC and bar, who commanded the Free French Wing, made the point that the French 345 'Berry' Squadron (ex-Vichy), and especially the personnel of 329 'Les Cigognes' (the Storks) Squadron who came from Algiers, felt superior to the early joiners of 340 and 341 Squadrons, whom they humorously called deserters from France, referring to their patriotic joining of de Gaulle's Free France in 1940. The amalgamated French squadrons were probably best held on course at that time by having a British wing leader in charge.

After the liberation of North Africa in late 1942, pilots arrived in numbers from Algeria, Oran and Casablanca. Many of them served in 329 'Cigognes' and 345 'Berry' Squadrons as part of the RAF's 145 Wing. The commanding officer of 145 Wing was very impressed with the way the new arrivals coped with the RAF routine, even managing to overcome the problems of the RAF slang terms used by radio operators to communicate with aircrew during missions. The English officer who so successfully commanded 145 Wing was Loel Guiness, a fluent French speaker who owned property and estates in France before the war. He was well respected and ideal for the command as he fully understood the problems and needs of the French pilots serving in the RAF.

These four Free French fighter squadrons, 329, 340, 341 and 345, flew Spitfires in the RAF's 145 Wing. In addition, 326, 327 and 328 Free French squadrons flew Spitfires.

The French bomber squadrons in the RAF included 342 'Lorraine' Squadron; Force Aériennes Françaises Libre (FAFL), flying Bostons and

Mitchells; 346 'Guyenne' Squadron (from North Africa), flying Halifax bombers; and 347 'Tunisie' Squadron (from North Africa), also flying Halifaxes. Many individual Frenchmen also served in regular RAF squadrons. One of those serving in the RAF who was later to become a French national figure was M. Mendès-France, Prime Minister of France from 1954 to 1955. He served in 342 Squadron.

On 16 December 1940 Sergent-chef Jacques Andrieux made his escape from Brittany to England on board a sailing boat. He was to serve with distinction in the RAF, being commissioned in 1942. He served in 130, 91 and 341 Squadrons. At the close of the war he had attained the status of an ace, with six enemy aircraft destroyed and four probable. He was also awarded the DFC and bar. After the war he served in the French Air Force and was eventually promoted to Général de Brigade in 1966.

Serving at various military airfields in North Africa and at the main Algerian fighter base at Oran, French pilots listened to de Gaulle's radio message broadcast from London on 18 June, calling them to arms. Many who were fired by his patriotic speech made secret plans to join the now forming Free French forces in Britain. Sergent Instructor Pierre Blaize and Georges Perrin, serving at Meknes in Morocco, decided it was their duty to answer the call from London. Without permission they took the personal aircraft of the base commandant, a Caudron Goeland Type C445M military communication aircraft with a crew of two and seats for six passengers. In total secrecy Blaize and Perrin took off with a full load of French Air Force pilots to make the flight to Gibraltar. On landing on the Rock they joined other French patriots who had already arrived. On 3 July they made up a party ready to sail in the French armed trawler *Président Houduce*. They found themselves in the company of other pilots who had also flown to Gibraltar in aircraft acquired from North African airfields. Some French pilots serving in North Africa had earlier taken aircraft to Casablanca and then sailed on by ship to Britain. One group boarded a ship in the south of France full of Polish soldiers making their way to Britain, all ready to carry on the fight against the German invader.

In January 1940 Sous-lieutenant Jean Demozay was acting as official interpreter to No. 1 Squadron RAF during the Battle of France. No. 1 Squadron's CO had been one of the first to install protective armour-plate sections behind the pilot's seat after one of his pilots had been shot in the back and killed during aerial combat. The squadron had lost seventeen

Hurricanes in battles over France. On 18 June, after a series of retreats through France, the squadron was finally ordered to withdraw from France. The pilots took off in their single-seat Hawker Hurricanes for England. Lieutenant Demozay was left on the airfield at Nantes with sixteen groundcrew. In its haste to get away from France, the squadron had to abandon a Bristol Bombay transport with full tanks of fuel after the discovery at the last moment of a smashed tail-wheel, which would not allow take-off. The Bristol Bombay had the capacity to carry twenty-four passengers plus crew. With some urgency, Demozay organised the mechanics to do an emergency repair job on the tail-wheel. When the makeshift repair was completed they flew the aircraft to England with all the trained groundcrew on board.

In the early months of the war many of these same French pilots fought and died fighting the Luftwaffe in aerial combat in the skies over Britain. These air battles fought by the RAF in 1940 were described in a moving broadcast by Winston Churchill as 'the Battle of Britain'. (Those fighter pilots who were engaged in combat with the enemy during the period 10 July–31 October 1940 were awarded the bronze Battle of Britain bar, worn on the ribbon of the 1939–45 Star. At least fourteen French pilots were awarded this prestigious bar.)

As 1940 drew to a close, more French Air Force personnel had made the decision to journey to Britain and join Général de Gaulle's FAFL. Typical of these staunch and determined patriots was Capitaine François de Labouchere, serving with the RAF in 613 Squadron. When asked why he decided to leave France in 1940 for England, Labouchere replied: 'Because I felt it was my duty. It was seeing where one's duty lay, not doing it, that had become so difficult.' (Labouchere was killed in action in September 1942.)

By 1941, with many colonies now pledging allegiance to Free France, Général de Gaulle's London-based authority had attained the status of an allied power. De Gaulle had assumed the sole mantle of French authority and made every command decision for those Free French who served the cause of freedom. Winston Churchill called him the Constable of France. After some sensible political advice from his allies, de Gaulle decided to form an administration whose character and responsibilities would command the respect and attention of all the allies. In September 1941 he set up the National Committee, a form of war cabinet whose decisions would be submitted for final approval to de Gaulle. The National Committee was formed from men who had stood by de Gaulle and Free France since the beginning. They were given the title Commissioner and each enjoyed clearly defined responsibilities: Cassin (Justice and Education), Pleven (Finance and Colonies), Dejean (Foreign Affairs), Legentilhomme (War), Valin (Air), Muselier (Navy and Merchant Marine), Catroux (High Commissioner in Syria), D'Argenlieu (High Commissioner in the Pacific). Diethelm, who had just recently arrived from France, was to be Commissioner for Labour and Information.

To further his cause, Général de Gaulle wanted the Soviet Union to recognise Free France and the role his newly formed National Committee could play in advancing a closer relationship between the two countries. Future agreements would extend to promoting positive military assistance. The French colonies were included in this proposed relationship. De Gaulle hoped this alignment would be beneficial for France in the future as a political counterbalance to the growing power of the alliance of America and Britain.

Stalin had responded coolly to the previous approaches from the Free French that had been made via the Soviet Ambassador Maisky in London. Things changed politically after the National Committee had been formed. The Soviets at once confirmed their recognition of de Gaulle as leader of Free France, and intimated their intention to enter into positive military relations with de Gaulle and promote Soviet collaboration with Free French overseas territories. Moscow accredited Bogomolov to the Free French National Committee in Britain; from this political recognition the seeds of Soviet–French military cooperation were sown.

TWO

GROUPE DE CHASSE 3, NORMANDIE, IS FORMED

In March 1942, after an exchange of telegrams between the French General Staff in London and the Free French Air Force in the Middle East, Commandant Tulasne, Commandant Pouliquen and Lieutenant Littolff were recalled to London for the most important operational instructions. They were to learn that an additional Free French Air Force Groupe was being planned. When this Groupe was operational it would be offered to the Soviets for active service in the Soviet Union.

Further details of Général de Gaulle's proposals were given by Commissioner of Air Général Valin on 15 May 1942 during his visit to French forces in the Middle East. Général Valin gave orders for the local command to start urgent preparations for the formation of a new Groupe de Chasse 3 (GC3). This new formation of Free French Air Force officers and men would have the chance to serve alongside the Soviet Air Force on the Eastern Front. The proposed force would shortly be offered to representatives of the Soviet government. Général Valin stated that de Gaulle envisaged that these volunteer Free French Air Force personnel would serve directly under Soviet command.

During this visit to the Middle East Général Valin was made aware by the command officers of Groupe de Chasse 1 (GC1) that the transfer of volunteer pilots and groundcrew from the Middle East Command to serve with the proposed Soviet Eastern Front GC3 would seriously deplete the abilities of the existing GC1. Général Valin's solution was to replenish the transfer loss by bringing French Air Force personnel over from Britain. It was at this time that Commandant Pouliquen, recently promoted, had his rank confirmed as permanent.

Général Valin as Commissioner for Air was to play a prominent part in the formation of the future Normandie Groupe. This officer had served France well ever since March 1940, when he was with the French military mission in Rio de Janeiro. In June that year he was promoted to lieutenant-colonel and then full colonel. In March 1941 Colonel Valin arrived in Britain entrusted with the responsibility of forming and directing the FAFL, and 1 July marked the official date of its formation. On 10 July Valin became Chief of Staff of the FAFL, forming in Britain the Fighter Groupe 'Ile de France' and in Chad the Bomber Groupe 'Brittany'. Next, he formed the Fighter Groupe 'Alsace' and the Bomber Groupe 'Lorraine'. In August Colonel Valin was promoted to the rank of général de brigade aérienne and on 24 September 1941 he was appointed Free French Commissioner of Air with the task of expanding the units of the FAFL. Under his direction units very quickly became operational in many theatres of operations. On 19 February 1942 Général Valin formally proposed to the Soviet military mission in Britain the formation of a fighter unit of the FAFL to operate with Soviet forces on the Eastern Front. The outcome of his proposal eventually resulted in the Normandie Groupe being formed for action in the Soviet Union. The French pilots who served on the Eastern Front were to attain eternal glory for France and themselves. At the end of hostilities Général Valin, having been bestowed with many decorations of honour, was placed on the active list for the rest of his life as a serving general.

The first designated volunteers for the Soviet Union were Lieutenants Préziosi, Poznanski, Derville, Colin, Louchet, and Lafont, and Sergent-chef Magrot. Unfortunately the North African aerial battles that took place in June 1942, prior to the battle of El-Alamein, were to deprive the future GC3 of three of these experienced pilots: Lieutenant Lafont was wounded in action, Lieutenant Louchet was killed in action and Lieutenant Colin failed to return from a combat mission.

During mid-August positive directives arrived for the proposed Russian venture. Capitaine Mirles, as the flying courier, brought to the Middle East base of GC1 the definite order to set up the new Groupe de Chasse 3. After a call for volunteers a list of sixty-two officers and men was drawn up. The names of these volunteers would later be submitted to the Soviet authorities for their comments and approval, and eventually the issue of visas for entry to the Soviet Union. The volunteers were now in a state of excited anticipation.

Orders signed by de Gaulle and dated 1 September 1942 confirm that Groupe de Chasse 3 was officially formed on that day. When the first elements arrived at the FAFL aerial base at Rayak, Lebanon, Lieutenant-Colonel Gence, commander of the base, welcomed them with a patriotic speech confirming the historical significance of this new formation now on parade before him.

After consulting the assembled GC3 officers and having taken advice, Commandant Pouliquen, perhaps anticipating the glorious role the French home province of Normandie was to play in history, requested that Général Valin give the new groupe the title 'Normandie'. It was envisaged that three escadrilles would form the Normandie Groupe and it was at this stage that their names were decided upon: Rouen for the 1st, Le Havre for the 2nd and Cherbourg for the 3rd. The Groupe would take the armorial bearing of the home province of Normandie: two leopards passant in gold, one above the other. The likeness for the motif had been drawn by an Armenian goldsmith from the souks of Damascus. The first issue Normandie badge depicted two gold leopards passant one above the other centred on a shield of plain red. The second issue badge had the addition of the word 'NORMANDIE'. This appeared at the head of the shield above the two gold leopards. The third and final Normandie badge had the new battle honour tile of 'NORMANDIE-NIEMEN' at the head of the shield above the two centred gold leopards. At the base of the red shield appeared a white lightning flash symbol. The same symbol appeared on the fuselage of the aircraft of the 303rd Soviet Air Division, the parent division of Normandie-Niemen Regiment.

It was from Rayak in Lebanon that Commandant Pouliquen was summoned to Syria by Général de Gaulle. Pouliquen had been informed that he was to receive his orders directly from the hand of Général de Gaulle. The orders came together with an official letter of command; the momentous occasion was marked with great dignity. Pouliquen was quick to notice the obvious pleasure of the moment shown by Général de Gaulle, who with great warmth presented Commandant Pouliquen with a signed photograph bearing the penned dedication: 'To Groupe de Chasse No. 3, in all confidence, 1 September 1942.'

At Rayak the Groupe was kitted out with new uniforms. The officers' and NCOs' uniforms were to conform strictly to French Air Force dress regulations, with smart walking-out uniforms together with working dress. For officers, battle dress was dark blue with khaki riding breeches; for NCOs it was khaki. The smallest details of the insignia, lanyard, pilots' badge, branch of service badge and gloves, all had to conform to dress regulations. It was considered necessary to standardise the uniform worn by the new formation.

Hitherto personnel had arrived wearing a mixture of French and British uniforms and desert equipment. Some pilots had taken a liking to RAF forage side caps, and the RAF Irvin flying jacket was a firm favourite among all pilots. The new ensemble now had great style; senior officers often said, 'you are not only aviators but also ambassadors who represent France abroad'. A campaign pack was issued on the base at Rayak; its contents (the same for everyone) included a lined haversack, mess tins, spoon, fork, water bottle and the famous French 'quart' (a mug that holds a quarter of a litre). The comings and goings in the corridors, with each man rushing about with his pack, reminded many of the feverish days of mobilisation. Général Catroux's wife was kind enough to donate three large packages of wool pullovers and suchlike as well as razors, toothbrushes, soap and towels. Colonel Cesari's wife surprised everyone with two immense cases each containing 1,500 packets of Zodiac cigarettes. News that 5 tons of special equipment had just arrived from London for the Groupe caused some excitement; the word went round that Normandie wanted for nothing.

On 23 September a coded message told of the expected arrival in Rayak of a detachment from London consisting of eight pilots, an interpreter, a radio engineer and the unit doctor. They were at their first stopover in Lagos, Nigeria, waiting to be flown to Cairo and then on to Rayak.

On 7 October the Lagos detachment arrived. Three of the pilots – Albert, Lefèvre and Durand – were a first-class contribution to the Groupe, known for their professional achievements. The other pilots had been considered above-average by the commanders of their British-based squadrons, but Commandant Tulasne and Capitaine Littolff decided that the piloting experience of the new arrivals fell short of the level expected for the new GC3. A decision had been taken to select only the highest calibre of pilots for the new GC3. The Soviets had asked the FAFL for experienced pilots to serve under Soviet Air Force command and had intimated a preference for officer pilots; hence the number of aspirants selected to join the Groupe.

The new unit doctor prepared for the expedition, administering to the reluctant squadron members who were sent along to him for their injections. Lieutenant de Pange fulfilled the role of deputy commander and did a good job with the movement arrangements. He was an experienced observer and had won the Croix de Guerre flying a Potez 63 during the Battle of France.

While awaiting movement orders, Capitaine Littolff succeeded in tuning one of the modern Dewoitine 520 fighter aircraft with the help of the ground staff on the base. As Commandant Tulasne made his first flight in the Dewoitine 520, a small crowd of personnel watched his aerial demonstration of boom and zoom passes and formed an excellent impression of his skill.

A clothing inspection parade was called on 18 October by Capitaine Littolff. The commandant looked over the assembled members and seemed well satisfied. The ensemble looked impressive, all its unofficial and desert gear now banished or hidden; France could be proud of her smartly turned-out sons. Commandant Pouliquen left for Damascus to say goodbye to friends in the parent GC1 on behalf of all those in the new GC3 in Rayak.

On 24 October, at a presentation parade before Colonel Corniglion-Molinier, Commander of Combat French Air Force, Commandant Pouliquen presented the new badge of the Groupe Normandie to each of its members; as already noted, the badge was in the shape of a shield with two golden leopards one above the other against a red background. This simple ceremony of presenting a badge to every member of the Groupe created a memorable occasion for all those on parade. The commandant told his men why they should be proud of this badge and what it represented, addressing the parade:

Officers and men of the Groupe de Chasse 3. I shall give you the insignia of our Groupe with the arms of Normandie. You will wear it with pride and dignity. It will represent for you the image of France itself in one of its most beautiful and rich regions. It will evoke in your memory of our previously calm and restful countryside. At this moment the region of Normandie is suffering under German occupation; bombardments and frequent fighting are taking place on our coasts and in our skies. Our thoughts are with this corner of France, which our Groupe de Chasse 3 will honour by bearing arms and which its pilots will glorify by their victories.

The anticipation and waiting continued. To fill the time, courses in the Russian language were given each morning by Aspirant Stakovitch; talks were given also on various subjects, but these were not always well attended. Lieutenant Michel then considered organising hunts for the 'Dahu', a small creature abundant in the mountains of Lebanon. All tried to stave off boredom while waiting for news of the long-awaited departure. The commanding officer made arrangements for a delegation of GC3 to participate in a commemorative ceremony for the French war dead that were buried in Lebanon. An open-air mass was said by the base chaplain, Father

Legenissel, former chaplain to GC1. Visits were made to the cemetery at Rayak, where Lieutenant-Colonel Gence placed a wreath. The many graves of past comrades who had died for France were then decorated with chrysanthemums.

On 8 November news that visas to travel to Russia had all been granted caused much excitement. Then there was a great stir as the men were urgently called to hear over the radio the announcement of the landings by Allied forces in Morocco and Algeria, news they greeted with almost electric enthusiasm. Two days later, in the evening, the long-awaited telegram arrived from Moscow giving the Groupe its orders to set off. Lieutenant Derville was immediately dispatched to Cairo with the mission of using his diplomatic contacts with the Americans to obtain immediate air transport for the first stage of the unit's journey, which was planned to go via Baghdad. On the following day, 11 November, Normandie held the traditional march past in honour of the armistice of 1918, the ceremony made all the more poignant by the knowledge that the Groupe was about to fulfil its destiny. At midnight Capitaine Littolff received a telegram from Cairo confirming that three large transport Douglas DC-3s were due to arrive the following morning. So as to not waste time, it was planned that the aircraft would leave the same day, taking the Groupe to Baghdad.

At 11 a.m. the three expected DC-3s landed at Rayak. They were loaded and took off, but one of them remained behind until the final items were ready to travel.

A Franco-Soviet agreement was signed on 25 November 1942 setting out details for the formation of the French Air Force Groupe on Soviet territory. The Soviets could not break old habits and requested that they be given the chance to scrutinise the names of those Frenchmen who had volunteered to serve in the Soviet Union. It was arranged that Capitaine Mirles would personally fly the proposed list of volunteers to Moscow.

The French volunteers for the Soviet Union were now all gathered. Some had been released from RAF squadrons and others from combat duty with the Free French Groupe de Chasse 1 serving in the desert war of North Africa; others had recently escaped from occupied France or made the journey from North Africa. Now they were all in Lebanon they attended a parade at the Rayak air base, where Général Valin, the Commissioner for Air, inspected the volunteers in their new smart dark blue uniforms and peaked parade caps. To celebrate the formation of the Normandie Groupe, an official group photograph of the assembled personnel was taken on the steps at Rayak, and each member of the Groupe was presented with a copy.

By 28 November the Normandie Groupe had arrived at Ivanovo, a training base some 125 miles north-east of Moscow. A week later, on 4 December 1942, the Normandie personnel were officially incorporated into the body of the Soviet Air Defence Force. The Soviets offered the French flyers the choice of flying British, American or Soviet fighter aircraft. Without hesitation they chose to fly Soviet. After the Normandie Groupe had made its choice at Ivanovo, it soon became apparent it would be equipped with the new Yak-1 fighter. Although the aircraft's excellent combat abilities were known to some French pilots, the Yak variants and design achievements were generally little known outside the Soviet Union.

The Yak fighter took its name from Alexander S. Yakovlev, chief Soviet aeronautical engineer and designer, who had gained a well-deserved reputation for designing gliders and sporting aircraft between 1925 and 1935. In 1938 the Soviet government announced its special requirements for a new fighter aircraft design. During an earlier visit to the West, Alexander Yakovlev had been impressed with the design of the British Spitfire and the German Bf-109. He had returned with the concept of a small but powerful single-seat fighter, and with this design in mind he set to with his design bureau and eventually produced the Ya-26 Krasavyets (Beauty). First flown in March 1939, this model was constructed mainly of wood with a fuselage strengthened with welded steel tubing. It was to be judged the best of the competing designs. After some modifications, which led to a spectacular flight on 1 January 1940 when the I-26 attained a speed of 373 mph, the Soviet government ordered the new aircraft into immediate military production. It was not long before the Moscow state aircraft factory was delivering the aircraft in quantity, a few months before the German invasion of June 1941. Alexander Yakovlev's first fighter design had earned him the Order of Lenin and the 1940 Stalin Prize Gold Medal, along with 100,000 roubles and the gift of a black Zis limousine.

With fortuitous foresight, Yak aircraft production was transferred from the factory in the Moscow area to the safety of Kamensk, a town that lay far in the east beyond the Ural mountains. By the end of 1941, with the German invaders moving ever closer to Moscow, the output of military aircraft east of the Urals had overtaken the earlier Moscow production figures. Eventually, three massive aircraft factories in Siberia were turning out Yak fighters.

TRAINING ON THE SOVIET YAK-1 FIGHTER

The French pilots and groundcrew were made familiar with the two-seater training version of the Yak-1 fighter. The French personnel were assisted by Soviet air mechanics and Soviet liaison staff. With this band of experienced Yak mechanics came a mascot in the form of a three-coloured crossbreed dog named Zazoute and its Soviet boy soldier handler. At the training base pilots were provided with additional Soviet flying equipment and issued with the standard Russian pilot's log book. These small landscape books would eventually have service entries penned in French, set out under the printed Russian column headings. Some pilots who had been attached to RAF squadrons would continue for a time to enter flying and combat details in their original RAF logbooks. All entries would be confirmed by counter-stamping with French and Soviet official seals.

In the early stages of the formation in Soviet Russia, owing to the initial low staff numbers, the Groupe was referred to by the serving members as an 'escadrille', but this was to change. In July 1943 when at Orel, with two escadrilles now active, the Soviets gave the Groupe the official title of Regiment, not an aerial unit title used by British or French Air Forces. Later, when numbers had been increased considerably and four escadrilles were formed on active service, the term 'Normandie-Niemen Regiment' became appropriate.

YAK-1M FIGHTERS ARRIVE

On 19 January 1943 everyone was out on the base to watch as the first six Yak-1M fighters arrived for the Normandie Groupe. They were flown to the Ivanovo landing strip by ferry pilots. Immediately the mechanics took over, and after three days of extensive testing the first flights took place. All the pilots declared they were very satisfied with the flying qualities of the Yak-1M aircraft. The mechanics had spent long hours preparing the Yaks on the icy and snow-covered landing strip. Noses and ears had started to freeze, but the French doctor found no cases of bronchitis or pneumonia. Some mechanics who took part in the African campaign were found to be still suffering from malaria and had to take short breaks. The commandant was very pleased with the work carried out in really extreme weather conditions.

The next day another four Yak-1Ms arrived, bringing the total strength of the Groupe to ten machines. Orders arrived from the French Military Mission in Moscow instructing Commandant Tulasne to take command of Normandie Groupe. He quickly established an aerial training programme of exercises in patrolling and target practice on the ground and with towed objects. During the course of training one machine was destroyed and several propellers bent due to the bad state of the runways and in places the deep, soft snow. All the pilots involved in the accidents, including the one where an aircraft had to be written off, were unharmed.

With this training session completed, officers of the Groupe were given four days' leave in Moscow, where they had the luck to be staying at the National Hotel near the Kremlin. Commandant Pouliquen received confirmation that he had been assigned to the French Combatants Military Mission in Moscow. In the evening Général Petit of the Military Mission hosted a dinner at the hotel for the pilots, with an abundance of vodka, Caucasian wines and Russian champagne; the dinner ended with lively discussion. Normandie were in Moscow on 23 February, the anniversary of the Red Army, but because of the war there were no parades in Red Square that year. Instead, the men on leave were shown an up-to-date film with live footage of the victorious battle for Stalingrad, where the German 6th Army had recently been destroyed. In the evening the men were taken to the theatre to see a performance of the *Barber of Seville*, which was enthusiastically received by the audience. The following day a visit was organised to the Red Army museum, where the Soviet military guide pointed out to the pilots some captured German weapons; unfortunately, noticed among the collection were some Panhard and Hotchkiss machine guns together with other arms manufactured in France. The Groupe left Moscow on 26 February at 6 p.m., arriving at Ivanovo the following morning. The commandant arranged for a contingent of groundcrew to have four days' leave in Moscow.

The Soviet general commanding the aerial region of Moscow arrived on 11 March for an inspection of his French Groupe at Ivanovo. Commandant Tulasne had prepared an aerial exercise that displayed the level of training achieved. The programme consisted of combat formations, patrolling, target practice with towed targets, attacks on mock enemy bombers, and individual acrobatics. Commandant Tulasne then took centre stage with a Yak-1M and executed a reverse Immelmann, which had probably never previously been attempted in a Yak. The general then ordered close banking flying with guns in action and live firing; Normandie did everything required.

Some three days later, the last ten sous-officiers and caporals remaining in Tehran arrived at Ivanovo. The Groupe was complete, and numbered fifty-eight Frenchmen all raring to fight. With the party from Tehran came cases of goodies; the contents, which were divided up equally, included cigars, cigarettes, sausages, and wine, all gifts from Mme Clavier; more cases were apparently en route.

On 16 March the Groupe received another four Yak-1Ms, bringing its strength up to fourteen aircraft. It was soon realised that French groundcrew numbers would not be enough to maintain a force of this size, whereupon nine aircraft were assigned to French mechanics and five to the Soviet mechanics. Normandie's Soviet personnel numbered two officers and fifteen NCOs.

At 9 a.m. on 20 March Général Petit, who had arrived the previous day, reviewed Normandie before the Groupe left for active service; it was known that departure for the front was imminent. The officers and mechanics were drawn up in front of the aircraft. For the first time in the Soviet Union, instead of a colour ceremony a guard of honour presented arms. Later, at 2 p.m., the Groupe performed an aerial display with twelve aircraft, a repeat of the grand show that was laid on for the Soviet general, but this time acting as a final fly-past. After a very cordial lunch, the evening ended at the theatre in Ivanovo.

PART TWO

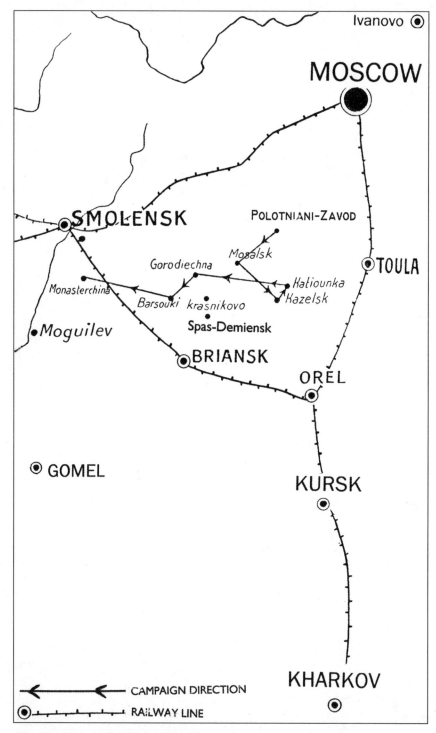

The First Campaign, March–November 1943.

THREE

FIRST CAMPAIGN,
MARCH–NOVEMBER 1943:
TOWARDS THE FRONT

Général Petit, after being taken for a demonstration flight by Commandant Tulasne in the two-seater Yak-7V, had a farewell drink of the recently arrived 'Tehran' vermouth and left for Moscow. As the Groupe was scheduled to depart for active operations the following day, it occupied itself preparing the baggage for the journey to the new forward airstrip. At 9.30 p.m. the traditional farewell banquet with the Red Army was held in the large refectory room, with French and Soviets gathered around a U-shaped table presided over by Colonel Schoumoff, who wished the Groupe well in the coming campaign. Commandant Tulasne made a heartfelt speech in which he expressed his pride in representing France side by side with the valiant Red Army.

At 11.40 a.m. on 22 March 1943, thirteen of the Yak-1Ms took off for the front, passing over the runway in formation, with a Pe-2 bomber guiding them to their theatre of operations. Three Douglas DC-2s were allocated to carry personnel and squadron equipment. One Yak was delayed for mechanical reasons and, together with the liaison aircraft, joined the Groupe later. Normandie was reunited on the ground at Polotniani-Zavod, ready for the important operations in this new sector.

On 9 May one page in the Moscow newspaper *Izvestia* was devoted to introducing the Normandie Groupe to the Soviet people. On Normandie's arrival, Lieutenant-General Khondiakov, Commander of the Soviet First Aerial Army, had received the Groupe and welcomed the French escadrilles into his army, wishing them every success. On 25 March the first reconnaissance of what was to be the Groupe's sector took place, again guided by one Soviet Pe-2 bomber. Twelve aircraft took part in a guided tour of Soukinitchi,

Kazelsk, Peremychl and Kalouga, and further reconnaissance was undertaken over the Malo, Iaroslavetz, Medine, Temkino and Iouknov sectors. Durand and Derville took off in pursuit of an enemy aircraft that passed about 5,000m above the landing strip. So it was on 26 March 1943 that Normandie's first wartime mission took place.

An important bombing mission on 29 March involved Pe-2 bombers that shared Normandie's landing strip. Normandie's task was to protect the bombers as they headed for enemy targets. Personnel were up at 3 a.m. The thaw had set in and the runway was covered in slush, making it difficult for the aircraft to get off the ground; at times the groundcrew had to lift the aircraft bodily to free the wheels. Finally, five aircraft were lined up ready to take off, but bad weather then forced the cancellation of the mission, which was the destruction of a bridge on the railway line from Spas-Demiensk to Smolensk. Intelligence had observed that this line was carrying much German equipment to the front. Despite bad weather, on 3 April five Pe-2 bombers, with four Yaks acting as escorts, took off to bomb the bridge, with satisfactory results.

FIRST AERIAL VICTORIES AND CASUALTIES

On 5 April two double patrols were sent out. One patrol accompanied three Pe-2 bombers to the Smolensk area, and encountered no enemy intervention. The second patrol, flown by Lieutenant Durand and Lieutenant Préziosi and accompanying two Pe-2s heading for the Roslav sector, encountered two German Fw-190s, which attempted to intercept the Soviet bombers. Préziosi swooped down and, attacking one of the German aircraft from behind at less than 80yd, scored a positive result; the Fw-190, with pieces of wing breaking away, went into a tail-spin and was seen to explode in flames on crashing. Durand attacked the other enemy aircraft from the rear flank; his fire tore into the Fw-190, which, immediately in trouble, crashed into the ground. All the Pe-2s and Yak escorts returned without a single bullet having struck them. These were the first two successes of the Normandie Groupe.

Next day General Khondiakov, Commander of the First Aerial Army, sent a telegram of congratulations and thanks. Later that day more patrols carried out escort missions and this time accompanied the bombers more than 100km behind enemy lines. As a result of this extended patrol,

Sous-lieutenant Albert and Sous-lieutenant Mahé ran out of fuel on the return journey and were forced to land well out in rough country. Albert landed on sodden, thawed ground and bent his propeller; Mahé found a rough dirt road and landed without any damage, taking off the following day to rejoin the Groupe. Protecting the Pe-2s was of the utmost importance, a grave responsibility that Normandie did not take lightly, such that on long hauls over enemy territory the Yaks stayed with their Pe-2 charges at all times. On the return journeys, even when low on fuel they did not leave the bombers, at times being forced to land in open country, often miles short of their landing strip. The Pe-2 bomber crews made known their appreciation of the protection afforded by their French comrades and the duty they performed.

As melted snow gave way to thick mud, the aircraft would become bogged down on the runway.

Three double patrols went out on 13 April: Commander Tulasne, Lieutenants Derville and Poznanski, Sous-lieutenants Durand and Mahé, and Aspirant Bizien carried out a mission in the Spas-Demiensk sector. As soon as they had crossed enemy lines they were attacked by at least eight Fw-190s; a whirling dogfight ensued, in the course of which Durand and Mahé scored some hits on their targets, though in the confusion of battle neither could claim definite victories, even though two Fw-190s were seen trailing clouds of smoke. Derville, Poznanski and Bizien did not return. Later, a report by Soviet infantry soldiers claimed that a Yak was seen to dive into the ground, but also that two pilots were seen descending gently by parachute towards Soviet lines. The report also confirmed that the Yaks had shot down three Fw-190s during the battle: three more victories for Normandie.

As a result of the first losses for Normandie, General Khondiakov visited Commandant Tulasne in person and expressed his sincere grief at the unfortunate event, but held out hope that the fate of the pilots would be known shortly. He said these losses, the first, must be the last; and he went on to say that the posting to Moukovnino had been necessary for the Groupe to become acquainted with activities on the front. He then announced that Normandie would shortly be attached to a combat regiment; he promised important missions for the Groupe and expressed his confidence that the pilots of Normandie would have the chance to avenge their missing comrades a hundredfold.

The next day two patrols commanded by Tulasne executed a mission in the sector where the three French pilots had been downed. The four Yaks in the patrol searched in vain for evidence of the missing aircraft. Other aircraft from Falianovo also mounted a search for the lost Yaks.

The Groupe sent six aircraft from Moukovnino to Mosalsk, the new centre of operations located about 40km from the front. Groundcrew and equipment were transported in a DC-3. It was decided that three Yaks that had to undergo mechanical work would follow later.

At dawn on 17 April General Khondiakov caused a surprise by placing a patrol of six Yak-7s of a Soviet Guards Air Regiment directly under the command of Commandant Tulasne, to whom he gave the following mission order: 'To prevent all enemy aircraft taking off from Secha, for the period 5 minutes before, during and after the bombing of the area by Soviet bombers.' Commandant Tulasne took command of a total of twelve planes: six of Normandie and six of the Guards Air Fighter Regiment, ordering Soviet Kapitan Siberine to head the protection patrol. Bombing raids were launched simultaneously on four enemy airfields, with about 500 Soviet aircraft taking part. Tulasne's mixed group provided cover for about 17 minutes above Secha at an altitude of 1,200m. No enemy aircraft took off; two Fw-190s were seen but did not intervene, and four Ju-88s drawn up on a landing strip were destroyed by Stormoviks. All aircraft returned unscathed. The aircraft of the Guards Air Regiment that had been placed under Commandant Tulasne's command were from an illustrious unit that had seen much combat action. The name 'Guards Regiment' was a group or unit honorary title awarded for exceptional battle achievements. Each member of the Regiment was awarded a Guards badge that he wore on his right chest below any decorations and retained for the rest of his military service; it proclaimed that the wearer was serving or had served with a crack unit. Guards Regiments or Units had their insignia painted on their aircrafts, tanks or ships, as the service branch determined. From the date of the award every serving member of the unit carried the prefix 'Guards' before his rank: Guards Captain, Guards Sergeant, and so on. So for Commandant Tulasne to be given command of these Yak-7 fighter of the Guards Air Regiment was an honour indeed; it demonstrated the confidence of the Soviet general in the Normandie command.

In April 1943 Normandie Groupe became operationally assigned to the Soviet 303rd Air Division of the First Aerial Army. Its pilots flew Yak-1Ms, escorting Soviet bombers on their combat missions; another duty was assisting the Red Army troops by executing ground attacks against heavily defended enemy positions. The markings on the Yak-1M flown by Sous-lieutenant Marcel Albert carried the expected Soviet red star markings on fuselage and tail fin; the French red, white and blue roundel was painted just below his cockpit.

NORMANDIE SUFFERS ITS FIRST NCO CASUALTY

Since their arrival in Mosalsk the unit's personnel had been lodged in a hamlet situated in the woods close to the airfield; the inhabitants had long since been evacuated. Normandie went on missions hunting for German troop convoys along the road to Warsaw. On 26 April a strange incident occurred on base. Caporal Benoît Saliba, an experienced armourer, was working on the weapons of a Yak-1M when one of the machine guns accidently fired, causing a rather serious flesh wound in his arm with a 7.62 calibre machine-gun bullet. The precise details were difficult to establish, but it would appear that Caporal Saliba was setting the convergence of the guns for the correct cone of fire when a second member of the armourers' service team inadvertently fired the gun. The doctor attended to him straight away; he was sent to hospital and eventually made a full recovery. Experienced pilots had specific preferences for the converging distance of the cone of their machine-gun fire; in this instance the armourers were aligning the guns according to the pilot's instructions. Commandant Jean Tulasne, who commanded Normandie from 22 February 1943 until his death in action on 17 July 1943, was informed of the incident. After investigating the circumstances surrounding the accident, he was impressed by the soldierly manner in which Caporal Saliba had behaved immediately after he was shot, noting in his report how Saliba had borne his wounds with fortitude. On 30 April Tulasne submitted in a document to Général Valin a proposal that Caporal Saliba be considered for the Croix de Guerre for his fortitude in carrying out his duties while being wounded on active service. Although the original Tulasne document to Général Valin has been located and confirmed, the general's decision remains unknown.

On May Day there were sorties over the road to Warsaw. In the evening Aspirant Lefèvre on a hunting mission attacked a Henschel 126 at 2,500m above the front line. He saw this high-winged monoplane go into a terminal dive as it tried to turn back over the German lines, trailing dense black smoke. As a celebration for May Day, the Soviet Commissariat sent the Groupe several very welcome bottles of red wine. During 3 May, towards 5 p.m. a patrol by Lefèvre and de La Poype was attacked by four Fw-190s and two Bf-109s. Lefèvre opened up his throttle and with great speed turned towards the enemy aircraft and fired a short burst of gunfire at the startled pilot of one of the Bf-109s, which dived towards the ground and crashed. De La Poype succeeded in disengaging from the other four Fw-190s by spiralling upwards into the clouds. Both aircraft return safely to base. Lefèvre had scored the seventh victory for Normandie. An hour later two double patrols left on a hunting mission and encountered a Henschel 126 watching activity over the lines within the Spas-Demiensk sector. Littolff, commanding, manoeuvred to place himself between the Henschel and the enemy lines, and executed with Castelain a very academic pincer attack. The Henschel was hit and dived, trying to escape, but Durand finished it off with a final burst of gunfire, sending it vertically into the ground. This was the Groupe's eighth victory.

At 11 a.m. on 6 May nine Yaks accompanied and protected Soviet fighters that were to attack enemy aircraft on the tarmac at Spas-Demiensk. Several enemy aircraft on the ground were set ablaze. At 6 p.m. eight Yaks accompanied nine Pe-2s to Secha. The bombs hit the buildings beside the runway and caused much damage. During the mission anti-aircraft fire was again very heavy; one of the Pe-2s was hit and fell in flames. All the Normandie Yaks returned safely to base. Early the next morning the Yaks went on a mission to shoot up any enemy aircraft at the Spas-Demiensk aerodrome. Several aircraft on the ground appeared to be destroyed or damaged. At mid-morning eleven Yaks left on a sortie to attack German-held villages near Spas-Demiensk; buildings were hit and Germans were seen running in all directions. Vehicles and the nearby station were also attacked; a train was hit and ground to a halt in a cloud of steam. The mission continued to Loubinka, where enemy aircraft on the runway were strafed. In the course of the sortie Mahé, an ex-RAF pilot, while hedge-hopping indicated he was damaged and would be forced to land. He was seen to come down in a clearing; the Yak's tail broke off as the aircraft finally came to a rest on its belly. The patrol returned and informed the commandant of Mahé's crash; it was hoped he had remained belted up, since if so he would have had a good chance of surviving. He was the fourth member of the Groupe to be posted missing.

On 13 May at 4.30 a.m. eight Yaks accompanied nine Pe-2 bombers on their way to attack the station at Ielnia. The mission was successful; the station was left heavily damaged and on fire. Later that morning the Yaks flew escort for another six Pe-2s whose target was the same important railway line moving German equipment to the front. On both raids the Normandie Yaks had kept the Soviet bombers safe from attack and all returned safely to base. The next day nine hunting sorties were undertaken in the sector from Kirov to Mouliatino. Bernavon, on a training session, was let loose with a Yak-1M, but on his first trip down the runway the compressor broke. He drew up his undercarriage and landed belly-down in a field, struck his head on the instrument panel and broke his eyebrow bone and his nose. The aircraft was written off and Bernavon spent two weeks in the base hospital. A broken compressor would take the mechanics a long time to repair or replace, and usually kept the aircraft grounded and out of action for some time.

A few days later, on 15 May, a patrol made up of Capitaine Littolff and Lieutenant Castelain spotted a Bf-110 that tried to lure the two Yaks over enemy lines. Littolff suspected a trap and decided to wait over Soviet lines; the heavily armed twin-engine Bf-110 then returned with a Bf-109. Littolff chased the Bf-109 while Castelain engaged the Bf-110; after a burst of fire into its belly the German aircraft spiralled down and crashed. These Bf-110s were heavily armed and well protected by steel armour-plate but were vulnerable to attack in their soft underbelly. Castelain left the patrol looking for traces of his crashed enemy. Some 800m from the German lines several eyewitnesses confirmed the Bf-110 had crashed. The liaison aircraft came from Moscow with Aspirant Maurice Bon, who had just arrived from Madagascar. After some very rapid training on the Yaks he took his place with the Groupe. Aspirant Alexandre Laurent, who had also come from Madagascar, arrived from Moscow and began his training on the Yak-7.

Under orders to change landing strips, Normandie left Mosalsk in late May for its new base, which was to be Kazelsk. Several Yaks stayed behind for mechanical work and would join the Groupe a few days later. The personnel went in trucks. Two new interpreters joined Normandie: Caporal Noel and Caporal Truco. Both had been captured in Belgium in May 1940. Taken as prisoners to East Germany, they made their escape and headed for the Soviet frontier, crossing it before the German invasion on 22 June 1941. Since that time they had worked on Soviet factory production in plants beyond the Urals, where side by side with Soviet workers they soon acquired a good basic knowledge of the Russian language, which was to prove useful.

AT KATIOUNKA WITH THE
18TH GUARDS FIGHTER AIR REGIMENT

On 29 May patrols flew a protection mission covering for a Douglas DC-2 transport aircraft, this particular one not American-supplied but built in the Soviet Union under licence from the Douglas Corporation in America. Normandie Groupe personnel were lodged some 2km from the airstrip in a village. They shared their surrounds with a Soviet cavalry detachment which had taken part in the Stalingrad offensive during the previous winter. Friendly understanding grew up between Normandie and the Soviet detachment, which told staggering tales of the battle and the German defeat. For the first time the Groupe experienced close and violent noise from the local anti-aircraft batteries, which opened fire on marauding enemy reconnaissance planes. The landing strip was now only 28km from the enemy lines. The Groupe moved to Katiounka, situated about 5km to the north, and shared an airstrip with the famous 18th Guards Fighter Air Regiment. Pilots were lodged in a peasant village 4km from the landing strip; the mechanics were in crude shelters consisting of huts made of branches and leaves that they had to construct for themselves. In the first week twenty-four hunting missions were dispatched, intended to catch any German aircraft flying over the sector: orders were to deny the enemy local airspace. Lieutenant-Colonel Pouyade arrived from Moscow on 9 June in a Douglas DC-2, along with eight pilots (de Forges, Léon, de Tedesco, Boube, Barbier, Vermeil, Mathis and Balcou) together with Corot, who was to act as an interpreter. They told of amazing adventures; Pouyade had recently escaped from Indochina; de Forges, Barbier, Vermeil and Mathis had within the previous few months escaped from occupied France. They detailed the serious problems of the occupation and how the established interior (partisan) forces were helping to get people over the border to Spain.

The following day four hunting sorties were sent out. At 7.30 p.m. eight Yaks commanded by Tulasne took off as escorts for a special bombing mission by eight Il-2s, 'Stormoviks', their target Oerskarp. On their return the news came that Petrov, adjutant to the commander of the Pe-2 regiment at Polotniani-Zavod, had been killed in action. He was flying his Pe-2 bomber when it was struck by anti-aircraft fire during a bombing mission. His observer tried to bring the aircraft back to base; he managed to fly the badly damaged plane for some while, almost reaching the regiment's base, when the plane went into a dive; the observer at the last moment parachuted out. Tulasne and Littolff went to Polotniani-Zavod for the burial. The commandant arranged for four Normandie Yaks to fly several times in tight formation above the airstrip: a symbolic gesture of support that bore witness to the brotherhood that united French and Soviet aviation in the struggle against the invader. This traditional gesture of brotherhood between pilots was often practised during the First World War. Tulasne and Littolff were dedicated and aggressive pilots who had an overwhelming need to get into combat and achieve victories. One veteran told me they were fighters first and foremost and not fun guys.

On 12 June a patrol by Lefèvre and de La Poype encountered a Fw-189 at 3,000m. It dived towards the front line followed by two Yaks some 200m behind it in hot pursuit; the shooting went on for some 10km, hedge-hopping well into enemy territory until the enemy was lost from view in the forest. An observation post that had followed the fight said that the Fw-189 was shot down. De La Poype returned with a painful burst eardrum which was caused during the fracas; he was sent to hospital in Moscow for treatment.

A few days later a patrol by Littolff and Castelain attacked an Fw-189 at 3,000m. It dived down to escape; the attack continued at low altitude and definite hits were observed. The action took place 15–20km from the enemy lines. The guns of one of the Yaks jammed but not before the Fw-189's damaged engine faltered and the pilot had to crash-land. The patrol returned to base, refuelled and took on more ammunition, then set off with another patrol that included Risso. It intended to search for the crashed enemy aircraft, which they eventually found burnt out in a field. In the course of the sortie Risso's aircraft in a steep dive lost panels (fairling) on the left side of the fuselage, but managed to land on a strip in the area. A couple of days later the patrol of Albert and Préziosi attacked an Fw-189 over the front line. The German pilot appeared to be badly hit and smoke streamed out from the engine; the aircraft headed for its lines in a shallow, slow dive, but Soviet army observers on the ground confirmed it had crashed in a pine forest.

At 5 a.m. on 23 June Tulasne and Béguin encountered an Fw-189 protected by two Fw-190s. Tulasne attacked the two enemy fighters while Béguin went in against the Fw-189 and executed three backward passes. During this diving attack Béguin's aircraft lost its covering panels, which were torn off along one side of the fuselage. At this crucial and vulnerable moment another Fw-190 came in to attack and pursued the handicapped Yak; Béguin withdrew and the Fw-190 did not persist. Meanwhile, Tulasne fired on the two Fw-190s with good results; one of them with its tail shot to pieces crashed to the ground. Back on the base training flights continued while at the same time several combat sorties were carried out. Poor Lefèvre suffered badly from jaundice; as he looked terrible and quite yellow, the doctor sent him for treatment to a hospital in Moscow.

In the course of a hunting sortie the patrol of Tulasne and Béguin encountered two Fw-190s. Béguin engaged in battle with one of the enemy fighters, the other disappeared for no apparent reason. The battle took place almost above the village where the pilots were billeted. The chaps were awakened by the blasts of anti-aircraft fire and came out to watch it all in their pyjamas. Béguin's guns jammed so he had to break off the engagement very quickly; he was at the end of his mission and had only a few minutes of flying time left in his tanks. Immediately Tulasne came to the rescue; at the very moment when Béguin was attempting his landing, the Fw-190 swooped down and threatened to attack him, but automatic fire from the ground guns forced this determined Fw-190 to break off its attack. Both Yak aircraft landed safely back on the strip.

Pravda newspaper published on 8 July the names of five officers of Normandie who had been awarded Soviet decorations. The Order of the Patriotic War 1st class, in gold, was bestowed on Commandant Tulasne and Capitaine Littolff, and three officers – Aspirants Durand and Lefèvre together with Adjudant-chef Duprat – were awarded the Order of the Patriotic War 2nd class, in silver. These were the first Soviet decorations gained by Normandie. The commandant received a telegram of congratulation from General Gromoff, Commander of the Soviet First Aerial Army.

FOUR

THE KURSK AND OREL OFFENSIVE, 5 JULY–23 AUGUST 1943

Wishing to avenge the defeat at Stalingrad and at the same time show the German nation that its armies could triumph over the Communist hordes, Hitler ordered the German High Command (OKW) to prepare an attack against the Kursk salient, an operation that would carry the code name 'Citadel'. With orders to go back on the offensive the German Army started a massive build-up of men and *matériel* in the Kursk region in preparation for a major pincer attack against Soviet positions in the Kursk and Orel salient. Soviet intelligence had already gained information from its 'Lucy' spy ring, a group of Soviet spies operating from Switzerland. They had informed Stalin that the Kursk operation Citadel was planned to take place between 3 and 6 July. Then on 4 July 1943 a reluctant Yugoslav draftee from the German Army deserted to the Russian lines and informed his Russian interrogators that a massive German attack was due for the next day (5 July) at 2 a.m. He also identified the location where the main armoured force was gathering for the big thrust forward. The Soviet Army, already well prepared, now knew the actual time and place where the main enemy attack would start.

The German offensive in the Kursk salient would be the last major tank battle of the Second World War. It was to be the largest clash of armour ever to take place; it has been described as the biggest land battle in history. At the start of the battle the German forces consisted of 900,000 men, 2,700 tanks and 1,800 aircraft. The Soviets had over 1 million men, 3,300 tanks and over 2,000 aircraft. Both sides would send in heavy reinforcements as the battle progressed; in one instance a German train full of new factory-delivered tanks was caught by the Soviet Air Force and destroyed before its cargo could be unloaded. It was here the new Ferdinands, heavy-calibre guns mounted on massive tank chassis, would be given their baptism of fire. As well, the updated Tiger tanks would be deployed for the first time in large numbers; over 100 would go into action at Kursk. The Soviets deployed the new Yak-9T attack aircraft, which were to prove that the Red Air Force had yet another superb aircraft, this time with a heavy-hitting 37mm cannon firing through the aircraft's nose cone.

By 7 July the Germans had penetrated about 7 miles. Then after a long dry period the rain started to fall during the battle fought at Prokhorovka, where the Germans lost 400 tanks and 10,000 men in one day. Guderian, the German general, watching from his command vehicle, remarked that he could see the Soviet T-34 tanks streaming like rats over the battlefield in numbers that were simply overwhelming. Another black day for the enemy was 10 July, when the Germans lost 200 tanks and over 25,000 infantry killed. The Kursk battle continued with unabated ferocity. On 12 July the Soviets launched a counter-offensive in the north on the right flank against Orel where they were facing Model's 9th Army with 3rd Panzer Corps and numerous infantry divisions. To the south of Kursk, Hoth's 4th Panzer Army, which included Hausser's SS Panzer Corps, was heavily engaged. It was near the town of Prokhorovka that a further 400 German tanks were destroyed during this desperate and determined clash with Soviet armour. Overhead the battle for control of the sky had become an important part of the overall conflict. Just as the ground battle below was being determined by the numerical might of the Soviet's heavy armour, so the aerial combat strength of the Soviet Air Force was proving to be a decisive factor as the Soviets sent in mission after mission of bombers against the German tanks and massed infantry forces. Soviet covering fighters stormed in against the attacking Bf-109s and Fw-190s; the enemy had put up a massive aerial protective shield to assist their advancing ground forces. It has been estimated that 65 per cent of the Luftwaffe in Russia were involved in the Kursk battle, but what turned out to be the real disaster for the enemy was that 70 per cent of his tank forces on the Eastern Front were now engaged in this greatest of all land battles.

The Soviet Air Force was determined to defeat the enemy and win control of the sky over the battle area of Kursk and Orel. This it did, in the process destroying over 200 Luftwaffe aircraft on 10 July alone. During combat missions flown over the battle region, Normandie was constantly involved in escorting and protecting Pe-2 and Il-2 bombers. These heavily armoured aircraft had orders to attack the German forces around the Orel salient, where Model's 9th Army was leading the attack in this northern sector. In the course of these covering missions Normandie was continually in combat with large groups of German fighters over the whole Northern Front. Normandie's aggressive and successful fighting abilities were to prove second to none, although the price paid was high, with six pilots lost in combat during the Orel campaign. Kursk was a terrible and wasteful defeat for the Germans; their entire tank reserves were spent in this futile battle. Their tank production was never to make good these massive losses. The Soviets claimed 70,000 German dead and the destruction of 3,000 enemy tanks. The Soviet tank losses were equally heavy, but Soviet factory production was geared to replace them. The Germans claimed they had destroyed 1,800 Russian tanks in the southern sector alone.

At the end of the battle the Soviet forces had captured more ground and were poised to advance into the Ukraine. By 6 August they had liberated Bielgorod. On the 23rd the city of Kharkov was liberated. The Normandie Groupe was mentioned in the Soviet 'Orders of the Day' for its successful part in this momentous battle. For its contribution to the victory, Normandie gained the battle honour OREL, an honour title that would now appear on its regimental colours.

AERIAL RAMMING OF ENEMY AIRCRAFT

It was at this time that the French pilots started to hear of startlingly heroic actions undertaken by individual Soviet pilots during the air battles above Kursk. A new form of ferocious aerial combat was taking place that involved ramming enemy aircraft. The main aim was to slice the tail off the German aircraft with the propeller, a procedure that was to be known as the 'falcon or taran attack' (sokolnyjudar). All Soviet air regiments kept a record of these heroic and drastic events. During the Kursk campaign, which lasted eight weeks, aerial ramming of German aircraft was successfully carried out on forty-seven occasions. If the 'falcon' ramming attack was executed at sufficient altitude, there was always a chance for the Soviet pilot to parachute to safety. Of the forty-seven successful falcon attacks during the Kursk campaign, fifteen of the pilots did actually get their aircraft back or made forced landings, and nine managed to parachute to safety, but records show that twenty-three pilots were killed after these dramatic engagements. This form of aerial attack was not new to Russian aviation; in 1915 Kapitan Pyotr Nesterov rammed the German aircraft flown by Baron von Rosenthal, both pilots dying in this falcon attack.

The Soviet statistics for these heroic attacks are quite staggering: 595 confirmed falcon attacks took place during the Second World War: 558 by fighters, 19 by Il-2s (Stormoviks) and 18 by Pe-2 bombers. One Soviet ace of twenty-eight victories, pilot B. Kovzan, was the leading exponent of this feat; he had accomplished no fewer than four successful taran attacks. On his last ramming he lost his left eye, but after surgery and recovery he went back on combat missions to claim a further six German aircraft destroyed, shooting them down in traditional combat. Records confirm that two pilots each performed three successful taran attacks, and thirty-four pilots accomplished this form of deadly attack twice. Some of these rammings took place after guns had jammed or ammunition had run out; the frustration caused in the heat of the moment could lead to these heroic last-ditch actions. Eventually this form of suicidal attack was forbidden by direct orders from Stalin. In 1994 the Russian Federation struck a Nesterov medal to be awarded to Air Force personnel for exceptional service; on the obverse of the medal is the portrait of Kapitan Nesterov.

NORMANDIE'S INVOLVEMENT IN THE OREL OFFENSIVE

The Normandie Squadron Diary written at the time tells that from 10 July, starting at 10 p.m., an artillery bombardment of great violence was unleashed on the Orel front; bombers passed over all night long and the sky was illuminated by large explosions and flares. Artillery bombardments lasted all the next day and the following night; explosions formed a continuous rumbling. A truly big offensive was under way. At 8 a.m. on 12 July Normandie sent up fourteen Yaks; they were split into two groups and accompanied eighteen Pe-2 bombers, while a further 28 Pe-2s joined the mission, which was to bomb positions just a few kilometres behind enemy lines. The pilots reported that the anti-aircraft fire was still very heavy and German lines were hidden under a cloud of smoke. From the Soviet side of the lines Normandie pilots saw dozens of artillery blasts occurring at the same time. At the first passage of the bombers the anti-aircraft fire was very violent as the armoured Stormoviks, which were flying at low altitude, attacked the enemy batteries; at the second passage the Pe-2s found that the anti-aircraft fire was now much weaker. All the aircraft returned without having been hit. Enemy fighters did not intervene. Towards noon, shortly after the Pe-2s' attack, artillery fire ceased and the Soviet counter-attack with tanks and infantry was unleashed. As the tanks rolled forward they were covered with Red Army soldiers, who clung to any hand grip available around the tanks' turrets.

During the Orel offensive on 12 July, a German fighter pilot, who appeared to be suffering from exhaustion and combat fatigue, came in to land and surrendered his Fw-190, which was in perfect condition. This small drama took place on the landing strip immediately next to Normandie, whose French pilots on the strip at the time were amazed by the unexpected visitor. Later, those who were interested in the German Fw-190 went over to examine the enemy aircraft closely. Early that evening the same Fw-190 was taken up and flown by an experienced Soviet pilot, who executed combat exercises in company with two Yak-9s flown by pilots of the 18th Guards Air Regiment serving on the strip next to Normandie. On 31 July this same German Fw-190 was extensively comparison-tested against a Yak-9 at Katiounka.

In the evening Normandie sent up fifteen more Yaks to accompany ten Il-2s that were heading for the bridge at Tsin, which was being used by scores of German tanks and heavy equipment moving into action. This important objective was covered and defended by about twenty-four Bf-110s forming two defensive circles, one above the other, and circling in opposite directions. The Bf-110s got ready to attack the Stormoviks but the Yaks attacked first and forced the enemy to break the circle, after which the Bf-110s became vulnerable. And so it was that Littolff, Castelain and Durand each shot down a Bf-110. The Normandie pilots observed the Stormoviks successfully attacking enemy troop concentrations in and on the edge of the woods. All the Il-2s and Yaks returned to base safely. On 12 July the Red Army claimed that more than 300 German tanks had been destroyed during the day, and Normandie was told the Soviet counter-attack was going to continue throughout the night.

KURSK: THE TIDE IS TURNED

The battle for Kursk had taken a massive toll of German men and armour. With the best part of 3,000 tanks destroyed and reserves now depleted, Hitler was forced to order a halt to the offensive. The enemy started pulling troops and equipment out of the salient. It appeared that the Wehrmacht needed to redeploy troops and tanks to Italy. As the Allies had just landed in Sicily, Italy was going to become another front, forcing Hitler to deploy his extended forces. During the last days of the battle a train-load of German reserve tanks including some Tigers arrived straight from the factories to reinforce the crumbling front line, but this much-needed delivery was caught while it was being unloaded from flat railway wagons. Soviet bombers found and destroyed them before they could even leave the railhead.

Hitler's gamble of a pincer movement around the Soviet forces at Orel and Kursk had failed and, with his dwindling reserves of heavy armour now further depleted, Hitler had no option but to end the battle and withdraw. This failed operation had lost so many tanks that factory production, suffering from Allied bombing and material shortages, would never again be able to catch up with operational needs. Although the Soviets lost about the same number of T-34 tanks, the Soviet factories were in full production and, not suffering from air attacks, made up the losses within six weeks. The destruction of German tanks had become such an important objective for Red Army tank crews that drastic measures were taken to achieve this end. Some individual tank crews, out of ammunition or with guns disabled, would ram the tracks off German panzers; they would do anything to stop the German tanks advancing. Here again Red Army foot soldiers took heroic risks to destroy the advancing enemy tanks. At the Anniversary Victory celebrations in Red Square in June 1985, Viktor Kanoyev reminisced, his story reflecting the heroic determination of the ordinary Red Army soldier during those crucial days. While Kanoyev was serving in the defence of Stalingrad, he used a desperate method of dealing with advancing German tanks when anti-tank guns or ammunition were not available. Placing himself squarely in front of an approaching tank in a crouching position, at the last moment he threw himself on his back between the two massive tracks, and as the tank passed over he attached a heavy limpet mine to the underside; a few yards further on the tank blew up. He repeated the same procedure on a second tank. His commander awarded Kanoyev the Order of the Patriotic War 1st class. He was wearing that same decoration forty years later at the soldiers' tomb beside the walls of the Kremlin.

On 14 July at 7.30 a.m. a parade took place on the base in honour of the national day. French and Soviet personnel were gathered together in a clearing beside the landing strip. Paul de Forges read a fine order of the day from Commander Tulasne. Because of Normandie's busy activity during the Orel offensive, the simple ceremony lasted only 10 minutes; on this day the tricolour flew over this little corner of French soil. The new dining room was inaugurated and, thanks to Aspirant Corot, the menu was varied and copious. In the afternoon seven Yaks commanded by Pouyade left to fly escort protection for Stormoviks that were going to attack enemy troop concentrations in the Balkov region. Four Bf-110s that were covering the enemy positions were immediately attacked by Pouyade, Préziosi, Béguin, de Tedesco and Albert. As a result two Bf-110s were shot down, one jointly by Pouyade and Béguin, the other by Albert; these two victories were confirmed by Red Army troops on the ground. Lieutenant de Tedesco did not return from the mission. A Yak-9 was seen by Albert to dive towards the ground trailing smoke, but searches in the area have so far not had any positive results. All the Stormoviks returned safely to base.

Castelain (Littolff's winger) was attacked by three Fw-190s and was separated from his patrol chief. He assaulted an Fw-190 that spiralled upwards into the tail of an unknown Yak, whereupon it was fired on and exploded in a ball of flames. Castelain also attacked a Ju-87, part of a formation that was bombing Soviet troops. Castelain had to break off the engagement as he was very low on fuel, and was forced to land some distance away from the strip. He was collected and returned to base in the much-used U-2 liaison aircraft. Thus on 14 July Normandie honoured France with three certain victories and twenty-five combat sorties. Unfortunately, on this festive evening Lieutenant de Tedesco was not among his comrades; his gaiety and spirit were missed. General Zakharov, Commander of 303rd Air Division, together with about twenty Soviet officers were invited to dinner. During the evening Zakharov read a telegram of congratulations from General Gromoff, Commander of the Soviet First Aerial Army, addressed to the Normandie Groupe.

The next day, during late afternoon, eight Yaks commanded by Durand flew protecting escort with six Il-2s in the Krasnikovo region. The Stormoviks attacked convoys of armour and mixed vehicles travelling along roads heading for the Orel front, also hitting some that were returning. There was no sign of any enemy aircraft. At 7 p.m. eight Yaks commanded by Tulasne accompanied Stormoviks to the Balkov region, north of Krasnikovo. On arrival at the target the Stormoviks were attacked by two Bf-110s coming in from the front at low altitude. Tulasne and de Forges dived at them and opened fire. The Bf-110 attacked by de Forges left his mate while trailing smoke; the commandant pursued the second, which was hedge-hopping, for about 10 minutes until finally it landed on its belly in a cloud of smoke and dust some 4km north-east of Orel. All the Yaks and Il-2s returned safely to base.

At 10 a.m. on 16 July, twelve Yaks left on a covering mission for troops on the ground in the Krasnikovo region. Three Bf-110s were spotted and attacked by Littolff and Castelain; Littolff shot down one, which landed on its belly. Castelain assaulted the second several times; the Bf-110 was hit and crashed to the ground in multiple pieces. During this time Pouyade, Préziosi, Béguin, Durand, Risso and Vermeil attacked a Fw-189 as it bombed Soviet troops. The assault of the six Yaks continued for quite a while and finally the Fw-189 was shot down, as confirmed by the troops in the area. All the fighters returned without having been hit. At 2 p.m. eight Yaks commanded by Tulasne left on a covering mission in the Krasnikovo area. On arrival in the region they noticed a group of fifteen Ju-87s heading for Krasnikovo. The Littolff, Castelain and Léon patrol, with the sun behind it in a classic attack mode, fired into the last group of the Ju-87s; the Pouyade and Bernavon patrol also attacked the Ju-87s; the Tulasne and Albert patrol stayed alert as protection at a higher altitude. The Littolff and Castelain patrol was attacked by three Fw-190s and three others made a strike on Léon, who turned in time and brought one down in a shower of sparks and flames. Léon was drawn upwards by the two remaining Fw-190s and found four Fw-190s awaiting him. He escaped by diving and returned towards Soviet lines by hedge-hopping, pursued closely by the four enemy fighters, which attacked him in turn. In the course of these assaults Léon succeeded in shooting down his second Fw-190 in the same sortie and returned safely to ground. On landing the groundcrew pronounced his aircraft a real mess, having been hit by so many bullets.

In his strike on the Ju-87s Pouyade shot one down in flames and was in turn attacked by an Fw-190, but although damaged he escaped by diving and was forced to make a heavy landing. At the moment when the Littolff–Pouyade and Tulasne–Albert patrols attacked the Ju-87s, they were in turn attacked by two Fw-190s coming from below. Tulasne climbed fast towards the sun and shot one of the Fw-190s down in flames. Attacked once again, he dived towards the ground and assaulted another Fw-189, without obvious results. Finally on his return he met four Fw-190s, attacked one without observing any results, and returned to the ground. In the course of these battles de Forges, now isolated, met two Bf-109s; he fired on one of them, which seemed to have sustained damaged. Littolff, Castelain and Bernavon did not return. Searches the next day did not disclose to the Groupe its comrades' fate. The battle for Orel was increasing Normandie's total of victories and also its casualties, which mounted day by day.

At 5 a.m. the following day, 17 July, nineteen Yaks took off to escort and protect nine Pe-2 bombers, which were part of a group of thirty-six bombers and thirty-eight fighters whose target was the railway station at Biela–Berega on the railway line from Briansk to Orel. The bombing of heavy armour moving along the railway to the Orel front was very successful; the bombs hit the loaded flat railway wagons. During this mission fifteen Bf-110s were spotted but for some reason did not intervene. Tulasne attacked one of them without obvious results. The anti-aircraft fire defending the rail target area was very heavy, but all the aircraft returned safely. At 8.40 a.m. ten Yaks left on a covering mission for troops in the Iagodnaia and Krasnikovo region. An engagement took place with some Fw-190s. Albert fired on three and shot one down in a ball of flames. All the fighters returned safely. At 1 p.m. ten Yaks executed a new sorties to protect heavily pressed Soviet ground forces. No enemy aircraft were encountered during this action.

At 5.10 p.m. nine Yaks took off to accompany Stormoviks in the Znamenskaia sector; these ground assault aircraft were ordered to attack lines of vehicles on the road from Boloto to Orel. Léon was attacked by two Fw-190s that he succeeded in escaping. Albert and Préziosi came to his aid, shooting down one Fw-190; Aspirant Bon attacked an Fw-190 without apparent results. At the moment when the Fw-190 appeared, Tulasne was seen for the last time gaining altitude; thereafter no information reached the Groupe about his fate. The patrol of Béguin and Vermeil, providing protection of the rear, was attacked by six Fw-190s. At the first burst of gunfire Béguin's plane received a shell in a wing near the fuselage and another in the horizontal tail fin. Wounded by a shell splinter in his thigh, Béguin manoeuvred and succeeded in firing a burst of gunfire for two seconds at an Fw-190 from 50m behind. He was attacked again and, despite receiving a shell in the engine, returned by hedge-hopping. As he made his way back, in pain from the shell splinter, he was amazed at the sight of the massive Orel tank engagement taking place below him. Because of severe damage to his aircraft he was forced to fly at only 40 feet above the battlefield. His mind was briefly taken off the pain of his injury as he became aware that the ground below him was covered as far as the eye could see with the black shapes of endless German tanks, each followed by clouds of smoke and dust, yet not one of the many enemy guns only feet beneath seemed interested in his failing Yak. As he made his way further forward another spectacular sight presented itself: the German tanks were being engaged head-on by what seemed like several hundred Soviet T-34 tanks, all moving forward at speed through a blue haze of smoke, heading for the advancing enemy panzers. With his aircraft badly damaged and losing height, Béguin at last gained friendly lines but was forced to land his Yak just behind the Soviet advance. His damaged engine had forced him to fly so low over the battlefield that he probably had one of the best close-up sightings of this massive historic tank battle ever recorded.

Vermeil, lost from sight at the start of the battle, did not return and there was no news of him. At the time of these hectic aerial battles, Normandie was facing about thirty Fw-190s in this sector.

Commandant Pierre Pouyade, known in the Regiment as 'Pepito', had luck on his side when he survived a crash landing on the evening of 16 July 1943. After his aircraft had been badly damaged in the engagement he was forced to put down on very rough land. In the five days of furious action at Orel and Kursk, with 112 sorties carried out, six of the Groupe had been lost or killed: Commandant Tulasne, Capitaine Littolff, Lieutenant de Tedesco, Sous-lieutenant Castelain, Sous-lieutenant Bernavon and Aspirant Vermeil. Every day the Groupe hoped to hear news of them but, alas, no information about what had happened to the missing pilots was forthcoming. The Normandie victories included 9 Bf-110s, 6 Fw-190s, 1 Fw-189, and 1 Ju-87; of the 109 enemy aircraft entered in the log as damaged some would later be confirmed by Soviet ground forces as destroyed. These victories cost the Groupe dear, with six Normandie pilots missing in action during the first five days of the Orel–Kursk battle.

At 7.50 a.m. on 19 July seven Yaks commanded by Pouyade executed a covering mission for advancing troops in the Krasnikovo region; no enemy aircraft were encountered. At 12.30 p.m. six Yaks commanded by Albert once again left on a covering mission. Two Ju-88s were encountered; immediately Léon, de Forges. Albert, Risso and Bon attacked, one twin-engine Ju-88 burst into a cloud of smoke and flames before diving towards the ground, and crashed in a dramatic fireball. Troops watching the engagement from their positions confirmed the result. This was entered in the diary as the thirtieth victory for the Normandie Groupe on the Eastern Front. The next day General Zakharov, Commander of the 303rd Division, ordered Pouyade not to execute any battle missions without his direct authorisation for a period that was to be dedicated to rest and training.

Everyone was pleased to see Roland de La Poype return to the Groupe on 28 July. At 1 p.m. seven Yaks commanded by Albert took off to cover troops on the ground some 20km north-east of Karachev; no enemy aircraft were encountered. At 3.45 p.m. six Yaks once again commanded by Albert executed a similar mission, but this time a group of 30 Ju-87s protected by about six Fw-190s was encountered. A whirling battle began, in the course of which Albert, Durand, Risso and Mathis fired on the Fw-190s. No obvious results were confirmed. Préziosi was lost from view in the battle and did not return; there was no news of his fate. In the afternoon Lefèvre returned from Moscow, bringing with him Aspirant Largeau, a new pilot for the Groupe.

THE FRENCH MECHANICS LEAVE THE SOVIET UNION

On 30 July Michel, the officer mechanic, left the Groupe for Moscow and from there was posted to the Middle East. All the mechanics whose departure had been ordered by the Military Mission in Moscow handed over their aircraft to Soviet mechanics. The French mechanics would be travelling to Moscow and from there would probably be sent on to the Middle East. The departure of the mechanics was a strange decision, but not unexpected as far as the pilots were concerned. The mechanics in general had a rough time; on many occasions they were placed in less than adequate accommodation, and their food or the small rations issued were always causing problems. In an equal society it would appear some were less equal than others; the pilots were very much needed, as was reflected in their treatment by the Division, but one had the feeling that chaps with spanners were assumed to be always available. Again, the political liaison (commissar) officer probably did not like his good Communist mechanics learning the ways of the cosmopolitan French mechanics. Général Petit of the Military Mission in Moscow was aware of the situation and probably hastened the inevitable. The pilots had formed very good working friendships with their mechanics; they had grown to rely on and trust their dedication and ability to have the aircraft safe and ready for the next mission. It had not been easy to watch them having a rough time; on one occasion the mechanics had to build overnight accommodation from branches and leaves while the pilots were shown into wooden huts to bed down. Food was another problem. It was a point of honour to share everything in the Groupe, but the Soviet attitude to the lower ranks did not help. Hence rabbits were hunted and frogs collected when food was scarce. The Soviet mechanics fared exactly the same as the French groundcrew, so at least there was an equal society in this stratum.

The forty-two mechanics had served for eight months in the Soviet Union, a period that had included one of the bleakest winters in living memory. They had a superb record of dedicated maintenance of the aircraft, including serving through the successful campaign at Orel, the battle honour of which would be added to the regimental colours of Normandie. Their service was of the highest order, but only Adjudant-chef (Mechanic) Louis Duprat would receive a decoration from the Soviets, being awarded the Order of the Patriotic War 2nd class. It would be totally wrong to say the mechanics and the aircrew did not feel they were a single combined force; the commandant made sure that they shared duties and leaves on equal terms. It just so happened that the mechanics by the very nature of their jobs shared the same problems and living conditions as the hard-pressed Soviet mechanics. It was the French pilots who appreciated the Soviet Air Force supply units' different treatment of aircrew and groundcrew, a gulf that existed on all airstrips of the Division. The Normandie commandant did everything he could to promote a unified approach to conditions and equal social activities for all his Groupe, and in the main he was successful.

Pouyade was informed that the Division was soon to change its location and went off with liaison officer Kounine to the new airstrip being considered for Normandie. At noon on 3 August General Levandovitch, Commandant Mirles and a general representing General Gromoff, Commander of the Soviet First Aerial Army, arrived on the airstrip at Katiounka for the ceremony of awarding decorations to the Normandie Groupe. At the same time a Douglas DC-3 landing from Moscow brought six new pilots as reinforcements. These were Lieutenant Denis, Sous-lieutenant Astier, Aspirants Foucaud, Rey, and de Sibour, and Sergent-chef Fauroux; several of them had recently escaped from occupied France. At 1 p.m. the entire Groupe was assembled in front of two Yaks. The French flag with the cross of Lorraine and the Soviet red flag with hammer and sickle now flew side by side in the centre of the square.

General Levandovitch gave a short speech to the Normandie Groupe in the course of which he summoned in turn the officer pilots who were to be decorated with the Order of the Patriotic War: Commandant Tulasne, Capitaine Littolff, Sous-lieutenants Durand and Lefèvre, and Adjudant-chef Duprat. The decorations for Tulasne and Littolff, who were lost on recent missions and now presumed missing in action, were placed with their personal effects that would be sent on to the Mission in Moscow. The following day at 5.30 a.m. General Levandovitch and Commandant Mirles left for Moscow in the Douglas DC-3, along with the first detachment of fifteen mechanics commanded by Adjudant Morisson.

Numerous training flights were arranged for the recently arrived pilots, who were introduced to the two-seater trainer Yak-7. Durand and Lefèvre were the instructors. In the late afternoon Pouyade and Laurent left on a navigation exercise. Between Soukinitchi and Iouknov Pouyade was obliged to make a half turn for mechanical reasons. Laurent continued alone but did not return; the base anxiously awaited his arrival but received no news of him. A search was mounted for Laurent in the U-2 liaison aircraft, but after an extensive search nothing of him or his aircraft was found. In the morning Normandie took delivery of some additional aircraft that brought its strength up to fifteen Yak-9s. The new aircraft were particularly well cared for and were completely satisfactory. The 1st Escadrille was commanded by Léon and the 2nd by Béguin. Training flights commenced; the newly arrived pilots were introduced to the Groupe's system of training and learned rapidly. Laurent was finally found and returned to base on board the U-2 aircraft, receiving a joyous reception. He had landed out of petrol near the village of Rokonovo in the Koulikovo area, having managed to get his aircraft down on a rough field without any damage. Local soldiers and villagers had received Laurent in a most charming and hospitable manner; the next day when Durand was sent to collect the plane he took along cigarettes and tobacco to thank them all for their kindness.

Over the next few days more training was undertaken, eighty-one hours in all. Lieutenant Jeannel and Sergent-chef de Saint-Phalle arrived to reinforce the Groupe; both had recently escaped from occupied France. A patrol was sent out to reconnoitre the new landing strip that the Groupe was destined for the next day. In the evening all made preparations for the departure. The Yak-9s would carry the mechanics squeezed in the back. Part of the baggage left by vehicle; the most urgent equipment was sent on by an R-5, the sturdy biplane that was used as the Division's work horse. It had an open cockpit and a two-man crew. The same type of aircraft had been used in the Spanish civil war, and later saw service in Manchuria as a reconnaissance bomber. Although the R-5 first went into service in 1930, it gave sterling service right through the Second World War.

On 18 August the Groupe departed for the new airstrip. That day all the cringers (non-flyers) had to fly. Brave doctor Lebiedinsky left on the Yak-7 piloted by Lieutenant Denis. The squadron's two dogs, Zazoute and Boby, previously examined by the doctor and found to be in good health, were to travel in luxury, piloted by de La Poype and Foucaud. At the new base all were received very amicably by the Soviet officers of the regiment and profoundly touched by their attention. After being conducted to the future dormitories the pilots were gratified to see at the entrance to the rooms two magnificent banners bearing the following inscriptions: 'To the brave sons of the people of France who with our valiant allies will conquer the detested enemy.' All were grateful for this cordial gesture of welcome. At dinner in the evening the good cheer, the vodka and the cinema session were an agreeable surprise and much appreciated.

After a night of recovery Normandie was given three missions for the following day. The whole Groupe was detailed to fly protection cover for a large formation of 35 Pe-2s on an important bombing mission but, despite giving close attention, Normandie mourned the loss of one bomber, a Pe-2 shot down by enemy anti-aircraft fire.

During a mission covering ground troops on 21 August, Lefèvre shot down an Fw-190; at the same time Largeau attacked a Stuka and scored some well-executed hits, probably destroying it. The next day during training an accident left one Yak aircraft burnt out on the ground. Normandie was ordered to send some aircraft to a landing strip only 5km from the front; on arrival they were well received by the Soviet officers and men. All day the pilots were on stand-by ready to go into action.

TO SPAS-DEMIENSK

On 26 August the 2nd Escadrille proceeded to the advance base of Spas-Demiensk. In the evening Pierre Pouyade made a schedule of the combat missions accomplished in the week since arrival at the new base. Entered for the two escadrilles in the Squadron Diary were 112 combat sorties. In the course of these missions two German aircraft had been shot down: one Fw-190 by Lefèvre and one Stuka by Largeau. The Stuka had originally been noted as a probable, but was confirmed as certain a few days later by Soviet ground forces. The satisfied smile of the commandant showed that he was pleased with the Groupe's accomplishments. In spite of these missions and the relocation, training continued for new arrivals.

The 1st Escadrille, commanded by Léon, proceeded to the advance base. In the evening of 27 August, after an emergency scramble, two patrols – Léon, Albert, Foucaud and Fauroux – encountered two Fw-190s. Foucaud attacked one Fw-190 and brought it down, but in an excess of boldness continued to pursue it in a dive. The other Fw-190 followed Foucaud and, being in a good position, shot away the upper part of Foucaud's windscreen. Léon, seeing the danger for his comrade, attacked the Fw-190, scored some successful hits and forced the German to disengage rapidly. A good result for the two patrols, but on their return it was discovered that a Yak had crashed and another had bent its propeller on the runway while landing at Spas-Demiensk. The pilot of the latter, Aspirant de Sibour (son of the well-known long-distance aviator), was able to return with his aircraft after a truck had been sent with mechanics to straighten the propeller. Pouyade had flown in the U-2 to the scene of the crash and signalled de Sibour to wait for the truck.

On 28 August the commandant was called to Division and told that the Soviet Army was about to launch a far-reaching attack and would direct its efforts on Ielnia. All morning a continuous rumbling of artillery was heard while Pe-2s and Stormoviks passed by above in imposing waves. During the day patrols ensured cover over the front. In the evening on their return it was learned that the U-2 had left on a liaison mission to the landing strip that Normandie formerly occupied near Kazelsk, with Astier as pilot and Rey as navigator. Pouyade had just been informed that the aircraft had come down near Soukinitchi. The initial information was that Rey had been seriously wounded and Astier slightly wounded. All anxiously awaited further news. During the night Pouyade learned from a telephone call that Rey had been killed and Astier wounded. All were utterly crushed by this news. Pouyade left in the Regiment's U-2 for Soukinitchi intending to find out about Astier and Rey. During his absence the U-2 piloted by Astier arrived, bringing back the terribly mutilated body of poor Rey. The sight of this aircraft returning with the corpse was frightening. The mortal remains were taken immediately to the hospital. Astier explained what happened. Trusting in Rey's navigation, they had arrived by mistake at the German lines and had been welcomed with heavy anti-aircraft fire. Astier had been able to hedge-hop back to the Soviet lines and land near Soukinitchi, his aircraft riddled by shrapnel. Rey had been killed at the rear; the engine was not even touched by the missiles. Astier had been able to return the next day. Rey was buried that evening at 8 p.m. Six pilots carried his coffin of white wood from the hospital to the base cemetery, accompanied by Soviet officers and a duty guard. Before lowering the coffin into the ground Pouyade gave a short and moving speech, very heartfelt, and a salute of honour closed this poignant ceremony. Farewell, poor Rey.

On 30 August 2nd Escadrille left for the advance base. It was a day of magnificent work and Pouyade was radiant. At 6 p.m. all the aircraft were sent out on an important mission to cover a sector heavily bombed by the enemy. Three enemy aircraft were shot down in the course of this mission with a further two probables. Mathis, Béguin and Bon attacked and brought down three Ju-87s. Risso attacked another Ju-87 and probably destroyed it. Another Ju-87 was attacked by Largeau, another probable. It was a day of victories, the best the Groupe had had so far: three definites and two probables, accomplished without loss. The commandant could also report that the Ju-87s did not carry out their intended bombing, for on arrival their formation was immediately broken up. A splendid result without any losses! There was singing and rejoicing in the mess that evening. In the morning the 1st took off for the advance landing strip, but received an order to return. Later that morning two escadrilles were detailed on a covering operation over Ielnia. During the mission a hectic encounter took place with a formation of Ju-87s closely protected by several Fw-190s. Lefèvre and Risso collaborated to shoot down one Ju-87, Lefèvre shot down an Fw-190, de La Poype claimed a Ju-87, Barbier another Ju-87, Albert also destroyed a Ju-87, and two further Ju-87s were severely damaged by Béguin and Mathis. In the five months since Normandie was formed, it had achieved forty-two confirmed victories.

At 2 p.m. a covering mission was required above Ielnia. Ten Yaks were detailed for this operation; almost immediately Béguin returned with his guns jammed. At 3,500m above Ielnia the Groupe encountered more than a hundred Heinkel-111s protected by several groups of Fw-190s. The Yaks got in close and attacked the enemy, and in the course of the running battle five aircraft were shot down. Durand shot down a Heinkel in flames, and some of the crew of five were seen to escape by parachute. Foucaud shot into an Fw-190, which caught fire and exploded in the air. Léon shot up another Fw-190, which went spinning down in flames. Risso and Mathis combined to shoot down one Fw-190, which crashed after going into a steep dive. But Capitaine de Forges and Aspirants Laurent, Fauroux and de Sibour did not return. In the evening the duty officer was informed by telephone that Fauroux had landed at an aerodrome near Viazma and was wounded. At 7 p.m. six pilots took off on a covering mission above Ielnia. Béguin returned once again with guns that were not functioning and was furious. Together with Normandie on the same covering mission were four aircraft of the 18th Guards Air Regiment. During the mission, which lasted 50 minutes, frequent altercations took place with Fw-190s. A group of fifty Heinkel-111s protected by Fw-190s appeared at an altitude of 4,500m, but attack was difficult because the Guard's Yaks were below. Four enemy aircraft were hit and sustained damage.

1ST FIGHTER AIR REGIMENT NORMANDIE

Normandie had won its spurs and the Soviets recognised the Groupe's successful combat missions during the Kursk–Orel campaign. At the end of July 1943 they were formed into the 1st Fighter Air Regiment Normandie. From now on this was to be the Groupe's official title, although it still operated as escadrilles. It was after their part in the hard-fought and victorious battle of Orel during July and August 1943 that the Normandie received the first Yak-9Ts. The previous 20mm cannon had been replaced by a heavier 37mm cannon firing through the hub of the propeller. To allow room for the installation of this powerful weapon, the cockpit had been moved further back along the fuselage. Capitaine J.M. Risso (later Général Risso), recipient of the Soviet Order of Alexander Nevsky, told how the powerful cannon when fired at enemy aircraft caused the Yak-9T to experience a loss of speed. This phenomenon could at times be turned to the pilot's advantage: an aircraft that was landing too fast on short runways could be dramatically slowed by a burst of three shots from the 37mm cannon. Capitaine Risso described the Yak fighter in complimentary terms when he remarked that 'The aircraft's silhouette gave the impression of a great robustness, a solid charger.'

These Yak-9Ts armed with the 37mm cannon were to achieve excellent results against both aerial and ground targets. The Yak-9K, which had an even heavier 45mm calibre cannon fitted, was to prove devastating against enemy tanks and tracked gun platforms. Later in the war even heavier German tanks were to make their appearance on the Eastern Front, including such monsters as the Koenig Tiger with its 88mm gun and the Jagd Tiger with its 128mm gun. But these giants also became vulnerable targets for the Yak-9Ts; at one time it was only the Pe-2 and Il-2 bombers that could destroy these heavy-armoured monsters from the air.

At 7 a.m. on 1 September nine pilots took off on a covering mission above Ielnia. They encountered many patrols of Fw-190s, which resulted in continuous fighting engagements for some 30 minutes. Albert and de La Poype each shot down an Fw-190. When they got back to base it was discovered that Durand and Léon had not returned. A telegram brought good news: Léon had landed on an advance landing strip used by the Guards Regiment and was safe.

Normandie had orders to move to another landing strip. Those who did not leave by aircraft stayed and looked after the baggage and equipment. In the afternoon the commandant went to Katiounka to see the mechanics. Passing through woods he saw a Yak in a clearing, suddenly noticing that the Yak had a 'Casserole blanche' (white nose cone). With great pleasure he realised that it was Laurent's missing aircraft, the pilot affected by his first fight and the endless attention of two tenacious Fw-190s on his tail. Laurent had got lost and was forced to land when low on fuel. At 4 p.m. Schick returned from Viazma in a U-2 with Fauroux, who, although wounded and in a bad way, had succeeded in landing his aircraft intact on a distant landing strip. The next day the squadrons left for the new landing strip.

MOVE TO MICHKOVO

The Regiment departed for the new strip at 10 a.m. Ten aircraft went to Michkovo, which was situated 15km north-east of Spas-Demiensk. The new strip was of reduced dimensions, and badly fitted out, and full of German debris after the enemy had left the place in a hurry only ten days before. Wounded Fauroux left in the hospital aircraft for Moscow; all wished him well. At 1 p.m. eight pilots took off on covering missions above Ielnia. They encountered several Fw-190s, which left hastily before any skirmishes could take place. The commandant returned to Nielej and left again with de La Poype taking Léon in his aircraft. In further covering missions above

Ielnia, Fw-190s were seen but evaded engagement. All day those pilots without aircraft waited with their baggage for the trucks to arrive for the journey to the new base. Finally two trucks arrived. After loading the baggage and cases, the Soviet mechanics, the pilots without planes, and of course the two important non-flyers, the dogs Boby and Zazoute, climbed in. At 9.30 a.m. the caravan got under way over rutted roads, fording rivers without bridges. The trucks crossed the former front line before Spas-Demiensk; the Russian and German lines were 800m from each other. Minefields were everywhere, and along the road into the forest burnt-out enemy tanks and abandoned German corpses were encountered. After four hours of endless bumps they arrived at the Michkovo strip, surprisingly without a puncture en route, having covered a distance of only 20km as the crow flies.

At 8 a.m. on 4 September eight aircraft took off to cover the Ielnia area. The pilots were unable to gain any information on the combat situation as the radio was not working, and the mission leader had to return without having intercepted a formation of Ju-88s that would have been within striking distance had the Yaks been informed by control. At 1.30 p.m. eight aircraft took off to accomplish the previously aborted mission. At 5.15 p.m. six pilots were scrambled to rendezvous south-east of Ielnia, where a formation of about fifteen Ju-88s in three groups were accompanied by several Fw-190s. Lefèvre attacked in a classic dive; he raked with his fire the Ju-88, which burst into flames as a Fritz left by parachute. Largeau selected a Ju-88 and attacked; his first run in hit it full side on, the second attack hit it straight up the tail, at 300m the German by parachute left the crippled aircraft with its engine in flames. Bon and Mathis collaborated in attacking a Ju-88, each making two passes. The German aircraft was crippled, its engine smoking. De La Poype attacked right in front of the Ju-88 and, breaking away, fired on an Fw-190, following it to the ground where he saw it crash in a cloud of pieces. After the battle Léon did not return.

During the day seven new Yak-9s with 20mm cannons arrived. The following day, 5 September, the new Yaks were checked out and allocated to pilots. Stakovitch came from the radio post situated on the outskirts of Ielnia, completely covered in dust and grime. He was the bearer of sad news: Léon was seen from the ground being pursued by two Fw-190s and came down about 6km east of Ielnia. A shell had hit him in the middle of the body, killing him instantly. He was buried on the spot and the exact position would be marked later.

In the evening Denis went to Nielej to convey a Soviet mechanic and did not return as expected, causing some concern for his safety, but he arrived back in the morning in good order; he had been detained in Nielej by a puncture. At 6.30 p.m. seven Yaks took off to cover Ielnia. Some Fw-190s attacked and fired on a patrol of the 2nd Squadron. Mathis, who was hit by an Fw-190, was seen descending by parachute. A pilot of the 18th Guards Air Regiment reported having seen him reach the ground safely inside Soviet lines.

In the afternoon of 7 September the commandant took de La Poype to Viazma in his Yak-9; he would fly back with Fauroux's repaired aircraft. The last days of summer heat seem to push young Boby to precocious impulses towards poor innocent Zazoute.

The following day was set aside for the mechanics to overhaul all of the Yaks. There was still no news of de Forges, Sibour, Durand or poor Mathis, who had parachuted down two days before.

Lefèvre left for Moscow on 9 September in a U-2 with the Soviet liaison officer Kounine. The commandant also left for Moscow in a Yak-9. In the evening Stakovitch returned from his radio post near Ielnia with better news: it seemed that Mathis was wounded and picked up by the Soviets, who were looking after him.

Stakovitch left by car on 10 September to pick up details of and to locate Mathis. Towards 2 p.m. the commandant returned from Moscow with Corot and some cheering service notes from the First Bureau: one of these memos taught Normandie pilots the correct regulation way to dress 'like an American'.

In the morning Lefèvre returned from Moscow with Kounine. In the afternoon the commandant gave a lecture confirming the historic and current importance of the Guynemer citation, which was given to the assembled pilots. They listened attentively to the details of this outstanding ace of the First World War, a pilot who carried out his duties so resolutely and gave his life for France. The facts were well known to every French pilot, but even so the attention of all in the room was impressive. After dinner travelling artists gave a much-appreciated performance of music, singing and dancing.

At 3 p.m. on 12 September there was a regimental parade and presentation of awards by General Litvienenko, adjutant of the Soviet First Aerial Army. Those decorated with the Order of the Patriotic War 1st Class (in gold) were

Capitaine Préziosi, missing in action 28 July, and Sous-lieutenant Castelain, missing in action 16 July. Awarded with the Order of the Patriotic War 2nd Class (in silver) were Lieutenant Béguin and Sous-lieutenant Albert, who were present on parade. Short speeches by the Soviet general were followed by an acknowledgement from the commandant.

The following morning Lefèvre went to Nielej to pick up a Yak-9. Schick left in a U-2 accompanied by the 'doc' to visit Mathis, who was being cared for in a hospital 30km from Moscow. The commandant went to Moscow to see the five pilots who had already arrived as part of the reinforcement detachment of eight from London. He returned that evening with Corot. It appeared that among the pilots only two could join the Regiment as the others were not sufficiently trained: Lieutenant Mourier arrived in Moscow, Adjudant-chef Joire had arrived from Tehran. The commandant was furious and from his looks one could imagine how he must have made his feelings known to the Moscow Mission. During the day Stakovitch left on leave for Moscow in an R-5, taking with him the sad belongings and recent decorations of those who were missing in action. A change of location was imminent; luggage was secured and packed ready for instructions to depart.

By 14 September no move had taken place. A mission to accompany Pe-2 bombers was called for. At 1 p.m. fourteen pilots took off. They met the Pe-2s in five groups of nine; the Yaks and bombers totalled some hundred aircraft. The target was the strip at Borovskoie between Smolensk and Roslav near the railway and 40km behind the front line. The bombing was very successful. Some Fw-190s appeared, but they did not attack. Another successful mission with the same objective was flown at 5 p.m; this time numerous Fw-190s were encountered and many dogfights took place. Risso shot an Fw-190 and watched as it dived out of control, hitting the ground in flames. Lefèvre and Barbier fired together at an Fw-190 and confirmed it was badly damaged. Largeau did not return. Pilots had seen nothing of the results of his combat; they had little hope as the fighting took place some 40km inside enemy lines.

Change of location occurred at dawn on 15 September. The new airstrip was very dusty and without any facilities; it appeared to be covered in pine needles. It was near Barsouki, a region that had been occupied for two years. The offensive had now begun in the sector and all were on the alert. Lieutenant Mourier, a replacement pilot, had arrived late the previous night from Moscow. Towards the village the Normandie pilots saw, enclosed by armed Soviet troops, a large band of Russian collaborators and other traitors dressed in German field grey; they showed great fear as they were gathered up like animals for slaughter, their fate apparently having been quickly decided. It was the ugly face of war, but all understood how the Red Army soldiers must have felt about these Russian traitors in the service of the Nazi occupation forces, traitors who were often involved in fighting and killing of their countrymen. Russians who collaborated and chose to serve in the German Army wearing the hated field grey Wehrmacht uniforms were known as 'Hiwis', and by official Soviet decree were to be executed immediately on capture. The German infantrymen used to have a saying about the Hiwis – 'They only join to wear our boots' – meaning that they joined the German Army to be fed and clothed.

Schick left to replace Stakovitch in the radio post at the front. At 5.30 p.m. eight aircraft took off on a covering mission to the west of Ielnia. Lefèvre, whose guns malfunctioned during the operation, returned accompanied by Barbier after a clash with some Fw-190s.

On 16 September the commandant and Bon went out on a mission to assess the weather over the front lines. Bad weather with heavy rain and an overcast sky had set in. Some pilots went down to the village where they could relax and play cards in long-forgotten tranquillity. At 2 p.m. travelling artistes gave a performance in a vast barn, with songs, comedy, juggling and conjuring tricks, in all a very successful spectacle. After having swallowed dust the day before, all were now wallowing in mud. In the evening the commandant reported a very interesting conversation with local inhabitants: in two years of occupation German troops had effectively occupied Barsouki only for the month of April that year. The rest of the time the partisans had held the region and even twice recaptured the nearest town, Ielnia. The partisan forces behind German lines in Soviet Russia were numbered in tens of thousands; they had direct communication with and received weapons from the Red Army.

At 9.30 a.m. on 17 September, in a scramble to cover the Ielnia sector, twelve pilots took off. Albert and Foucaud surprised two Fw-190s and each immediately downed an enemy aircraft. At 12.30 p.m, in another scramble for the same type of sortie over Ielnia, no enemy was seen. The commandant went to Michkovo, then to Viazma, to transport a very sick Soviet mechanic. At 3 p.m. and 6.30 p.m. the Yaks mounted covering missions over the same area. Pilots could hear Schick's reports very clearly over the radio from his communication post close to the front.

TO FILATKI

Normandie was on the move, with more packing of equipment and luggage. At 1.30 p.m. a mission covered Ielnia, as did another mission at 5 p.m. At 6.45 p.m. the Regiment moved by aircraft to the strip at Filatki with the exceptions of Mourier, de Saint-Phalle and Astier, who stayed to complete training. The rest of the Regiment arrived at the new base at 7 p.m. on 18 September. It was a good, dry evening and most of the crews rested in the open and watched as the night sky was well lit up by Katyushas rockets and the glimmer of fire from the front, while above was the constant noise of aircraft as they droned into action.

The following morning the commandant left at noon with Laurent for the landing strip at Michkovo. At 1.30 p.m. eleven Yaks were scrambled, but they returned with nothing to report. The sector now stretched towards the west, going as far as the Dnieper. The Soviet advance was rolling forward at speed. At 4 p.m. Lieutenant Denis went hunting enemy aircraft towards Barsouki. On the way to Barsouki the commandant had worrying news: de Saint-Phalle reported that Mourier, having left on a training mission in a Yak-1M more than an hour beforehand, had failed to return. At that very moment a Yak passed vertically over the runway; the controller sent up signal flares for him, without success. The commandant took off in pursuit but the aircraft had already disappeared. Suddenly, when all hope seemed lost – the aircraft had now been in the air for over 1 hour and 45 minutes – suddenly the Yak appeared, lined up on the runway and finally landed. The commandant breathed a sigh of relief. According to the mechanics, there were only 2 or 3 minutes' flying time left in the fuel tank. At 5.30 p.m. ten aircraft scrambled and headed for the Ielnia sector. Two Fw-190s were seen above the clouds. The radio car informed that German bombers were in the area; nine Ju-87s were seen diving to bomb. Normandie pilots swooped in to attack. Barbier fired and brought down a Ju-87; Risso and Balcou together brought down a Ju-87; and Lefèvre, de La Poype and Béguin together attacked and brought down another Ju-87. Lefèvre did not return from the battle. At 6.45 p.m. six aircraft took off on a mission for the Ielnia sector, where all appeared quiet. At nightfall at 7.45 p.m., a Yak-9 turned above the landing strip; the controller fired signal flares; the doc, his hands trembling as he held the flare pistol, also fired flare after flare; then the Yak-9 landed in the middle of a firework display: it was Lefèvre. He had pursued a Ju-87 to the edge of the Dnieper, where he saw it come down. Then, after having gone astray, he had landed at Kloutchi on the former emergency runway before returning.

At 10 a.m. on 20 September the commandant and twelve pilots took off. During the sortie several Fw-190s were sighted and engaged. Bon did not return to base. At 3 p.m. ten Yaks were scrambled and sent to the Ielnia sector. During this mission several Fw-190s dived out of the sun, launching a surprise attack on the Yaks. Risso broke away but Balcou was hit and was seen falling in flames. A little after 4 p.m. Bon returned; he had lingered over the sector, lost contact with the patrol and landed near Ielnia. In the evening the Russians, full of goodwill, arranged a house for Normandie with wooden beds where the chaps could stretch out. But soon the roomful of pilots become agitated: bedbugs had taken over. Some brave souls, the tough nuts, stayed put; the rest retreated, led by the commandant, who decided to sleep in the open rather than spend the night with unwelcome guests, so the sleeping bags were placed outside on bundles of clean hay.

At 9 a.m. the following day there was an emergency scramble for eleven Yaks. They spotted four Fw-190s but the Germans decided to avoid combat. News came that Balcou had been brought down and killed at Kniaje-Selo; he had been buried in the middle of the village. The commandant went to Barsouki in the afternoon with Barbier, who brought back the Yak-4, then on to Nielej with Astier, who was to pick up a replacement Yak-1M.

NINE VICTORIES WITHOUT LOSS

At 1 p.m. on 22 September ten pilots and the commandant scrambled. About 30km south-east of Smolensk three groups of Ju-87s were encountered, escorted by ten or twelve Fw-190s. Risso fired a short burst of fire at a Ju-87; trying break away, the German Stuka in panic collided with its neighbour and removed its wing; the two Ju-87s exploded in mid-air. Risso had destroyed two enemy aircraft with one burst of fire. Bon, de La Poype, Béguin and Denis each brought down a Ju-87. Albert brought down an Fw-190, Lefèvre destroyed another. Risso and Jeannel each attacked separate Fw-190s, probably destroying both of them. Barbier damaged an Fw-190 and Jeannel a Ju-87. The commandant, who had manoeuvred with the Fw-190s, was most upset at not having got into a firing position for any of them. Foucaud did not return. The affray lasted only a moment but must have been spectacular; the pilots who were following Risso passed through the centre of a cloud of sheet metal pieces scattered by the explosion of his two Ju-87s.

At 4 p.m. there was another scramble by six aircraft, but they returned with nothing to report. At 6 p.m. a U-2 turned low over the runway; from the ground the passenger in the rear could be seen signalling with his arms. On landing Foucaud got out, looking all muffled up and covered in bandages. During the battle he had brought down an Fw-190, then with his guns jammed he was pursued by another two Fw-190s. He had succeeded in extricating himself and sought to land in U-2 territory, north of Ielnia. On touching down the machine turned over and ended up with its back broken. The Soviets on the ground freed Foucaud immediately; fortunately he only had superficial wounds to the head, a sprained thumb, numerous scratches and slight contusions. The Soviets, who knew of the Normandie Regiment, looked after him exceptionally well and tended his wounds, even dressing his bruises. They wanted to keep Foucaud with their unit and allow him to rest but, faced with his insistence on returning straight away to reassure the Regiment about his fate, a Soviet pilot brought him back in a U-2. This wonderful and momentous day ended with nine victories without a single loss.

Next day the weather was bad; the pilots rested and devoted their leisure time to clearing the sleeping area of bed bugs. Schick arrived back from the radio car stationed at the front.

In the morning Schick left again for the front, the journey lasting hours because of the damaged roads. On 24 September good news came over the radio: the Soviets announced the capture of Smolensk and Roslav. To reflect the victory celebrations the evening meal was enhanced with champagne. The pilots of the 18th Guards Air Regiment made up a choir with accordian. Enthusiasm was at its height when the colonel of the Guards Regiment made a speech, followed by a short and brilliant response from the commandant. The two orators found themselves thrown up in the air by the vigorous arms of the somewhat delirious audience.

The following day was overcast so there was no flying. Some bucolic souls who wished to clear their heads after the previous night went in search of mushrooms.

Next day the weather had cleared a little, and at 1 p.m. a patrol of four Yaks took off to cover the south-west of Smolensk. In an encounter with two Fw-190s, Béguin fired on one, which nose-dived. Then there was an altercation with eight Fw-190s that were attacking some P-2s escorted by

Yaks. Risso fired on an Fw-190 and probably brought it down. Bon fired on two Fw-190s; the first he had swooped on, the second he followed down in a dive but it escaped after hedge-hopping. Béguin fired on an Fw-190 and damaged it. Jeannel was hit during a dogfight but, with his aircraft in flames, managed to escape by parachute. At 3.15 p.m. seven pilots and the commander took off. Four German Bf-110s were spotted; at that moment several Fw-190s came in to attack, but they were quickly seen and achieved no results. In the afternoon the commandant returned from Barsouki accompanied by Lieutenant Mourier, de Saint-Phalle and Astier. Then Mourier, getting into a Yak-9, made a horrifying take-off followed by a hair-raising landing. The drama ended in a field beside the runway. Those watching learned with relief that Mourier had escaped without harm. On take-off his small tail-wheel had collapsed into the end fuselage, blocking the flying controls to the tail. At 6 p.m. six pilots took off and, hedge-hopping, flew over Smolensk. They noticed much damage and observed that some houses were still burning.

The weather was bad again on 27 September. Arriving on the strip, a U-2 ambulance brought Jeannel back. As his parachute had been ripped and torn by bullets during the aerial battle, he had been forced into a brutal landing and badly injured. Picked up by a T-34 tank crew, he was immediately attended by a medic serving with the tank regiment; then a captain from the same outfit took charge, looked after Jeannel, and accompanied him back to the base. The doctor, after examining him, declared he was suffering from concussion. A U-2 ambulance took him to hospital in Spas-Demiensk, from where he would be sent to Moscow. The commandant took off for Moscow with the Soviet political (commissar) officer Lieutenant Kounine. This Soviet officer was kindly thought of by his Normandie comrades, but as the Soviet authorities eventually thought he was not achieving the correct political results he was replaced by a hardline commissar by the name of Kapitan (later Major) Vdovine. This Soviet officer would monitor the political correctness of the ground staff, which would eventually cause great sadness on the base. The Red Army soldiers were allowed to send letters home free of charge, but to gain this privilege the sheet of paper had to be folded in a crude triangle without being sealed in any way to indicate to the postal authorities that the letter was to be delivered free. This unsealed letter was, however, also easy for the censor to read, and any doubtful security or political scribblings could be passed to the commissar for action.

The bad weather continued. Schick went to Division in the U-2. The 18th Guards Air Regiment, which had served alongside Normandie, departed for another landing strip near Borovskoie.

At 1 p.m. on 30 September the commandant returned from Moscow, where he had been discussing the future of the Regiment. He was disheartened by the lack of response from Algiers to the many requests for additional reinforcement pilots. The only sign of the existence of the authorities in Algiers was the memos they sent in ever-increasing numbers – which were to be used only for hygienic purposes. At 3.20 p.m. the Groupe sent up eight Yaks for covering missions over Krasnoie, a town about 50km west of Smolensk. The ceiling was 600m; the low-flying pilots could see villages burning, destroyed as the Germans retreated. On returning, aircraft could fuel up at Borovskoie, which was now in Soviet hands; earlier it had been bombed by the Pe-2s that Normandie accompanied on 14 September. The colonel of the 20th Infantry Regiment, stationed at Borovskoie, put a truck at the disposal of the Regiment, enabling the commandant to make a tour of the base to see the damage. The runway was full of bomb craters; debris from destroyed Ju-87s and Fw-190s lay everywhere. The Germans blew up nearly everything before leaving; only a few damaged buildings were still standing among piles of bricks and scattered debris. It had been a large and organised base, with a nearby hospital and large cemetery. At 6 p.m. a second mission took off, except for de La Poype, Risso and Denis, who had to return with mechanical trouble. Mourier, de Saint-Phalle and Astier spent the next three days training.

The weather broke at 11 a.m. on 4 October. Ten pilots and the commandant took off to give cover for troops on the ground involved in hard fighting around Gorki. The commandant had to land because of problems with the undercarriage. Several Fw-190s were seen but they made off. Pilots landed at Borovskoie to fuel up. The doctor, more aeronautical than ever, arrived with the commandant in a Yak-9. At 1.20 p.m. eight pilots took off to cover 60km west of Smolensk. A layer of cloud hung between 800m and 1,300m. Towards 2,500m a Henschel-126 was encountered, which was immediately fired on in turn by Albert, Foucaud, de La Poype, Denis, Bon and the commandant. Some Fw-190s rallied to defend this foolhardy Parasol-winged spotter aircraft, the 'flying motor scooter'. Albert, Foucaud, and Risso each took them on. Later Foucaud and Albert saw the Henschel-126 burning in a field; Foucaud confirmed that he had earlier seen the Henschel with its propeller jammed. With the rolling Soviet advance, the landing strip was now about 140km from the front line. Another change of location was ordered by Division for the following day.

TO SLOBODA

On 5 October everyone set off for the new base at Sloboda, near Monasterchina. The baggage and mechanics left in three trips by Douglas DC-3; then the Regiment departed, led by General Zakharov, who piloted his La-5. It is a credit to the organisers that scarcely two hours elapsed between Normandie ceasing to be available for missions and its arrival and resumption of operations at the new landing strip. Settling into the former village school, the chaps were very comfortable; the walls were whitewashed and no bed bugs plagued the sleepers. The food at the canteen was plentiful and excellent.

Everyone woke up fresh and rested. A fog had come down and good flying weather seemed definitely compromised. At 3.30 p.m. four Yaks took off on a hunting mission in the sector from Krasnoie to Tatarsk. At 4.30 p.m. another four pilots took off on a similar mission. On return de La Poype reported over the radio that he was having a problem with his undercarriage: only a single wheel could be lowered. Then he started to turn above the runway. The commandant took off to establish radio contact but one wheel was firmly stuck and the other one could not be retracted because of lack of compression. Everyone looked up. Emotions ran high and the doctor was very agitated as he stood on the running board of the ambulance. De La Poype made a last turn and came in at hedge high. The tender and emotional souls thought that this low approach was to let his comrades see him for the last time; others, less generous, said he did it to make sure the ambulance was on site. Finally, de La Poype made a perfect landing and the aircraft was not damaged; only the propeller showed signs of a permanent curve. In the evening there was dancing in the canteen to an accordionist.

At 11 a.m. four pilots took off, hunting over Krasnoie-Tatarsk. An Fw-189 was sighted, accompanied by two Fw-190s. Béguin and Bon attacked and both fired on the first Fw-190, which was left burning on the ground. Béguin fired on the second Fw-190. It was Astier's first combat mission; he was somewhat moved by the experience. At 3.15 p.m. four pilots took off on the same type of sortie, this time encountering no enemy.

At 10 a.m. and 11 a.m. the next day (8 October) similar hunting missions were undertaken, with four Yaks sent out each time. At noon four pilots took off on another hunting mission; above Gorki they spotted an Fw-189 accompanied by two Fw-190s at 2,500m. Albert approached in the clouds at 3,000m; the two Fw-190s noticed him and climbed. Then an attacking and wheeling battle began. The Fw-189 took advantage of the confusion and scuffle to disappear, zigzagging. Albert and Foucaud turned and attacked one Fw-190; Lefèvre and Denis fired on the other.

The next two days were set aside for mechanical activities on the aircraft. When the service work was completed the training flights resumed. A wager took place on Laurent's flight in a Yak-1M; Laurent bet 100 roubles with Béguin that he would bank in fewer than 16 seconds. The commandant got involved and made the same bet, but went up to 20 seconds. Laurent clinched his banking in 14 seconds, this silencing all the doubters! All day four pilots were on standby, ready to scramble. In the evening, the cinema in the barracks relaxed everyone.

On 11 October the aircraft were reviewed. All day four pilots were on standby. The salient event of the day was Laurent's wedding. Commandant Pouyade, in his capacity as registrar, performed the ceremony at 4 p.m. between Aspirant Alexandre Laurent and the Soviet base doctor, Lieutenant Valin. The tricolour was deployed, which impressed the young bride. But her surprise turned to anguish when the commandant applied the official military stamp of the Regiment to the marriage certificate. Learning that General Zakharov wanted to congratulate her, the young embarrassed bride ran off and the lonely Laurent did not see her again . . . until the following morning.

First thing the next day the commandant received the order to send four Yaks to Borovskoie to escort a Douglas DC-3, which was carrying on board Général Petit on a visit to Normandie. Lieutenant Béguin left with his patrol to look for the general. At noon eleven Yaks departed on a mission to cover Lenino–Baievo sector. As soon as they arrived over the sector two Fw-190s appeared but departed swiftly. After staying for about an hour over the area, the Yaks headed for home. On the way back the patrol of Albert, Foucaud and de Saint-Phalle (this was his first battle sortie) was attacked by two Fw-190s and de Saint-Phalle's Yak was hit. Albert saw it flying some 20m from the ground and it did not return to base. Towards 2 p.m. the Douglas DC-3 arrived with its escort of three Yaks. Général Petit, Mme Misraki, two representatives of the Soviet press, two staff officers and Général Petit's secretary disembarked from the aircraft. With them was Aspirant Stakovitch, who was due for posting, and also Adjudant-chef Joire and two interpreters, Adjudant Eichenbaum and Caporal Pistrack. Général Petit brought lots of good news. First of all the promotions: Lieutenant Béguin to Capitaine, Sous-lieutenants Albert and Lefèvre to Lieutenant, Apirants Risso (at last), Mathis and Schick to Sous-lieutenant.

Then came a touching letter of congratulations from Général Valin, which designated Normandie as 'the elite escadrilles among all the elite escadrilles which have ever been part of French aviation'. The evening before his arrival the général had received the second collective citation for Normandie, which gave the personnel of the Regiment the right to wear the 'fourragère' (aiglet or lanyard) in the colours of the Croix de Guerre.

Order No. 18, Award of the Croix de Guerre, citation reads:

During offensive operations carried out in the Ielnia region from 18 August to 4 September 1943, with the participation of sixteen then fourteen and later twelve pilots, the Normandie Groupe in fifteen days of tough battle, accomplished a remarkable task in shooting down twenty enemy aircraft, two other probables and damaging ten while preserving morale despite the loss of one pilot killed and three pilots missing in action. During the period the Groupe totalled 309 war missions, 220.25 hours flying time and were involved in fifty-nine aerial battles.

This citation requires the allocation of the Croix de Guerre with palm.

Algiers, 16 October 1943.
Signed: Giraud

Among the numerous telegrams received, one in particular touched all: the congratulations sent by Colonel Luguet, who had been the air attaché in the French Embassy in Moscow. He was originally responsible for the planning of the (GC3) Normandie expedition to the Soviet Union.

At 3 p.m. a second mission by eight Yaks was sent to the same sector. Foucaud and Albert attacked a group of Heinkel-111s protected by several Fw-190 fighters. The patrol attacked the He-111s then went for the Fw-190s. Foucaud and Albert shot one down. At 5 p.m. the third mission was sent to the same sector. At 8 p.m. everyone was gathered at the 'stalovaia' (canteen). There was lots of atmosphere, the entertainment repertoire was run through, but the major declined to perform his usual doubtful number; perhaps on this occasion modesty forbade him. After dinner the champagne flowed. The commandant proposed a toast to the health of the newly promoted. Général Petit rose and, after congratulating Normandie on its success, he once more celebrated French–Soviet friendship and unity, raising his glass to Général de Gaulle, Marshal Stalin and General Zakharov, followed by a toast to French–Soviet aviation. General Zakharov rose in turn, mentioned the great part played by the Regiment in victories at Orel, Ielnia, and Smolensk, and drank to the health of the heads of the Allied countries.

Just after 11 a.m. on 13 October, a U-2 brought back de Saint-Phalle, who, having been hit by an Fw-190, had his fuel tanks punctured and had to land in a field many kilometres away. His lip was cut as he landed against his joystick, but he had been very well looked after and returned with his lip stitched. At noon a mission of twelve Yaks left for the Lenino–Baievo sector, and the lower-altitude patrols saw action with Fw-190s. In the course of different engagements Risso and de La Poype shot down one Fw-190, and Commandant Pouyade and Mourier claimed one probable. Unfortunately, three aircraft were reported missing. Laurent informed the Regiment that Béguin, shot from behind by an Fw-190, had been obliged to put down, undercarriage tucked up, in a field 10km to the west. But Bon and Denis did not return and nothing was known about them as their action was hidden by clouds. Général Petit and his entourage set off again for Moscow, but this time no escort could be supplied because of a lack of aircraft and the heavy workload involvement. At 5 p.m. a second mission of eight aircraft headed for the same sector.

On 14 October there were no operations first thing, but at 1.30 p.m. eight Yaks took off to cover the same sector. All was quiet. At 4.30 p.m. a further eight aircraft were sent on the same mission. On his return Astier followed his patrol leader to the ground then left and went off into the blue. In the morning information was received that he had landed on his belly at Potchinok in the Borovskoie region.

At 8.30 a.m. on 15 October eight Yaks were ordered up; within 15 minutes the patrol intercepted a group of Ju-88s. Lefèvre attacked one, which broke away with its right engine shot out and headed for the German lines, losing altitude fast. Albert and Foucaud attacked a Ju-88, which was probably downed. Barbier shot another Ju-88 close-up at 20m distance and saw it crash and break into many pieces. After this interception, some Fw-190s preceded the Ju-87 by nose-diving. De La Poype and Risso attacked two of them and damaged both. At 11.40 a.m. a second sortie went up, still in the same sector. At noon they were attacked by four Fw-190s. Albert and Foucaud shot down one and damaged another. Mourier shot one, which crashed beside the one shot down earlier by Albert and Foucaud. Lefèvre fired at another, which left trailing a lot of smoke. Unfortunately, Barbier was not in the squadron when it returned. At 4 p.m. six aircraft were sent to the aid of Yaks of the 20th Air Regiment that were engaged in the same sector. Towards 4.20 p.m. Astier returned, his petrol gauge was at zero and while pumping he had lost sight of the runway and been obliged to land on his belly.

Normandie had been heavily involved in combat sorties for some considerable time, sustaining ever growing losses and injuries, so it came as a respite when on 16 October, after missions carried out between 9.50 a.m. and 4.30 p.m. – three sorties of six aircraft each in the same sector – the Division telephoned to say that no more missions would be demanded of the Regiment because of reduced effectiveness caused by casualties. During dinner the commandant was brought a telegram of congratulations from General Gromoff for the work and results obtained by Normandie since the beginning of the offensive to 14 October inclusive. The doctor departed for the front in search of those who had disappeared and to obtain confirmation of victories. On 17 October information from pilots of the 20th Regiment returning from the front confirmed the deaths of Lieutenant Denis and Aspirant Bon. On his return the doctor confirmed the deaths of the comrades. Bon, attacking an Fw-190, had been killed by another Fw-190. He struck the ground, where his engine buried itself up to 3m into the earth. Bon was laid to rest at Gorodetz (Central Front). Lieutenant Denis, hit by an Fw-190, jumped with his parachute but it did not open and he was killed on impact. He was buried at Kongress. Commandant Pouyade left for Moscow with Soviet liaison officer Kounine.

The doctor brought back confirmation of results of battles fought from 13 to 15 October, as follows:

13 October: One Fw-190 shot down jointly by Risso and de La Poype.
             One Fw-190 shot down by Commandant Pouyade and Lieutenant Mourier.
15 October: One Ju-88 shot down in collaboration by Albert, Lefèvre and Foucaud.

THE KURSK AND OREL OFFENSIVE

One Ju-88, a probable, by Albert, Lefèvre and Foucaud.
One Fw-190 shot down jointly by Albert and Foucaud.
One Fw-190 shot down jointly by Albert and Lefèvre.
One Fw-190 shot down by Mourier.

Aspirant Schick left for Moscow with the U-2 and took with him Astier, who was leaving the Regiment and returning to the Middle East. Schick returned from Moscow on 20 October. He told the commandant that when landing in the Moscow airport he was astounded to see a new Lockheed aircraft in French colours proudly showing the cross of Lorraine and with 'Paris' painted along the fuselage. It was the aircraft of Colonel de Marmier, which had just carried out its first transport link with Moscow. He had other very welcome news: he had brought with him 800kg of provisions sent by Mme Jean Helleu, wife of the French Resident-général in Syria.

Missions started again on 22 October. At 4 p.m. six Yaks were sent up on a protecting mission for twenty-seven Pe-2 bombers going to the front. The following day Pouyade returned from Moscow. He was to go to Algiers the following Tuesday, taking advantage of the 'Paris' plane. There was frantic activity in the regimental office, where everyone had to contribute to organising the documentation that the commandant had to take with him on his journey to Algiers for the 'paper keepers'. Algiers was now the administration centre for postings, pay and promotions; it carried out all the accounting for personnel of the Normandie Regiment. The commandant read a telegram from Général Bouscat which stated: 'Please convey to the Normandie my warmest congratulations. I have made sure our Air Force are well aware of your magnificent exploits, it will I am sure lead to noble emulation among our aviators, with the sole aim of liberating France.'

In the evening of 24 October a grand dinner was held in honour of Commandant Pouyade's departure. Many Soviet friends attended, including Colonel Goloubov of the 18th Guards Fighter Air Regiment. Many toasts were drunk. Colonel Goloubov proposed a toast to Normandie, the commandant in turn proposed a toast to the 18th Guards Fighter Air Regiment. Variations of these toasts were repeated several times, making it a lively evening. In the morning Pouyade departed, taking Corot with him, and the doctor and Béguin left for Moscow. In the evening arrived the official burial papers of Barbier, who had been interred at Ivanovka, in the village, at the foot of a birch tree.

Bad news was confirmed on 26 October, when the burial papers of poor Bon arrived. Mourier, Lefèvre and Pistrack went to plant a named memorial cross on Barbier's grave.

Later in the week the good comrades of the 18th Guard Fighter Air Regiment came to dine with Normandie. As was always the case, heavy drinking had become the expected norm.

Schick returned from Division on 3 November and announced a telegram from the army commander ordering departure further to the west. The ever-moving Soviet front line had once again left the Regiment too far to fly before getting into action. The first flakes of snow made their appearance. Béguin, Fauroux and the doctor returned from Moscow.

THE GROUPE CITATION FOR
THE CROSS OF THE ORDER OF THE LIBERATION

Béguin brought great news which overwhelmed all with pride and joy. By a decree of 24 September 1943, Général de Gaulle awarded the Cross of Liberation to the Groupe de Chasse Normandie. It was the first French aviation unit to receive this magnificent groupe decoration. Béguin also brought a telegram of congratulations from Admiral d'Argenlieu, Chancellor of the Order of the Liberation.

Général de Gaulle, President of the French Committee of National Liberation.

By reason of order No. 7, dated 16 September 1940, instituting the Order of the Liberation.

The Cross of Liberation is awarded to the Fighter Groupe 'Normandie' for the following reason: 'Engaged on the Eastern Front in 1943, under the command of Commander Tulasne, missing in action 17 July 1943, then of Commander Pouyade, has inscribed on its roll of honour from 1 April 1943 to 4 September 1943, fifty certain victories, four probable victories and fourteen enemy aircraft damaged. Normandie has lost seventeen of its pilots, half of its total strength.'

Algiers, 11 October 1943.
Signed: Charles de Gaulle

An ambulance plane had been requested on 6 November to transport de Saint-Phalle to hospital in Moscow; he had jaundice, probably caused by the wartime diet. Towards 10 a.m. an R-5 biplane with a crew of two arrived to take de Saint-Phalle. This gave Mourier, de La Poype and Foucaud an opportunity to go to Moscow. Towards 10.30 a.m. a Douglas DC-3 arrived to take personnel of the Regiment to Toula, where Normandie would have its winter refitting quarters. The Douglas DC-3 having to return to Moscow that same evening, it was decided that, after depositing the baggage at Toula, French personnel would continue to Moscow to celebrate 7 November, the Soviet national holiday, as it was the anniversary of the Soviet Revolution.

PART THREE

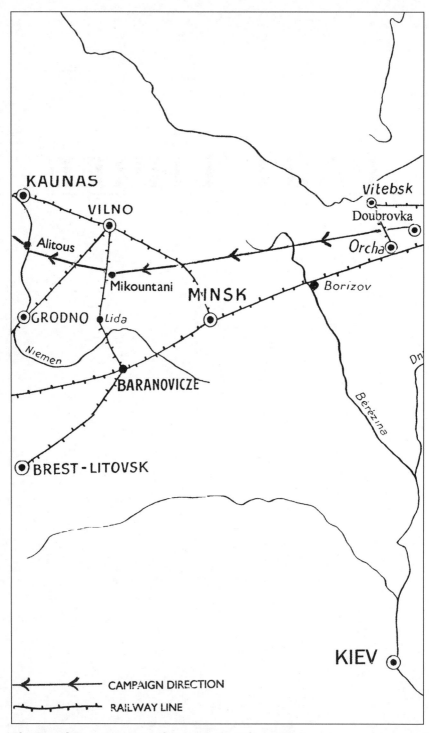

The Second Campaign, November 1943–December 1944.

FIVE

SECOND CAMPAIGN, 9 NOVEMBER 1943–6 DECEMBER 1944

On 9 November Général Petit organised a dinner at the Moscow Arakvi restaurant to celebrate the award of the Order of the Liberation to Normandie. The importance of this most senior Second World War award confirmed how Free France through Général de Gaulle acknowledged the patriotic achievements and sacrifice by the Normandie Regiment. It was a great honour and formed an exceptional milestone in the history of Normandie.

Tea at Général Petit's reception rooms was arranged for 17 November. Several Soviet personalities were invited, including General Levandovitch, Ilya Ehrenburg, J.R. Bloch and M. Ramette. Ilya Ehrenburg was probably one of the most famous journalists of the Second World War, writing articles for the hugely popular and hugely circulated Red Army newspaper *Krasnaya Zvezda* (Red Star). It was after this November meeting with Général Petit that Ehrenburg wrote in his newspaper that 'Normandie are Ambassadors of Courage'. He had a devoted following among the front-line troops, especially the rank and file, who avidly awaited every issue to read his comments and patriotic pronouncements. He made a habit of urging the defeat and punishment of the Fascist invaders; his articles were often bloodthirsty harangues against the German beast and spoiler. One of his sayings, 'Let us slaughter the Fascist beast in his lair', was to become standard official terminology in many Orders of the Day. His powerful rhetoric was to irk Goebbels, the Nazi propagandist, so much that Goebbels falsely accused him of writing an article urging Red Army soldiers to take German women as their 'lawful booty' and to 'break their racial pride'. Ehrenburg wrote in his reply in *Krasnaya Zvezda* to this piece of Nazi propaganda: 'There was a time when Germans used to fake important documents of state. Now they have fallen so low as to fake my articles.' One of his phrases for Germany, 'the Blonde Witch', was to become universally used by the Red Army soldier.

Movement within the Regiment continued with Joire going to hospital on 21 November. Then on the evening of 23 November the doctor, Laurent, Fauroux and two interpreters left for the winter quarters at Toula. Foucaud, who was suffering from his accident in September, had to return to hospital. Several seniors, including Lefèvre, Albert, Béguin, Risso, de La Poype and Mourier, stayed in Moscow. Although they enjoyed the time in Moscow other duties prevailed; they had been invited once again to call on Général Petit as an informal tea had been arranged on 2 December to meet the author J.R. Bloch, who had requested interviews with the senior pilots for his official book on the Normandie Regiment.

On arrival at the winter quarters at Toula on 5 December the Groupe was very favourably impressed. The escadrilles were lodged at the airport, in a completely new building. Mourier took off for Orel on 13 December in a Yak-9, taking as passenger the engineer who constructed the building that was now their living quarters. Over the radio the news was heard that commandant Pouyade had just been named Officer of the Legion of Honour, together with a magnificent citation. The Rosette would be awarded to him at the Summer Palace in Algiers by Général Giraud. Soviet liaison officer Kounine, returning from Moscow, announced that the five Normandie seniors – Capitaine Béguin, Lieutenants Albert and Lefèvre, and Sous-lieutenants de La Poype and Risso – had been nominated Knights of the Legion of Honour (Chevaliers de la Légion d'Honneur), the cause of great joy in the Regiment. Having the news second-hand from Kounine might seem a strange way for senior officers of Normandie to discover that they were to be made knights of France's top honour, but it confirmed that the Soviet and French commands were as one.

Over the next few days some pilot replacements arrived: Lieutenants Cuffaut, Bertrand, and Amarger, and Aspirants André, Casaneuve and Feldzer.

In the evening of 23 December Béguin, Mourier, Albert, Lefèvre, Risso, de La Poype, the doctor and Schick left once again for the short journey to Moscow. On arrival they found no room at the Savoy, so decided to invade the Military Mission at 7 a.m. Resident de Pange, woken with a start, had a comforting breakfast served to them. The général introduced the gallant band to Mme Petit and Mlle Petit, who invited them for lunch. In the evening a grand party was held and hosted by M. Garreau, delegate of France Combatants in Moscow. It was a very successful Christmas evening, at which two Czech officers were noticed wearing their gold stars as Heroes of the Soviet Union; they were well received by all. Then de La Poype, as clumsy as ever, with one deft movement overturned the Christmas tree, which had looked so pleasant and had occupied a place of honour in the room.

Normandie had been ordered to the new airstrip at Toula, well behind the front line, in order to allow training of the recently arrived replacement pilots. During 1943 Normandie had been continuously involved in front-line combat missions and accordingly had suffered casualties including the loss of many pilots and aircraft. The Regiment had ended the year under-strength and with tired aircraft. Toula would promote the opportunity to train the replacement pilots and take delivery of new aircraft. It must also be said that the Soviet High Command had no wish to see this French Air Regiment, with such an excellent combat record and high profile, ground down with losses without the chance to replenish and retrain ready to return to the battle.

At the base in Toula, now under snow, a big, festive Franco-Soviet meal was provided. The opportunity for the new arrivals to get to know the Soviet officers, resulted in good camaraderie and an excellent ambiance.

On 27 December all the pilots who were still in Moscow, as well as the doctor and Schick, got together in the evening at the Arakvi restaurant to celebrate the Legion of Honour of the five seniors. The following day they returned from their Moscow leave. At midnight a supper celebrated the New Year. Very ordinary food but the vodka made everyone euphoric. The brave ones went down to Toula, where a dance was planned.

STARTING THE NEW YEAR

Everyone woke up to the new year of 1944 with a hangover. Traditional wishes were exchanged. The training of the new pilots began. Albert and Lefèvre were instructors on the Yak-7, Cuffaut, Bertrand and André made their first flight in a Yak, and on 6 January Cuffaut and Bertrand flew solo on the Yak-9. The seniors were going to be busy with training schedules as fourteen new pilots were due to arrive on 7 January: Lieutenants de Seynes, de Saint-Marceaux, Verdier, de Faletans, and Douarre, and Aspirants Dechanet, Carbon, Mertzisen, Sauvage, de Geoffre, Penverne, Delin, Martin and Marchi. This would bring the Regiment back to strength after the losses and injuries sustained over the previous months. Toula, being well away from the front, would allow the various escadrilles to work up in safety.

Risso and Laurent left on 11 January to convey two problem Yaks to the factory near Moscow for a complete check and modifications. On take-off Risso made an exhibition that horrified the assembled pilots. It was learned later that his aircraft was not responding to the wing ailerons; Risso did well to get it up and away. In the afternoon a Soviet kapitan from the Division that was not accompanying the two pilots to Moscow informed the commandant that Laurent had had an accident 15km south of Moscow and had sustained a head injury. He was obliged to land on a rough field in the country because of fuel pump trouble. These two rogue aircraft had been causing problems for the Regiment for some while.

In the course of landing in a dual-control training Yak-9, de Geoffre ran out of runway and collided with a stationary La-5 and cut into it, but luckily the startled Soviet pilot, who was sitting in the cockpit awaiting orders before take-off, was not harmed. The decision of de Geoffre to land at this precise place had been taken at the very last moment, which meant that poor Lefèvre, who was the instructor, was not able to do anything to correct this somewhat doubtful decision.

Risso returned from Moscow on 13 January with the news that Colonel Pouyade had just arrived in Moscow with an aircraft carrying 1,500 kilos of various interesting items from his trip; at present these goodies were lodged in the Mission. The colonel also brought good tidings: Albert and Lefèvre had been appointed Companions of the Order of the Liberation.

Training continued. On 16 January Lieutenant-Colonel Pouyade arrived in Toula. The entire Regiment, in particular the seniors, were very happy to see him. He brought intriguing stories about his recent travels and meetings, then told the pilots he was the bearer of good news: the Regiment had been honoured with four collective citations, which gave the Normandie personnel the right and honour to wear the fourragère in the yellow and green colours of the Médaille Militaire.

Air Force, Order No. 14. Award of the Médaille Militaire, the citation reads:

Engaged since March 1943 on the front with the armies of the USSR, the Fighter Groupe Normandie was revealed immediately as an elite unit which by its ardour in battle and its faith in victory performs on this front France's desire to fight. Thanks to the moral force and energy of all its personnel, it had adapted rapidly to the particularly hard conditions of life and work on the Eastern Front. Under the orders of Commander Tulasne this unit, formed entirely of volunteers of an admirable buoyancy and audacity, displayed its expertise of aerial tactics in the accomplishment of numerous hunting missions and battle engagements that it was entrusted with. The Fighter Groupe Normandie distinguished itself particularly in the period from 1 to 7 May. Army Général Giraud Commander-in-Chief has decreed the unit will have the right, from today, to wear the fourragère in the colours of the Médaille Militaire.

Algiers, 12 January 1944
Commander-in-Chief Giraud

On 18 January Béguin, Risso and de La Poype departed for Moscow on leave. Béguin and Risso were particularly good friends, having earlier served together in Britain in RAF 253 Squadron. After Béguin had left Normandie and the Soviet Union in February 1944, he returned to Britain and flew combat sorties with the French 'Alsac' Squadron, and was later appointed Commander of the 'Strasbourg' Squadron. When on a sortie over Belgium on 26 November 1944, his aircraft was hit by an anti-aircraft shell and brought down west of Wesel. Béguin was killed.

On 20 January the colonel gathered the Regiment together in the large hall and wished all a happy New Year. He then presented the Soviet officers and NCOs of the Regiment with the insignia of 'Normandie'. On the occasion of the return of the colonel, the base organised a grand dinner with liquid refreshments for the thirsty. General Terapchine presided. Many members of the Division were present, adding to the spirit of comradely attachment.

On 26 January Capitaine Brihaye and Aspirant Pierrot arrived. Capitaine Brihaye brought a flag beautifully embroidered with the arms of Normandie, which Mlle Perigault had given him in Cairo. The next day saw dual-command flights in the two new Yak-7s that had just been received. Lefèvre and Mourier were the instructors. After three days' training on the Yak-7 the students were let loose on the impressive Yak-9. In the course of his first landing, Carbon was the victim of a curious incident. At the moment when he made contact with the ground, his undercarriage retracted, but with the impact the aircraft climbed again, during which time the undercarriage came down again and the aircraft landed normally. He rolled for about 500m and at the end of this half the undercarriage retracted. All ended well; there was only a slightly bent propeller. This malfunction of the undercarriage would continue to haunt the Regiment and would cause some hair-raising situations.

Training continued and on 1 February solo flights were undertaken by Capitaine Brihaye, Carbon, Penverne and Delin. The following day it was de Geoffre's turn to be let loose and fly solo.

At just after midnight on 3 February, while several players were gathered around a poker table and the colonel was watching the card hands, acrid smoke swept in from the colonel's bedroom and penetrated the card game. They rushed in and found the bed on fire. Blankets, sheets, mattress, pallet, everything was burning briskly. Quick action succeeded in bringing the danger under control. As for its cause, it was believed a cigarette butt that had been forgotten on the bedside table had fallen onto the bed. Just think: a disaster might have devoured all the passionate memos sent by headquarters!

Poker was the favourite card game played by pilots when not on duty. When one of the players did not return from a mission, the seat at the poker table would be taken by another player. Poker was played continuously all through Normandie's service in the Soviet Union; it soon became a floating poker game every time they had to move. In Toula the pilots played the board game Monopoly, using a British version obtained by one of the pilots who escaped to Britain during 1940. The idea of this capitalist-inspired board game being played in the heart of the Soviet Union during 1943–5 seems a little incongruous. The unit's Soviet political liaison officer would have found the whole idea of the game somewhat bewildering and politically incorrect.

Those serving with Normandie received no regular roubles or other cash to spend while in the Soviet Union. Pilots who had originally joined de Gaulle in Britain had their wages paid monthly into a London bank account. Later the accounts for the personnel of the Normandie Regiment would be managed in Algiers, including any new rates of pay gained by promotions or uplifted grades. This is not to say French pilots did not obtain roubles; as always in these circumstances a well-founded system of bartering sprang up. Surplus clothing was always most useful for local exchanges for goods or services.

On 5 February training flights took place in snow. Dechanet was let loose and flew solo. With only two Yak-9s, they managed only ten hours flying a day. The following morning six new pilots arrived: Lieutenant Moynet, Sous-lieutenant Le Martelot, and Aspirants Iribarne, Lebras, Bourdieu, and Bagnères. During the day there was some excitement as eleven Yak-9s with the heavy and powerful 37mm cannons arrived for the Regiment. On 7 February Schick returned from Moscow with the U-2 transformed into a delivery van. He brought some of the provisions brought by the colonel from Marmier. In the evening during a meeting the colonel announced the composition of the three escadrilles:

Commandant of the Normandie Regiment: Lieutenant-Colonel Pouyade.

1st Escadrille 'Rouen': led by Lieutenant Albert, with Lieutenants Cuffaut, Amarger and Bertrand, Sous-lieutenant de La Poype, Aspirants Foucaud, Fauroux, Casaneuve, Dechanet, Sauvage, Iribarne, de Saint-Phalle, Marchi and Bagnères.

2nd Escadrille 'Le Havre': led by Lieutenant Mourier, with Capitaine Brihaye, Lieutenants de Seynes, de Saint-Marceau, Verdier and de Faletans, Sous-Lieutenant Risso, Aspirants Laurent, Feldzer, Carbon, Martin, Lebras and Delin.

3rd Escadrille 'Cherbourg': led by Lieutenant Lefèvre, with Lieutenants Moynet, Sauvage and Douarre, Sous-lieutenant Le Martelot, Aspirants Joire, André, Mertzisen, Pierrot, de Geoffre, Penverne, Monier and Bourdieu.

After a while the crude landing strip covered in pine needles became so bad that on 12 February flights were halted. While rolling and sliding along on the snowy runway, Joire ran a magnificent Yak-9T with a heavy 37mm cannon into a pylon.

SOVIET DECORATIONS ARE AWARDED

In the afternoon of 12 February a Douglas DC-3 landed on the strip carrying on board the Red Army Air Force General Chimanov (member of the Higher Council of the Red Army), together with General Levandovitch and Général Petit. At 1 p.m. a regimental parade was mounted with all present. This took place in a clearing beside the wood; the aircraft were lined up for the occasion, and two flagpoles erected. Behind were the Normandie pilots, to one side the Soviet staff. Having received the generals in front of the parade, Colonel Pouyade ordered 'to the flag'; at this moment there rose simultaneously into a cloudless sky the French tricolour with the cross of Lorraine pendant and the Soviet red flag with the hammer and sickle. The Marseillaise and the Soviet national anthem rang out. Normandie's hearts were gripped on hearing for the first time the Marseillaise in a foreign country. Then the ceremony took place for the awarding of Soviet decorations.

Decorated with the Order of the Red Banner: Lieutenant-colonel Pouyade, Capitaine Béguin, Lieutenants Lefèvre and Albert and Sous-lieutenant de La Poype.
Decorated with the Order of the Patriotic War 1st class: Sous-lieutenant Risso. Decorated with the Order of the Patriotic War 2nd class: Aspirants Foucaud and Mathis and Lieutenant Jeannel.
Decorated posthumously with the Order of the Patriotic War 2nd class: Lieutenant Léon, Aspirant Balcou, Lieutenant Denis, Aspirant Bon, Aspirant Largeau and Sous-lieutenant Barbier.

Finally the parade heard the names of the five seniors who were awarded the Legion of Honour. Général Petit then embraced Béguin, Albert, Lefèvre, de La Poype and Risso. A final Marseillaise and Soviet national anthem marked the end of the military ceremony. The heroes of the festivities were the prey of journalists, photographers and film-makers. A large banquet where the vodka flowed freely gathered everyone together. Towards 4 p.m. the generals boarded a DC-3 for Moscow, but the festivities continued with an evening of dancing with the charming young ladies of Toula, who gave everyone the pleasure of attending. Under the enlightened direction of Capitaine Brihaye, choruses of old French songs brought a little melancholy to the close of the enjoyable celebration.

In the evening of 16 February Capitaine Béguin, former commandant of the 2nd Escadrille, left for the last time. All regretted his departure, which deprived them of an excellent comrade. The doctor and de La Poype were also departing, but they would return after their leave.

In the course of a training flight on 19 February Joire misjudged his height, pancaked his aircraft at 10m, crashed in the snow and nearly flipped over on his back; the aircraft was much damaged, Joire just shaken. Risso left in the evening for Moscow to fetch the 2nd Escadrille's fourth aircraft.

The following morning the Regiment received a magnificent Yak-6 liaison aircraft. In the afternoon the colonel and Brihaye did a double act in the Regiment's new aircraft and tried out this prize addition.

Despite continuing snow, Schick, Mourier, Albert and Lefèvre did their double tutor stint in the Yak-9. With training flights for the new arrivals progressing well, all would soon be ready to bring the Regiment back to strength, ready for a return to front-line duty and action. On 22 February two aircraft piloted by Fauroux and Iribarne did not return; everyone was very anxious. Telephone calls to different bases yielded no news of the missing two. About 3.30 p.m. the colonel decided to search the region with the U-2 and left with Albert. Meanwhile, everyone awaited the return of the searchers: 4.30, 5, 5.30, 6 p.m., with still no sign of the colonel, anxiety was mounting. At 5.45 p.m. Capitaine Brihaye took off with Bertrand and Schick to continue the search. At 6.15 p.m. he landed; no sign of the missing airmen. Towards 8 p.m. a car brought the colonel and Albert back to the aerodrome. Engine trouble had forced them to land in the open and they had been able to regain the base only after more than an hour sledging in deep snow over rough country. Almost at the same time they learned that Fauroux and Iribarne had landed belly-up in the Stalinovgorod region about 40km from Toula. A collective sigh of relief.

The twenty-sixth anniversary of the foundation of the Red Army was on 23 February. General Terapchine came to the landing strip and in a meeting with the colonel and the three escadrille commanders repeated to all assembled what was known already: that incidents such as that of Fauroux and Iribarne were unacceptable. In the afternoon, he telephoned to invite the colonel and the three commanders plus a few senior members of Normandie to the festivities at the theatre for the anniversary of the Red Army. The guests made their way to the ceremony and underwent an hour and a half of politically slanted lectures of which they understood nothing. From the first interval it was a case of who would dare to be the first to slope off for lighter rejoicing.

The following day four new pilots arrived: Lieutenant Charras, Sous-lieutenant Castin and Aspirants Schoendorff and Monier. At 2 p.m. the colonel gathered the Regiment together to drink the health of the newcomers. The colonel gave them the insignia of the Regiment and welcomed them. Then in a brief talk he expressed displeasure and concern at the recent incidents. If such things happened again, the result would be immediate recall of the Regiment.

In the afternoon of 27 February twelve Yak-9s with 20mm cannons were delivered. In the evening Colonel Pouyade and Lefèvre left for Moscow. In the morning Capitaine Delfino arrived; he was to prove to be an excellent commanding officer of Normandie. Training flights continued. In the course of a flight in a dual-seater Yak, Monier, with Le Martelot as instructor, landed a little far out and, after rolling along, came gently to rest on its nose: an accident that would not be too much time or trouble for the mechanics to rectify.

CAPITAINE ALBERT'S VICTORIES REACH DOUBLE FIGURES

Capitaine Marcel Albert, who on 12 February had been awarded the Order of the Red Banner, was achieving an imposing score of enemy aircraft destroyed; his victories had now reached double figures. The Order of the Red Banner, which was suspended from a red and white ribbon, was the most important Soviet honour yet bestowed upon any member of the Normandie Regiment. The Soviet general had congratulated Capitaine Albert with a traditional Russian bear hug. Later in the year General Zakharov would submit the name of Capitaine Marcel Albert for the highest honour, 'The Gold Star Medal, Title: Hero of the Soviet Union'. This simple 24-carat gold five-pointed star suspended from a crimson ribbon proclaimed the recipient as worthy of the highest degree of battle merit. To reinforce the importance of this decoration the recipient was also awarded the Order of Lenin, the Soviets' highest award of resolution.

It was a tradition in the Soviet Air Force that pilots who shot down a multiple number of enemy aircraft or destroyed important enemy installations could be considered for the award of the Order of the Red Banner. In the early days of 1941 the decoration was bestowed upon pilots for destroying three or more enemy aircraft, but as the war progressed the number of enemy aircraft destroyed deemed necessary to earn the Order of the Red Banner increased considerably.

On 7 March the landing strip was at last completely clear of snow, and was used for the first time. On landing Iribarne, who had no hydraulics, came down without flaps or brakes. He was a little long and after a fast taxi along the strip went straight into a pylon. The following morning Colonel Pouyade and Lefèvre returned from Moscow. Colonel Pouyade brought good news: Lieutenants de Pange, Challe and Mourier had been promoted to Capitaine, Sous-lieutenants de La Poype and Le Martelot to Lieutenant. All the promotions dated from 25 December 1943. In the afternoon, General Terapchine came to tell the Regiment that as a security measure the military commander of Toula had forbidden the Normandie pilots to stay in town after midnight. However, if permission was requested 24 hours in advance, they could stay there and if 'assassinated' it would then be legal!

In the course of a training session on 13 March, the Regiment of La-5s, which was now using the same landing ground as Normandie, put two of their fighter aircraft into the dreaded pylons: the fate that had dogged the Regiment recently had now passed to the neighbours. Without any sign of modesty all felt vindicated, including the colonel.

On 18 March Capitaine Challe arrived with eleven new pilots: Aspirants Génès, Pinon, Lemare, Challe, Émonet, Perrin, Manceau, Querne, Menut, Miquel and Gaston. Aspirant Taburet was still in Teheran; an error had delayed his Soviet visa. These new arrivals were destined in principle for a second groupe, which was to be commanded by Capitaine Delfino, but while waiting they did their training with the rest of the Regiment. Capitaine Challe brought to Joire the long-awaited news of his promotion to Sous-lieutenant. Training flights were in progress. At 11 a.m. the colonel was informed by telephone that a collision had just taken place between two Yak-9s about 70km to the north. There was great anxiety. The order was given by radio for all the aircraft to land immediately. Everyone returned except the Joire–Bourdieu patrol. At the moment when the colonel was about to set off to the location of the accident, an ambulance brought back the bodies of the two unfortunate comrades. From the information that the Regiment was able to gather, it seemed that the two aircraft had collided as they came out of a cloud. Joire had succeeded in jumping out with his parachute but on his descent he had been caught by the tail of his own aircraft, which tore off his parachute, and he crashed to the ground. Bourdieu, meanwhile, had dived to the ground in his aircraft. This lamentable and stupid accident dismayed everyone; once again it was the cruel irony of fate that brought death to the ill-fated Joire on the day he had learned of his promotion.

The general, informed of the accident by telegram, arrived at Toula in a Douglas DC-3 for the funeral of the two unfortunate comrades. The funeral took place on 19 March at 3.30 p.m. The cortège moved towards the little wood where the aircraft stood and where a grave had been dug. In front of the grave Général Petit said a few words; Colonel Pouyade bid a final farewell to the two comrades and read the citation. The two coffins were then lowered into the grave where the Normandie comrades would sleep their final sleep.

Foucaud rejoined the Regiment on 26 March after an absence of four months spent in hospital and convalescing. M. de Carbonel, First Secretary of the French Embassy in Moscow, and Mme Lucette Moreau arrived on the same train as Foucaud; they had come in the name of the delegation of France Combattante in Moscow to lay a sheaf of corn on the graves of Joire and Bourdieu. At 1 p.m. the ceremony took place in a snowstorm. Colonel Pouyade thanked the delegation for the gesture and asked all those present to observe a minute's silence in memory of Joire and Bourdieu and all those Normandie comrades fallen in battle. In the evening Albert left for Moscow. The next day Marchi took M. de Carbonel and Mme Moreau up for a flight; they would be leaving for Moscow in the evening. On 28 March, in the course of a training session, Aspirant Émonet landed to the left of the runway and his wing clipped Laurent's aircraft, which was positioning for take-off. As a result both aircraft had their wings damaged and had to be repaired.

On 30 March M. Pierre Cot, who had done much to smooth the way for Normandie's integration within the Soviet military and political administration, visited the Regiment. He arrived in a Douglas DC-3 accompanied by Capitaine Fouchet of the Military Mission and several Soviet personalities, among them the famous journalist Ilya Ehrenburg, a good friend of Normandie. General Zakharov, who commanded the Division at the front, had arrived that morning in his La-5 fighter to visit Normandie. All these persons attended a training session in the course of which they were, alas, witnesses to a horrifying accident. Suffering a hydraulic failure, Monier, with his undercarriage retracted, collided with a tree beside the runway and catapulted himself out. The aircraft struck the ground with its wing, the engine became detached and bounced for 20m, and the plane was pulverised. Everyone assumed that the pilot was in small pieces, but happily he was not. Monier, whose fourth accident of this type it was, walked away with light bruising and a gash to his right cheek. In the afternoon before the departure of Pierre Cot, Marchi gave a dazzling and reassuring exhibition of aerobatics in a Yak-7; Pierre Cot was highly impressed.

Training continued to have its moments of unexpected tension and excitement. On 1 April Schick landed with his undercarriage up; he had simply forgotten to put it down. André and Penverne caused some concern. After one and a half hours of flying they had not landed; the weather was bad, so the worst was to be feared. Eventually they arrived back. It appeared that André, having climbed above the clouds, had got lost and landed on another strip before returning. Albert returned from Moscow, bringing with him Aspirant Taburet, who was destined for Capitaine Delfino's new groupe.

The next day Colonel Pouyade left for Moscow on official business. Capitaine Brihaye and Sous-lieutenant Eichenbaum, fluent in the Russian language, went to Tambov on duty and would return the following day. On 10 April the Regiment received eight new Yaks; two were to be assigned to each escadrille, the future groupe of Capitaine Delfino's counting as one escadrille. From that day and every day, one escadrille had been ordered to be on standby. Four aircraft of the 1st scrambled and took off in 1 minute; four aircraft of the 2nd took off in 5 minutes. The standby status lasted from dawn to dusk. On 16 April news of the Red Army's capture of Yalta filled all with joy. This town on the southern tip of the Crimea had been a summer Black Sea resort for the Czar. In February 1945 it was the site of the 'Yalta Conference' where Roosevelt, Churchill and Stalin made the final decisions on how after the war some countries would be distributed among spheres of influence.

On 21 April, while returning from an exercise, Foucaud did a roll 50m from the ground; ending up on his back, he tried to right himself but sadly the aircraft crashed into the ground and poor Foucaud was killed. At 6 a.m. the coffin containing the remains of the unfortunate comrade was carried by the pilots to the edge of the wood, where he was buried beside Joire and Bourdieu. At the grave Colonel Pouyade said some very moving words recalling Foucaud's life: 'A great Frenchman, a great pilot, a great hunter.' That same sad day a Stormovik leaving the runway ran into one of the standby aircraft of the 1st and seriously damaged it. During lunch there was a great commotion as anti-aircraft fire opened up; the Yaks were now on an alert ready to scramble in what could not be filthier weather. The Toula batteries fired; flashes and shrapnell fell on the runway. The standby pilots were forced to shelter under the wings of parked aircraft. In the evening Mourier, Lefèvre, Risso and Schick went to Moscow on leave. On 25 April Charras, having lowered his undercarriage, noticed that the mechanical indicator had remained in the retracted position. He assumed that only half of his undercarriage had descended and retracted the whole, hit the runway and collided with a vehicle on the edge of the strip.

On 28 April Lieutenant-Colonel Pouyade created the 4th Escadrille, 'Caen', commanded by Capitaine Challe. Brihaye and Pistrack left in a Yak-6 for a destination 100km from Toula to pick up two Russians who had drunk caustic soda mistaking it for vodka. Two others died outright. Drinking to excess was prevalent among the ordinary Red Army men; they would try any spirit available to quench their thirst for alcohol, often with dire results. A technical commission came to check over the equipment before the departure for the front; it recounted marvellous things about the new Yak-3.

On 4 May those on leave came back from Moscow and brought with them de Pange and de La Poype, returning from leave in Cairo. They announced that the doctor, returning from London, was in Moscow as well as Capitaine Matras and four other pilots. Through him the pilots learned of great news obtained from sources in London: Derville was alive and a prisoner of war in Germany.

On 6 May twenty new Yak-9Ts with 37mm guns were delivered. On arrival one of the ferry pilots lost speed and crashed the aircraft at the edge of the runway. The rate of accidents happening on this training base, although worrying, did not exceed that in other training areas or indeed other air forces. Even under the most secure training control, accidents and malfunctions had to be expected. After the Second World War the RAF published a list of all aircraft written off in accidents; it ran into many hundreds.

On 7 May Mahé and Risso teamed up for a patrol. They encountered enemy aircraft and their determined attack stung the Germans, who became very active but then decided to make their escape. A single Yak-9T with a 37mm gun arrived to replace the one that had been damaged the previous day by the Soviet ferry pilot. Another Yak-9 with a 20mm gun also arrived. The four Normandie escadrilles were now up to strength and complete.

Capitaine Matras, Lieutenant de La Salle, and Aspirants Bayssade, Versini and Lorillon, destined for Capitaine Delfino's groupe, arrived at Toula. The doctor returned from his leave in London. At midday the pilots met and were given information about the sector of the front that they were to occupy. On 11 May de Seynes and Bagnères went to hospital in Toula to get rid of a tapeworm. Two days later Eichenbaum left for Moscow taking the pilots' surplus baggage, including that of those listed as missing in action. De Seynes and Bagnères rejoined the Regiment having won a stunning victory over the tapeworms!

On 14 May there was some excitement on the base. In the course of the morning's flight, a Stormovik, supposedly impeded in its landing by Capitaine Challe's aircraft, crashed to the ground. The wings were useless, the crew undamaged. With training of the new pilots completed and the Regiment with a full complement of pilots and aircraft, the 1st and 2nd Escadrilles performed a successful demonstration on the morning of 16 May. They made sorties of twelve and eleven aircraft. Normandie now felt confident and ready to enter the fray once more.

On 19 May there was a visit to Tolstoy's house, only a few kilometres from Toula. The Germans spitefully burnt down this historic place in their retreat. The commandant and pilots enjoyed a lovely walk in an enchanting setting. The colonel wrote suitable words in the visitors' golden book at the house. They saw Tolstoy's tomb, where the Germans had buried eighty of their own; the Soviets had just exhumed and transported them to other places. The retreating invaders had sawn through the fruit trees a metre from the ground in an act of vandalism. A vocational school opposite the Tolstoy Museum had been burnt down and the village destroyed. The museum's two caretakers, who spoke very correct French, had done their utmost to replace the objects that had been misappropriated by the Nazi barbarians. The destruction of dwellings and local facilities and even the cutting-down of fruit trees were standard vindictive practice of the Germans whenever they were forced to withdraw from a village or town they had occupied.

On 20 May Général Petit came to inspect the Regiment before its departure for the front. The 2nd Escadrille carried out aerial antics to impress him. Risso and Lefèvre left for Moscow as delegates to the Anti-Fascist Congress. These two senior officers were well thought of by the Soviets for their battle attainments; both had achieved considerable scores, so the commandant considered that these two officers should represent France and Normandie at this politically important conference. Meanwhile, there were feverish preparations for departure, with fond farewells to the young ladies of Toula amid floods of tears, and drinking on the base at midnight.

At 7 a.m. on 25 May General Zakharov arrived in his La-5 fighter and told the commandant that the Regiment would leave in the morning. At 10 a.m. they took off from Toula with 15-minute intervals between escadrilles. Their destination was Borovskoie, where the Regiment gained an idea of the destruction carried out by the Germans as they were being forced out; they found piles of ruins at the base and the village had been dynamited. The colonel and the escadrille commanders returned after having reconnoitred the battleground at Doubrovka. The Regiment moved in and everything went very well, it had a good impression of the base, with its proper quarters and good canteen. Here Normandie would start combat missions in what was to be known as the 'New Fighting' Second Russian Campaign.

SIX

'NEW FIGHTING' SECOND CAMPAIGN

The training of replacements was complete and Normandie's 'New Fighting' Second Campaign began. The Regiment was operating for the first time with a complement of four escadrilles, all fully equipped with new aircraft. Their additional hitting power now included twenty newly delivered Yak-9Ts, each armed with the potent 37mm heavy cannon. By the end of the year the Regiment would have 200 confirmed victories and their aces would have been decorated with the highest French and Soviet honours.

On 26 May the 4th Escadrille was on standby and made the first sortie, scrambling to chase some Ju-88s. The patrol comprised Capitaine Challe, Querne, Pinon and Perrin. The 1st and 3rd went to reconnoitre the sector. It had been decided that these sorties were to be carried out twice, as this would allow all the pilots to participate and gain immediate experience. The 1st Escadrille noticed in the distance some Fw-190 bombers, but they were too far away for an interception. In the evening, by trucks they reached by means of a badly rutted road 'their' village, which was 1km from the base. The escadrilles settled into their respective quarters and made them as comfortable as possible. The first night was spent in bug clearing. The regulars comforted the new ones by announcing that in the future the bites would no longer wake them!

The next morning the 3rd was on standby cover ready to scramble; this happened three times during the day. The first mission, by the Challe–Miquel and Mertzisen–Monier patrols, covered the front. Four Yaks undertook the second mission, then, 5 minutes later, four others undertook the third. A call warned control that three bombers had been sighted; two were confirmed seen, but at such a distance any attempted pursuit would have been fruitless. Shortly after the enemy aircraft were identified the clouds closed in and the two patrols landed.

The weather was fine on the Whit holiday of 28 May. Sixteen sorties were undertaken. Lieutenant-Colonel Pouyade, Lieutenant Lefèvre, Aspirant de Geoffre, Lieutenant Douarre, Aspirant Bayssade, Lieutenant Sauvage, and Aspirants Pierrot and André carried out a reconnaissance mission over the sector. On seeing his fuel gauge fall to zero, Lefèvre decided to return to base, but at about 10m from the ground his aircraft caught fire. He crashed the aircraft into the ground, immobilising it within a few metres. Unfortunately, petrol fumes accumulating in the cockpit had soaked his clothes. Lefèvre managed to get out of the aircraft on his own, but was obviously badly burned on hands, face and legs. At 3 p.m. the Yak-6, piloted by Capitaine Brihaye, took off for Moscow carrying Lefèvre, the doctor, Lebiedinsky, and a Soviet nurse. The departure of Lefèvre was to be a great loss for both his friends and for the Regiment of which he was one of the pillars. The 4th Escadrille carried out sector reconnaissance; the 1st was on standby. Shortly before Lefèvre's accident, fire had taken hold of one of the huts in the village serving food. Helped by the wind, three other huts quickly caught fire; with great difficulty the men on the base, including those of Normandie, managed to limit the fire damage. Capitaine Matras now took command of the 3rd.

By 29 May life at Doubrovka had got organised. On a day with fine weather with strong northern winds, the 2nd was on standby duty at 3.45 a.m. but did not need to take off. Escadrilles 1, 3 and 4 made two sorties with six aircraft. In the course of one of them Capitaine Delfino pursued two fighters which rushed west, crossing 60km into enemy territory. At a distance of 300m the pilots noticed that they were Yak-9s. Kapitan Kounine of the NKVD thought that they were Germans flying captured Yaks, as it was known that the Germans had got their hands on some Yaks that had come down behind enemy lines.

The 2nd rejoined its new base at 9 a.m. The base at Izoubri was hidden coquettishly in clumps of pine trees but infested with mosquitoes. At 8 p.m. General Zakharov and Colonel Orlof studied with Colonel Pouyade the measures that needed to be adopted to get the best out of the Regiment's work in the sector. The runway was rough and battered because of the poor state of the landing surface. Aspirant Bagnères and Miquel each damaged a propeller while taxiing along the strip. The 1st Escadrille diverted its audience on the ground with a humorous brawl on the radio between 'Muche' (Bertrand) and Cuffaut. The latter, being unable to catch the control instructions, complained that Muche was talking too quickly, but Muche made the Russian sky resonate with his Burgundian Rs and continued on his way. Soviet anti-aircraft fire brought down a Heinkel-111 to the south of the sector at 9 p.m.

On 30 May the 4th was on standby. The 1st Escadrille sent out two patrols; Lieutenant Bertrand, Aspirants Casaneuve, Iribarne and Marchi executed a reconnaissance mission over the sector and above the German lines. Shortly after take-off Iribarne experienced some mechanical trouble and returned to base. He was a little short of the runway and tried to increase the engine speed, but it did not respond and, with his undercarriage still up, he landed heavily 300m beyond the runway. Iribarne's face was injured and he had to spend several days in the hospital. The other three aircraft continued their mission and were caught by light enemy anti-aircraft fire 400m above the lines. Aspirant Marchi lost his leader and landed on a nearby Stormovik landing strip south of Smolensk, returning to the base a little later.

The next morning clouds were drifting at 100m. The 2nd and 4th flew short missions, then the weather closed in. The arrival in the evening of travelling entertainers was a pleasant surprise. A great artistic performance was announced for 8 p.m. in the village hall. With the help of bad weather, all Normandie attended. Due to lack of space some spectators made themselves comfortable on the stage and even began the show while waiting for the lights to go up; the songs by Laurent were much applauded. In the hall the general's wife was much admired. Finally everything was ready. 'Boum' (Eichenbaum) translated the first part of the show, consisting of poems about Stalingrad. The second part comprised Russian songs, music and dances. In spite of the limits and lack of space, the show was a success. The troops of the regiment of Border Guards fired all with enthusiasm with their liveliness. All in all it was a very good evening. Afterwards the 1st organised a game of poker in the mess.

A STORMOVIK IN A FRIENDLY FIRE INCIDENT

The 1st Escadrille was on standby on 1 June. Numerous clouds lay towards the east, but the pilots of the 1st were ready, sitting in their aircraft awaiting any Germans who might come to spread their wings in the immediate sector. From 8 a.m. a group of Ju-88s flew over the Dnieper, but disappeared very quickly towards their own lines. Two patrols took off without making contact with them. In the afternoon the Soviet Polkovnik (colonel) made a visit, followed by three pilots of the 4th who ran after his shadow. His visit had been reported by the officer of the day, but this was 20 minutes after he arrived! Bertrand dreamt the previous night of the He-126 that he hoped to bring down very soon, if he did achieve this it would not be his first as he had already downed three in the Battle of France. During this time a mass of official memos had been in the process of production in the Zemlienka (dug-out bunker), destined to increase the efficiency of the standby patrols. The serious training of the young ones was about to begin, to their great joy. The U-2 had gone to fetch Risso from the 2nd Escadrille's ground. Service finished at 10 p.m; and despite the fatigue of the day the room of the 1st was transformed into a poker den. Life in the village was very monotonous. Widowhood locally had begun to make itself felt, but the pilots' pretensions in this matter seemed to decrease at the rate of their advance to the west!

The next day the 2nd was on standby; the pilots rose for duty at 2 a.m. Four patrols, despite desperate appeals over the radio, could not intercept the numerous 'pointy ears' (Germans) who were crossing the lines at high altitude. But, not despairing, the patrol of Lieutenant de Seynes and Aspirant Lebras took to the air and, after an intrepid course towards the buttocks of the invisible 'Fritz', spotted two aircraft at low altitude. Listening only to their courage and taking advantage of the altitude, the pair of intrepid aviators launched themselves at their prey, which they suddenly identified as being friendly. But all was not over, for the machine-gunner of one of these famous Stormoviks, seized by panic, opened fire on one of the Yaks and then, judging the affair a little too serious, left his aircraft for more hospitable places by parachute! Having landed safely near the landing strip, the machine-gunner was taken to the base by the service jeep. There he swore that a brutal manoeuvre by the Stormovik pilot, to his surprise, allowed him to know the joys of a parachute jump.

A double patrol of the 1st Escadrille went up at 9.50 a.m. A little later an He-126 was recognised over the lines, but as the German pilot had completed his mission of making a visual study of the area, he disappeared. A large group of German aircraft were spotted; a double patrol on standby took to the air but did not make contact. Through the calm afternoon the pilots waited, but the ops room was silent. At 6 p.m. a triple patrol went up but encountered nothing. At 9 p.m. the officer of the day returned to ground in the U-2.

On 3 June the 4th was on standby, and the pilots were at their post from dawn. The weather was overcast, the ceiling low and falling. Those patrols out hunting returned without seeing any enemy. The weather deteriorated, and rain fell on the standby patrol still waiting on the ground without taking part in any action.

The 4th was on standby again the following morning. The weather was foul, with drizzle. Nevertheless, in the morning a Yak-6 left for Moscow piloted by Capitaine Delfino with Commissar Kapitan Kounine and the Russian-speaking Eichenbaum as passenger. At 6 p.m. a wide rift opened in the cloud, and at 6.15 p.m. an Me-110 came in from the west, passed vertically over the runway at 5,000m and veered towards the north-west. Since no report had reached the control dug-out, the standby patrol waited in vain for an order to take off. But the Bertrand–Marchi patrol that was preparing to leave on a hunting mission activated its departure and took off after the Me-110 intruder. Unfortunately, Marchi's patrol was forced to abandon the chase because of a serious fuel leak and returned after 25 minutes of flying.

On the morning of 5 June the weather was overcast, the ceiling at 200m, with rain. There were no missions until 3 p.m. At 3.10 p.m. the standby patrol of Bertrand, Aspirants Casaneuve and Marchi took off after two Fw-190s reported in the region to the north, but returned without result after 30 minutes. Towards the end of the evening the weather broke; the ceiling was at 3,000m with windows in the clouds. At 5 p.m. a patrol of the 3rd comprising Capitaine Matras and Aspirant de Geoffre took off on a hunting mission. Capitaine Matras returned alone at 6.10 p.m., making everyone anxious. On landing he informed the Regiment that de Geoffre left the patrol having been fired on by anti-aircraft fire at Vitebsk. His comrades waited and hoped it was nothing serious. At 6.15 p.m. Le Martelot and Monier carried out a second hunting mission, returning at 7.45 with nothing to report. Towards midnight a dance was organised at the officers' mess; it was a great success. The Don Juans of the squadrons renewed their attacks on the pleasing blondes of the technical section – perhaps hoping to score.

REJOICING AT THE ALLIED LANDINGS IN NORMANDY

On 6 June the 2nd Escadrille was on standby. Towards 5 a.m. a magnificent interception was spoiled through a mistake by the tawny-haired telephonist, who had piled up messages without communicating them to the drowsy officer on standby duty. Attracted by the noise, the latter finally left the control post to witness the line of enemy aircraft reported. At 6.40 a.m. Division requested protection missions: the serious business was beginning. The standby 2nd Squadron stationed at Izoubri was called up urgently and landed 5 minutes later in Doubrovka to await an Il-2. This expected aircraft got lost, mistook the strip and finally arrived three-quarters of an hour late. At 7.30 a.m. a Pe-2 heaved into sight; a little hurried in the landing, it overshot the runway by quite a margin and went into the soft, wet ground. Finally, at 8.40 a.m. the Il-2 took off, protected by a patrol. After ten minutes mechanical problems forced everyone to land. At 9.30 the Pe-2, now unstuck and lifted out, took off and reached an altitude of 4,000m to photograph Baranovicze-Bogouchevskoie. It was protected by a double patrol. The mission lasted for 35 minutes and proceeded without incident. At 10.50 the Challe–Querne–Pinon–Perrin patrol took off and gathered up the Il-2, which had returned to the strip and was rushing towards the lines. The mission was to protect the Il-2, which would be taking photos at an extremely low 20m, following the railway line Orcha-Vitebsk. The mission lasted 35 minutes. The pilots returned from it somewhat excited. They had wandered at 400m above the German lines and had encountered one aircraft about whose nature there was some conjecture. The old hands agreed it had probably been an Fw-189, which on a protecting mission was wise to abstain from engaging.

At 3.30 p.m. the incident of the day exploded as twelve Fw-190s attacked the station at Krasnoie. Mourier took off with his patrol – Brihaye, Martin and Versini – and made contact with the Fw-190s, which dispersed without a result. The patrol of Verdier, Delin, Risso and Laurent arrived to the rescue; only Martin had been able to fire. Both patrols landed after 45 minutes of flying. Shortly afterwards, Lieutenant-Colonel Pouyade came to the strip at Izoubri by jeep to meet Colonel Stalin, the son of the Commander-in-Chief of the Soviet Armed Forces, Marshal Joseph Stalin. At the time the pilots were told nothing of this historic meeting between Pouyade and Colonel Stalin; later all were saddened to learn that this only son of Stalin had been captured during combat. He was to die at the hands of the Nazis in a prisoner of war hell camp, one of 2.3 million Red Army prisoners to die in German captivity. At 7.30 p.m. a patrol took off and landed after 35 minutes' flying without incident.

A memorable event left its mark on 6 June: the opening of what the Soviets would term the long-awaited 'second front' with the Allied landings in Normandy. The invasions of North Africa and then Italy had taken place earlier, but did not appear to count in the Kremlin as 'second fronts'.

On 7 June Commandant Pouyade, Mourier, Albert, Sauvage, de La Poype, Risso, Fauroux and Laurent in a U-2 reached the landing strip at Smolensk, where a Douglas DC-3 was waiting to take them to Moscow for a funeral service. The telegram from the Military Mission was confused and the chaps supposed that it referred to a funeral service in Moscow of comrades Bourdieu, Joire and Foucaud, who were killed at Toula. Towards 8.30 a.m. the standby 4th Squadron took off to escort a Pe-2 that had orders to take photographs above the lines near Vitebsk. The mission was successfully accomplished. Three times the standby escadrille took off to pursue imaginary bombers. At 9 p.m. a Douglas DC-3 landed bringing the comrades back from Moscow. The news they brought crushed everyone. Their dear comrade and brother-in-arms, Lieutenant Lefèvre, who through his qualities as hunter and leader, his numerous victories, and his total self-sacrifice had carried to such heights the fame of the French cockades, had succumbed to his burns, being attended to at his last breath by Capitaine Delfino. The Regiment, aviation and France had lost a great patriot; the sadness felt by all was exceptionally deep. But there was some good news: Aspirant de Geoffre rejoined the Regiment. Hit by anti-aircraft fire at Vitebsk, he had landed on his belly deep in the country and survived uninjured.

On 8 June, as usual when the 3rd was on standby, the weather was rather bad, but it cleared quickly. German aviation was showing signs of great activity all along the front between Vitebsk and Orcha. Unfortunately, Soviet reconnaissance had not yet been carried out, leaving gaps in the operational intelligence. Towards 1 p.m. a standby patrol took off to protect a sensitive position at Serokorenie. To the south-east of the area some Me-110s had been spotted, but they quickly headed for their lines. At 4 p.m. another patrol took off to protect the same position. After patrolling for a while, it was directed to Roudnia, where some Fw-190s had been spotted and where a patrol of the 18th Guards Air Regiment also found itself undertaking a similar mission.

On 9 June the 1st was on standby. At 7.15 a.m. a patrol took off after sighting a Ju-88, which they could not engage. At 3.15 p.m. there was an emergency scramble, which seemed to be serious. The standby patrol took off and landed after an hour. In the evening Bertrand went for a spin in the

Yak-6; he was training for a highly confidential mission with which he would be entrusted the following day. Several senior members – Commandant Pouyade, de La Poype, Schick, Mourier, Risso and Albert – appeared on the strip in their parade uniforms, then proceeded to the base of the Regiment's close comrades, the 18th Guards Air Regiment to attend the funeral of Guards Lieutenant Arkhipov. This was a sad affair made worse by the fact that Lieutenant Arkhipov had been shot down during a friendly fire incident. So many of the 'top guns' of Normandie made a point of attending the funeral of this Soviet pilot because one of their own, Aspirant Challe, had mistaken the Soviet flyer for an enemy and shot him down. These accidents of mistaken identity took place in the heat and confusion of combat, but when they happened to a known comrade hearts were especially heavy.

The return of the three Yak-9s and the U-2 from the funeral was accompanied by a great launching of flares. All partook of a welcome 100 grams of vodka (though some felt it could have been more), but still it rounded off the sad day with a little compensation.

On 10 June 2nd Escadrille was on standby. The confidential mission was revealed when Bertrand took Mme Zakharov to Moscow in the Yak-6; Marchi also took his place in the aircraft for support and a chance to see Moscow. Jeannel accompanied them as 'guide'. The day passed in perfect monotony. The Yak-7 took advantage of the calm to take to the air. The next day the 4th was on standby. An emergency take-off by the double patrol of Capitaine Challe had no result; the Yak-6 returned from Moscow; and there were some training flights. All awaited news of the Allied landings, the Soviet comrades were overjoyed at the second front opening at last. On 12 June the 3rd Squadron was on standby, with uncertain weather. The only activity of the day consisted of finding a means of transport between the mess and the strip; the motorised 'tombereau' (tip-cart) had carried out sixty trips. At the very moment when Igor Eichenbaum was finishing or thinking of finishing the Normandie diary, an He-126 was signalled in the immediate area. A patrol took off at 8.45 p.m. and landed 40 minutes later, with an empty bag.

On 13 June 1st Escadrille was on standby. Enemy reconnaissance aircraft were much in action; then there was an emergency scramble and two patrols took off. Enemy activity intensified towards 9 a.m.; orders came in to undertake a patrol at 5,000m from Roudnia to Izoubri. An He-126 and a twin-engine machine were identified over the lines, but lost from sight on account of very poor visibility. On the roads from Smolensk to Orcha and Vitebsk much activity was noticed; trucks, tanks, guns and other heavy equipment were being transported, the prelude to a great Soviet offensive in the sector for which Normandie would be required to provide cover. From 5 a.m. on 14 June the 2nd assured a permanent presence at 5,500m between the landing strip, the Dnieper and the front line. Towards 10 a.m., this presence having ceased on orders of the Division, German reconnaissance aircraft were very active. A double patrol took off headed by Risso and missed a Ju-88, which was imprudent enough to circle above the strip with a trail of condensation. The 3rd and 4th Escadrilles carried out three fruitless missions. The following morning the 2nd had a busy time carrying out twelve covering missions; then the 3rd carried out four more. The chaps of the 1st were told that vaccinations would be administered. Albert at the front of the queue made a nervous joke to the doctor, who totally ignored it as he gave the injection with medical determination.

In the evening Colonel Goloubov of the 18th Guards Air Regiment shot down a Bf-109 and then within minutes a Ju-88. The pilot of the Bf-109 parachuted down inside Soviet lines. The all-action General Zakharov pursued him in the U-2 and took him prisoner. The German for some strange reason was wearing civilian trousers. He implored his captor not to shoot him. It might seem strange that a captured German airman should plead for his life. This enemy pilot may have felt he could be guilty under a Nazi directive that anyone bearing arms against the Reich while wearing civilian clothes could be considered beyond normal military justice and executed. The knightly tradition of First World War air combat had not survived on the Eastern Front. Air combat had become a ruthless type of warfare; the Germans had on many occasions strafed and killed Soviet pilots after they left their burning aircraft, while they were vulnerable and swinging beneath their descending canopies. This was illustrated by Alexander Pokryshkin, Ace of some fifty-nine victories and commander of an illustrious Guards Fighter Air Division, when he reported: 'In the morning we received a phone call telling us that the pilot Ostrovskij of the 16th Guards Fighter Regiment was interred near a hamlet on the Kuban. Enemy fighters had shot him down while he was returning home. Ostrovskij managed to get out of his burning aircraft but was killed by a burst of German aircraft fire. I was upset. How many times had I shot down a Messerschmitt and seen the pilot bale out. But never had I thought of shooting him.'

The fine weather continued and the 4th carried out six covering missions. Photographs were taken of the Regiment, the escadrilles, the pilots and the mechanics: amateur photographers were numerous. In the evening they enjoyed dancing to the sound of the accordion at the canteen. Rumours circulated that two additional fighter groupes would soon join Normandie.

On 17 June heavy rain prevented flying. Engines were overhauled in preparation for the expected offensive, for which about 600 Yak and La-5 fighters and 400 Il-2 bombers were assembled between Orcha and Vitebsk. For more than a year Normandie had been in action on the front and for more than a year the Regiment had been following the steps of the 'Grand Armée': Polotniani-Zavod, Ielnia, Smolensk. During the afternoon the runway unfortunately grazed the propeller of the Yak-9 taking the colonel to Moscow; this time nothing was said.

In the evening of 21 June Normandie received orders to carry out two covering missions the next morning protecting Pe-2s on reconnaissance missions over the lines and at the same time they intended to transport some fresh vegetables to the isolated Soviet infantry. Protection was also required for Pe-2s going to bomb Borizov, an important airstrip 120km behind the German lines. These two sorties announced the forthcoming offensive. The following day would be the third anniversary of the German invasion of the USSR, ensuring that a major action against the enemy would take place. On that day the great offensive would begin that in three weeks would lead the Red Army to Poland. It has been said over the years that Orcha and Vitebsk are the gates of Moscow and likewise the gates of Berlin. In the morning the first of these two missions took place. At 7 p.m. eight aircraft of the 4th Escadrille and four aircraft of the 3rd were protecting twelve Pe-2s. The Germans were pulling back fast and had abandoned their once-defended positions; information from partisans confirmed that the enemy was evacuating Vitebsk.

VITEBSK: THE CRUCIAL OFFENSIVE

On 23 June all were woken at 6 a.m. by the start of the artillery preparations. The rumbling was uninterrupted and the ground trembled. From daybreak Soviet air traffic was intensively active. Stormoviks and Pe-2s by the hundred, surrounded by Soviet fighters, reached the front. The weather clouded over towards 11 a.m. but improved later and at 6 p.m. aerial activity resumed. Protection was given to an expedition of Pe-2s whose mission was to bomb Bogouchevskoie, the railway station between Orcha and Vitebsk. Twelve Yaks of the 1st provided protection, accompanied by the colonel in an aircraft from the 3rd. German air activity was non-existent.

Three young interpreters were allocated to Normandie; they came from Moscow University and spoke academic French. The 18th Guards Air Regiment arrived to take up residence on the same shared landing ground; they had been working with Normandie since the previous year. Colonel Goloubov informed the commandant that, after the successful campaign and mentions in 'Orders of the Day', Normandie and the 18th Guards Air Regiment had gained the right to call themselves 'Regiments of Smolensk'. As with the French Regiment, the Soviet veterans were thin on the ground; the pilots who came as reinforcements were all very young, while the pilots who had come to Normandie from Algiers were of mixed ages. The aircraft received by Normandie six months previously were now well worn, old and tired.

On 24 June fourteen aircraft of the 3rd and the Commandant Delfino–Charras patrol carried out protective missions for Pe-2s going to bomb Bogouchevskoie. The village having changed hands several times, the mission had to be cancelled at the last moment until it could be established whether Soviet troops were back inside the village. Aspirant Fauroux received the Medal of the French Resistance; Capitaine Matras received the Medal for Escaped Prisoners. He had crossed into Spain from France in 1943 to reach Algeria and to serve the cause of freedom.

Next morning three protective missions were flown accompanying bombing expeditions to different strategic objectives. In the course of the last mission Vitebsk was seen on fire as the smoke rose to 2,000m. There were two night scrambles. German aircraft were signalled but the squadrons found that the enemy and flak were non-existent. At 7 p.m. there was a theatrical performance at the base; the weather was cold and the performance also!

The following day, 26 June, was to be notable: thirteen protective missions were flown for a bombing expedition. At 4.30 p.m., in the course of a covering mission, Capitaine Challe brought down a Bf-109, and the same patrol brought down another. These were the first two victories of the Regiment that year. At 6 p.m. Borizov, on the right bank of the Berezina, was covered. The colonel directed the first group of eleven aircraft from the 1st Escadrille and ten from the 2nd. The second group, composed of eight aircraft from the 3rd and nine from the 4th, was commanded by Delfino. A dozen Fw-190s attacked the Delfino group. Lemare had the controls of his Yak hit and severed, but he managed to return safely to the ground. His team member, Gaston, was hit and brought down. Normandie counter-attacked and the Moynet–Taburet patrol brought down the two Fw-190s that had just attacked the Lemare–Gaston patrol. 'To each his own.' Aspirant Challe brought down an Fw-190. His team member Miquel was hit and lost altitude. Iribarne and Casaneuve each brought down an Fw-190. Lieutenant Risso, as member of Zakharov's team of 'eyes', reconnoitred over Vitebsk. He recounted the scene: 'Destroyed tanks, overturned lorries, Fritz killed in hundreds, bodies floating in the Dvina, houses on fire.' The Regiment rejoiced in his sightings and the fate of all these filthy Boches. A beautiful day for Normandie: seventy-three sorties accomplished, seven victories. Unfortunately, Miquel was missing and Gaston had been shot down.

At 7 a.m. on 27 June two aircraft of the 4th took off; the sector appeared cleared of the enemy. At midday General Zakharov, on patrol with Lieutenant-Colonel Pouyade and Albert, made a reconnaissance of sectors and landing strips. From 2 p.m. protection of Pe-2s was carried out. As on the previous day, the patrols giving protection took off when groups of Pe-2s appeared over the landing strip. At 4.15 p.m. eight aircraft of the 1st protected eight Pe-2s on reconnaissance over the River Berezina, which the Germans were crossing in disarray. Before take-off one of the Pe-2 pilots took out his map and showed some of the French pilots the extraordinary progress of the offensive. Orcha, Vitebsk and Moguilev were taken; Soviet infantry were 50km east of the Berezina; and the Red Army was rolling at speed over the retreating and beaten enemy.

On departure visibility was very poor; the last two patrols of the 2nd failed to catch up with the Pe-2s and abandoned the mission. At 8 p.m. six Yaks from the 1st carried out repeat missions. Miquel came back that morning, parachute and equipment under his arm. He had fired seven or eight shells at an Fw-190, which escaped, trailing smoke: another victory for Normandie. Then he himself was hit when banking. He hedge-hopped to the east and had to make a pancake landing. In the afternoon the colonel assembled the pilots; he was pleased to announce that General Zakharov had ratified Miquel's victory. Then the Order of the Day was read:

Death to the German occupier. ORDER from the General High Command Bagramian and Chernyakhovsky. Today, 26 June, troops of the 1st Pribaltic front and the 3rd Belorussian front, after a hard attack, have liberated the town of Vitebsk, important knot in the German defences. In the battle for the liberation of Vitebsk the pilots of General Zakharov's Division distinguished themselves. Eternal glory to those heroes dead in the battle for the liberation and independence of our country. Death to the German invaders.

Supreme Commander, Marshal of the Soviet Union. J. Stalin

The battle for Vitebsk was an outstanding victory; 20,000 Germans lay dead and a further 10,000 were taken prisoner. This victory would pave the way to the Baltic and eventually lead to the encirclement of the German Army Group North.

At 8 a.m. on 28 June six Yaks of the 1st Escadrille protected a photographic mission carried out by a Pe-2 over the Berezina. At 10 a.m. fighters were ordered to carry out protection for groups of Pe-2s going to bomb Borizov. The four aircraft of the 3rd had difficulty finding their charges and went hunting while hedge-hopping to the east of Borizov. The 4th carried out a flight of one and a half hours and succeeded in its mission; the group of Pe-2s being protected was flying at 1,000–1,500m. At 3 p.m. Commandant Delfino and three aircraft of the 4th protected four Yaks of the 18th Guards Air Regiment that were on reconnaissance on the right bank of the Berezina. At 7.30 p.m. eight aircraft of the 2nd undertook a similar mission; at the same time twenty-eight aircraft took off from the landing strip as well as twelve Yaks from the 18th Guards Air Regiment to protect groups of Pe-2s going to bomb Borizov, the station from which the Germans were trying desperately to evacuate their heavy armour and field equipment. Confusion was at its height; two patrols returned without finding their protégés. Certain groups of Pe-2s were protected by only two Yaks, others by five patrols instead of three. Capitaine de Pange remarked that the events and these 'clangers' would lead to more gold braid being issued.

On the runway the dust whitened the colonel and his aide André, who had come to direct departures from the starting point. In the morning a party of the 1st, covered in grime and dust, presented itself at the communal bathroom. But it was occupied by some very well-built military ladies in the process of washing away personal sweat and toil. It was Maurice Amarger, with everything at the ready, who braved their hostile reluctance to allow the pilots to share the ablutions; he bravely thrust himself forward and joined the ladies in the wash area. He was then quickly followed by all the other, shyer squadron members. After some negotiations a non-aggression pact was concluded and the cleaning carried out without further incident.

At midday an air ambulance brought in Colonel Goloubov. Having attacked two Bf-109s and shot down one of them, he was hit by Russian anti-aircraft fire. His aircraft in flames, he looked to land but was blinded by the fire. Heading for the runway at 200mph, he had to jump; he came round to find a soldier in the act of tearing off his fine boots. He was burnt on the face and had several serious fractures all over his body. At 4 a.m. a Douglas DC-3 arrived to fetch him and take him to hospital. All the Guards Regiment and some pilots from Normandie lined up to bid him goodbye. He found the strength to say that he regretted leaving his regiment just as the Soviet Army was delivering the decisive blow to the German Fascist usurper; he would return soon for the Soviet victory. His deputy, in the name of his regiment and on behalf of his French comrades, swore to him that both regiments would do their duty. What strength in this man: with such leaders the Red Army had conquered and would continue to conquer.

In the evening pilots were involved in strategic discussions. During this assembly Capitaine de Pange remarked, 'If during the last war the infantry did not manage to follow the tanks, during this war it is aviation which cannot keep up with the infantry.' It was true that, after this lightning advance of 200km in five days, bombers and fighters with bases far back had trouble keeping up, only those aircraft that carried 600 litres of fuel could accomplish these long-range missions. To keep near the front some groups had already moved ahead, but the number of serviceable airstrips was insufficient. After dinner all relaxed in the canteen with comrades of the 18th Guards Air Regiment. There was plenty of singing and dancing, broken only by friendly conversation, all this helped by red wine. Noticeable by their successful performances were Risso, Carbon and the colonel. Finally a general chorus struck up 'Tatania'.

At 8 a.m. on 29 June four aircraft of the 1st Escadrille took off in fine weather to protect reconnaissance by Yaks of the 18th Guards Air Regiment. Their mission took them to the east bank of the Berezina. The Yaks went hell for leather, the Guards showing off their speed with engines turning at 2,500 revs. At 1 p.m. a similar mission was accomplished, this time by four aircraft of the 2nd. At 3 p.m., 5 p.m. and 9 p.m. fighters carried out similar missions. The cook had made a fine sponge cake in honour of the Regiment's victories of the previous few days: it was destined for the conquerors. Some mischief-makers reported that certain people choked themselves while eating it; perhaps it had a quality expressly for those who deserved it!

On 30 June the weather was again hot. At 11.30 a.m. and later at 6.20 p.m. missions were flown protecting Pe-2 bombers going to bomb the three great roads that left Borizov for the west. At the beginning of the afternoon, General Zakharov came to give the order to depart the following day at dawn for the new base near Borizov. Normandie completed effective duties using aircraft of the 18th Guards Air Regiment, whose pilots had gone to fetch the new Yak-3s from the factories at Saratov. It was at Saratov that the production and service facilities for the Yak aircraft were situated, and also a ferry park for the collection of new and reconditioned aircraft ready to be flown to the front. Bruno de Faletans had left in a Yak-7 with his mechanic, heading for the spot where he was forced to land and leave his unserviceable aircraft. They had been expected back soon but, worryingly, there was no sign of them.

The Normandie Regiment had by now established a reputation for achieving a commendable success rate protecting bombers during their missions over German lines. General Zakharov once remarked that half of all Pe-2s missions in his sector were protected by Normandie, during which time not one bomber was lost to enemy fighters. Also, the Regiment's achievements when ordered to attack enemy targets, both on the ground and in the air, had been excellent. The pilots' outstanding skill in destroying German aircraft was to become legendary; only one other Soviet Air Force Fighter Regiment was to better their final total of 273 enemy planes confirmed destroyed. At the end of June 1944 Normandie had a full complement of forty-seven operational pilots.

At 10.30 a.m. on 1 July a covering mission was flown protecting Pe-2s going to bomb the crossroads 60km west of Minsk; one of the patrols went to Molodetchno, a large village in former Poland. It was a great distance, making it a very long mission, which the pilots would repeat at 3 p.m. The Pinon–Perrin patrol shot down a Ju-52. Up to that time the Normandie Regiment had protected 45 per cent of the bombing missions without losing a single bomber under its protection. The pilots had been told by Division they would receive the personal thanks of General Zakharov.

On 2 July there were no missions other than protecting the Douglas DC-3 which was taking mechanics and baggage to the future base at Dokoudovo. Operating from a strip closer to the front would make it possible to remain longer over the battle area, which had become crucial. The new base was occupied by three combat regiments, one of them the 523rd Guards Air Regiment. The Smolensk–Orcha–Minsk road was traversed by unbroken lines of trucks and numerous columns of prisoners, some in bare feet, heads bowed, clothes in tatters. What had happened to the Germans who had been seen in the past parading for news films on the squares of conquered towns? Their corpses and those of their vehicles and tanks now testified that their defeat was total.

On 3 July news arrived that the Soviet advance had captured Minsk; further advances by Soviet troops already threatened Vilno. The German rout was becoming more marked, the retreat was growing apace.

In the afternoon of 4 July a great storm refreshed the atmosphere. The 2nd Escadrille was on standby; the others were bathing and fishing for crayfish. De Pange and Pistrack went to Dokoudovo with numerous mechanics and the personal effects. En route they searched for the remains of Gaston's aircraft; Division had a report of a burnt-out plane in the area. They therefore landed near a village; the entire population turned out and surrounded them. De Pange requested information from the crowd about the aircraft's location; information was given, but unfortunately it was not Gaston's Yak. His search completed, de Pange decided to continue the journey and started up the Yak's engine, whereupon two Soviet soldiers, one armed with a sub-machine gun with drum magazine, the other with a Tokarev pistol, come running up. The latter jumped up on the aircraft and ordered de Pange to get down. De Pange, punctilious as ever and following the aircraft manual instructions, revved the engine before cutting it off. But that was not what the soldier ordered; and de Pange felt an immediate response in the form of a cold pistol barrel on his temple. He cut off the engine straight away. Then he and Pistrack, despite the latter's explanations in fluent Russian at the same time showing their Soviet identification cards to the keen guards, were led away to the village and detained for a good hour before being released after a Soviet officer was summoned to sort things out.

News that Vilno had been captured confirmed that the mighty Red Army was rolling west at a fast pace. As of 8 July the Regiment was still resting at Doubrovka. Training of young pilots continued. The other old hands walked along the river banks, where they surprised bathing beauties who, naked as Eve, were relaxing from their military duties. Taking advantage of the absence of its master, de Pange, the U-2 had been borrowed by Aspirant Fauroux, who took it to caper about over Smolensk. In the course of this flying adventure an accident put an end to this courageous and much-liked 'taxi'. It had served Normandie well and had carried out more than 400 hours of flying. It had been badly damaged at the end of August the previous year, but it was Fauroux who gave the U-2 the *coup de grâce*.

On 10 July the colonel accompanied General Zakharov on a trip to Lida. They went to the airstrip that the Regiment would soon occupy. The war trophies Normandie had obtained were many, and included an enormous stock of genuine cognac. Zakharov asked whether it was poisoned, and was told, 'We don't know, but we have been drinking it for a week.' There were now five German prisoners working under guard at the base. Some pilots overheard the Soviet guard instruct the prisoners to repeat 'Hitler is a filthy . . . Yes Hitler is a filthy . . .' 'You are German pigs.' 'Yes we are German pigs.' After this interlude, it was suggested that all German prisoners should be used to repair the damage done to towns and buildings. The time of the arrogant prisoner had now gone.

On 11 July, some brute had broken the record 'Tangerine'. Eichenbaum, Querne and Miquel, who left two days before in a jeep to tidy up the graves of lost comrades Léon, Balcou, Denis, Barbier and Bon, killed the year before, returned after a round trip of 600km. On each grave they had erected a white cross. On each cross was a bilingual inscription giving the name of the pilot and the date of his birth. In addition, the Soviet villages had given a certificate and a commitment to maintain the graves.

The national holiday was celebrated: true, a day early, but all were preparing to depart the following day. Unfortunately, a great storm broke and dinner was served in the mess, where it was crowded. On the menu were the starter (zakouski), pork ribs, potatoes, sweets, cakes, sugared almonds, vodka and wines, followed by some impressive entertainment: the colonel in the 'Tonkinoise', then the commandant in the 'Metinge du Metropolitain'. Sauvage embellished a story, told with a knowing air, of a certain mission by the Cuffaut–Amarger patrol. But the pilots, somewhat stupefied by fifteen days of inaction, showed little reaction, and the evening ended early, though not before Capitaine Matras had entertained the chaps with his good humour.

MEMORIES OF NAPOLEON

On 14 July was the departure for the strip at Mikountani, which lay halfway between Vilno and Lida. Léon Cuffaut, while out walking in Lioubavitchi, met the 'pope' (senior clergy) of the local Orthodox Church, who had been restored to his original function now that his flock had been liberated. His church was now full of the faithful attending services. He produced the obligatory vodka and offered it generously to the pilots. In his village, 150 Frenchmen of Napoleon's Grande Armée had been killed during the 1812 campaign. The grassy mound where all the French soldiers were buried was known by the inhabitants of Lioubavitchi as 'the Frenchmen's mountain'. A selection of their uniforms and arms were preserved in a small building known locally as the museum. The Boches had spitefully burnt the display; they left nothing intact in their desperate retreat.

At 9 a.m. on 15 July a mission by the 1st Escadrille was followed after 20 minutes by another by the 2nd. Several minutes after their departure, the de Seynes–Lebras patrol returned. De Seyne's aircraft had a bad fuel leak and de Seynes was trying in vain to land. Probably overcome by petrol fumes, he lined up twice, opened the throttle while elevating the aircraft in an exaggerated way, went past several times inverted while straightening, dived and crashed to the ground. With him in the back of the aircraft was his mechanic Bielozoube who, known as the 'philosopher', had been with Normandie for a year. With the responsibility of his mechanic behind him, it was obvious de Seynes did not want to jump by parachute, as he should have done; instead, he had fought bravely to overcome the fumes and save both of them. What a charming comrade the Regiment had lost in him, full of imagination, simple, frank and honest. The Soviet groundcrew fully understood that de Seynes had stayed with the aircraft in the hope of saving both lives. From that day an even firmer bond had been drawn between the Soviet and French members of Normandie. The 2nd Escadrille had been hit hard: de Faletans, who disappeared two weeks before, and that day de Seynes. Lieutenants Sauvage and Lebras attended the funeral near the mess at Doubrovka, while at Mikountani the colonel asked for a minute's silence from the squadrons.

The new base was more than 400km to the west, in pre-war Poland or present-day Lithuania. En route, from the heights of Viliena the pilots could see the end of the immense, monotonous, exhausting Russian plain with which they first made contact when crossing the Volga. Many enjoyed and applauded the sight of the first church in pretty red brick, surrounded by pleasant meadows. The move west was bringing Normandie closer to home.

The weather was hot and sultry on 16 July. The Regiment was staying in a large farm, roofed in tiles, and part of a substantial property. In the centre of the farm was a pump like those in France, with kerbstones bordered by smooth pebbles: the first stone pump and pebbles Normandie had encountered since arrival in the USSR. In the vicinity was undulating countryside with fields, meadows and woods; here the horizon was limited to 500m.

The pilots now had the chance to make contact again with individualism. Up high in a fir tree some storks had made their nests. Beautiful trees bordered the roads. The inhabitants, many of whom were young Polish men, were pleased to see the French pilots. On their lips was always the same nervous question: will we have the Kolkhozes (collective farms) here? Countless flies were accompanied by fleas and other devourers. It was so isolated there that the aircraft fuel supply had not yet reached the landing strip, giving the chaps a chance to relax their vigilance. Fortunately, the resources of the country were many: hunting wild duck around the pond and strawberries in the woods. There was a lovely kitchen-garden; the salads were magnificent.

The Regiment was stood down while awaiting delivery of the new Yak-3s. To occupy themselves, the pilots cooked. The market was held in the courtyard of the farm every morning. Since the German mark was banned and the rouble valueless, it was bartering that allowed procurement of the ingredients for any feast. It was found that an RAF-type shirt was worth eight small chickens, a sweater 2 litres of local brew. In each squadron there were master-chefs: Dechanet, Verdier, and Émonet. Sweet-smelling omelettes preceded pork on skewers, duck, geese or guinea fowl surrounded by salad, followed by bilberries with fresh cream. For months they had not known what it was to digest copious meals, after which they contemplated their lives under beautiful trees.

The Regiment took on two new flyers on 20 July. The 1st Escadrille adopted a young stork abandoned by its mother, and de Pange was given a magnificent new U-2, with style and youth. It was doubtful whether he would allow it to be used by anyone who was not considered careful! Each evening at 6 p.m. Commissar Kapitan Kounine held a political meeting: 'On the Origins of the Revolution and this Revolution', certainly not riveting stuff. Kounine was the friendly Soviet liaison officer serving on the base; later he would be replaced by the less flexible and decidedly hardline Commissar Vdovine.

On 23 July the commandant made arrangements for each escadrille in turn to go by car to Vilno, a distance of some 50km. The journey took about two hours and the car was forced to leave the good metal road to skirt round two bridges that the enemy had blown up. On the road were numerous houses surrounded by fortifications, where the Germans lived perpetually threatened by attacks from partisans. Also seen in Orcha were houses barricaded in this same way. Superb Vilno, built in the valley of the Vilna, standing on a bend in the river, looked like a French town in the east, Commercy or Bar-le-Due, with its lovely main street with fine hotels, and beautiful wide pavements planted with trees; all marvelled at these carefully regulated things.

On 24 July the 18th Guards Air Regiment celebrated the anniversary of its nomination to the title of 'Guards'. On this occasion the Regiment received a group award of a single Order of the Red Banner for its colours. Eleven Normandie pilots had been invited to the ceremony. General Zakharov pinned the decoration on the regimental colours, then decorated numerous pilots and mechanics with combat awards. This symbolic and festive occasion commemorated three years of war, 10,300 combat missions and 370 victories. In the mess the Normandie pilots found decorations of foliage and portraits of the Guards Regiment's honoured aces. In the centre were big tables covered with zakouski, vodka and wine. After the second toast the ambiance was warm and vibrant. With so many memories in common during the years of combat, it was time to remember the landing strips on which they had served together, fighting for the common cause of victory.

When an Air Regiment gained the title 'Guards', its aircraft carried the 'Guards' badge painted in red and white on the engine cowling, usually below the exhaust. All officers and senior NCOs were addressed with the prefix 'Guards' before their rank. All personnel, irrespective of rank, were awarded an identical badge to signify that they had served in a unit that had been awarded the group title Guards. The oval Guards badge design showed a large central red star on white enamel surrounded by a gold wreath and surmounted by a red banner emblazoned with the title 'Guards'. This badge was worn on the right breast below any decorations. When General Zakharov decorated his pilots and mechanics with the orders and decorations, at the same time he also presented squadron members with the red and white enamelled Guards badges. During the same anniversary ceremony the 18th Guards Air Regiment was awarded the Order of the Red Banner; this was a unit award to the Regiment. The single Order of the Red Banner would then be attached to the regimental colours and displayed on all future parades. It was a custom for a representation of this decoration to appear painted on the aircraft fuselage, usually immediately to the right of any painted Guards badge emblem.

Numerous Germans had been sighted in the woods, survivors of the battles of Minsk who were trying to reach their retreating comrades. Many were captured when they were out looking for food near the villages. The R-5s stationed nearby had captured two the day before. The doc was going to interrogate this pair and would show them the newspapers, in which was an appeal by captured German generals to those of their men still fighting to surrender to any member of the Red Army.

On 27 July, the 2nd Escadrille, on the occasion of the birthday of its comrade de Saint-Marceaux, gave a magnificent banquet with twenty-four roasted chickens, stuffed mutton, salad and potatoes, chocolate cream and bilberries, followed with Benedictine, which put the finishing touch to this succulent meal. At 6 a.m. Loiseau Paul, a Frenchman sent as a forced labourer to Germany, arrived at the Regiment's landing strip. At the end of April 1944 he had fled from Brunswick and by chance transport took him to the east. Finding himself in Vilno at the moment of the town's capture, he heard that French flyers were at the front. He was 33 but looked 50. This was the first free Frenchman, without a German uniform on his back, to have come here from the west. What emotion for all to learn of so much tenacity and courage! The Soviets allowed Normandie to hold him until he could be sent on.

On the command of the colonel, missions resumed on 28 July. At 6.30 a.m. eight aircraft of the 3rd went on a sortie to protect the passage over the River Niemen of Soviet troops who were facing very stiff enemy opposition. At midday eight aircraft of the 1st ensured mastery of the skies over Kaunas and to the south of this town. A similar mission was carried out at 6.45 p.m. by the 4th, commanded by Capitaine Challe; it passed over and through heavy flak, and the well-aimed shots forced the Génès–Manceau patrol to return to the ground: Génès' Yak had received a shell burst in the left wing. Anti-aircraft fire also scored a direct hit on an aircraft of the de La Salle patrol. The pilot, Charras, jumped by parachute as his plane was terminally damaged; de Pange would pick him up the following day in the new U-2. What a blessing were these useful 'taxis'.

In the morning eight aircraft of the 2nd flew a covering mission in the sector west and south-west of Alitous. At 3 p.m. a similar same mission was carried out by seven aircraft of the 4th, which landed at the new strip at Alitous. At 4 p.m. the Regiment set off for Alitous. The 2nd Escadrille's mission was to protect a Douglas DC-3 transport which was conveying the mechanics in several trips. The Yak fighters gave tight and constant protection to this important DC-3. The twin-engine Yak-6 liaison aircraft made the journey alone. By 7 p.m. all the aircraft were at Alitous. From 8 p.m. until nightfall the 2nd kept up constant covering protection over the new airstrip with two double patrols.

Notable in this change of location was the aerial animal transportation by the DC-3: Dechanet with his cow, Raia the bitch dog, de Saint-Phalle with his chickens, the squadron's adopted stork and many frogs. One might ask why Normandie travelled with such a strange wartime menagerie to forward airstrips. It appears that the cow, chickens and frogs had for some time been a necessary addition to their table needs. One Normandie veteran explained the problems experienced in the early days in the Soviet Union; with food so scarce it had become necessary to try to supplement the diet by the best means available. In the early days supply problems at times left the Regiment's mechanics woefully short of food, and they had taken to catching rabbits, fish and frogs to supplement their mealtime fare. In most Russian villages would be found a pond, muddy pools that were an excellent habitat for large frogs. The pilots remembered how surprised they were to find that the local population had no interest in cooking or eating rabbit, which often meant that wild rabbit could be added to the squadron's menu. These shortages had recently been overcome; a well-supplied canteen, bartering and provisions via Moscow had made supplies very much better.

At 4.30 a.m. on 30 July the dawn patrol took off. At 11 a.m. a patrol of the 4th Escadrille responded to an alert. At 12.30 p.m. eight aircraft of the 3rd flew a covering mission to Souvalki, made up of patrol leader Matras–de Geoffre, patrol Challe–Bayssade and, high above, the patrols of Le Martelot–Monier and André–Penverne. While banking the upper patrols missed the patrol leader, they headed for four enemy aircraft seen a few kilometres away. They turned out to be Fw-190s. A serious very close engagement took place; it was noticed that this group of Boche appeared to be all moustached. Matras and de Geoffre arrived as reinforcements, just in time to see one of the Fw-190s attacked by André dive to the ground, while the pilot jumped with his parachute. Le Martelot, after several turns passed into the clouds, shot at an Fw-190 and probably brought it down. During this time Challe, who had lost Bayssade, found himself alone in the middle of nine Ju-87s, which he attacked with machine guns, probably shooting one down. The patrol André–Penverne regrouped in pursuit of a Ju-87 that they shepherded to the Soviet strip at Souvalki, where the German was welcomed by violent anti-aircraft fire that forced it to retreat. André brought back his aircraft with a hole as big as a man on the right wing; he was also hit on the left wing-tip and the tailplane. Monier and Bayssade were missing; none of the pilots knew where they were or what had happened to them. At 1 p.m. and 4.15 p.m. two patrols were scrambled. Taburet's aircraft had a serious fuel leak; the pilot, blinded by fuel as he came in to land, switched off, bounced to the right and came to a halt, causing grave concern to the spectators around the strip. Perrin, his team member, continued alone and joined Pinon and Schoendorff; all three then witnessed a fight between Bf-109s and Stormoviks, which ceased as soon as the Yaks joined the fray, but not before Perrin had fired on a Bf-109, thus freeing the Stormovik. At 8 p.m. a covering mission was flown over the Simno–Mariampol sector by patrols of the 1st; they noticed eighteen Fw-190s bombing the battlefield but did not succeed in catching up with them. Two patrols of the 4th carried out the dusk patrol. It was a bad day for the Regiment: two pilots, Monier and Bayssade, missing and three aircraft badly damaged, for two Fw-190s shot down and probably two Ju-87s damaged.

The Alitous strip was a former Lithuanian base but its buildings had been almost completely destroyed in June 1941. The Stalovaia (canteen) was situated in the barracks. The pilots lived in the suburbs of the town of quite clean and pretty houses. The air base was on the right bank of the Niemen, on a bend in the river. It was a scenic runway that ended at a cliff overlooking the river. The town was on the left bank; the modern port was destroyed by the Germans a week beforehand. Thus, those who wanted to go to town had to swim across the Niemen. The town looked like many small German towns. It had been completely ransacked, if not destroyed. So well, that the trophies there were of little value – some books, newspapers, and stamps.

Bayssade, who was listed as missing in action on the recent mission, was shot down inside enemy lines and captured. He survived his time in enemy hands (see Chapter 9).

On the foggy morning of 31 July, the 3rd Escadrille carried out the dawn patrol. Another patrol took off at the sight of a German reconnaissance plane 6,000m above the runway, which made off quickly. From 10 a.m. to 12.30 p.m. the 3rd flew hunting patrols. On his return from Moscow, the colonel informed the Regiment that the body of de Faletans had been recovered, as well as that of his mechanic. This news had an emotional effect on all the pilots, as they knew their well-loved comrade de Faletans could have saved his own life had he decided to abandon his mechanic and bale out. But such was the close bond between the pilots of Normandie and their Soviet groundcrew that this heroic action strongly reinforced the existing comradeship.

The colonel read out the honours list of victories for June 1944. The Regiment was in second place with eight-six confirmed victories. Attached to the honours list were two bulletins, numbers 9 and 10. Bulletin No. 9, published by the French Air Force fighter section after the French campaign of 1939–40, concluded with the following paragraph: 'At a time when combat aviation closes its wings, while awaiting better days, it can be proud of the task accomplished.'

Bulletin No. 10, published in June 1944, began with the words: 'French Air Force fighters have reopened its wings; this task, of which it can be legitimately proud, has resumed.' Thus Bulletin No. 10 ignored the fact that, after the publication of Bulletin No. 9, the French Air Force had already reopened its wings on 21 July 1940, above Germany! And it was thanks to the French Navy and Air Force that Général de Gaulle could affirm that France had never left the war.

Colonel Pouyade informed the assembled Regiment that a committee of anti-Fascist youth in Algeria had sent Lefèvre a letter and a purse, thanking him for his brave and victorious energy in the struggle against the invader. Learning of his death, these young people had asked for their gift to be passed on to a friend of Lefèvre or to the first pilot to have shot down a German aircraft that year. The colonel had therefore given it to Capitaine Challe.

ASPIRANT PINON EXECUTED ON CAPTURE IN
EAST PRUSSIA

On 1 August 1944 the weather was fine. The 1st Escadrille, which was on standby, sent up two patrols at dawn. Four aircraft of the 1st provided a covering mission over Sterki. Followed by Commandant Delfino and three aircraft of the 4th, on take-off the leader of the patrol, de La Salle, scraped the runway with his propeller, and patrol member Charras, not to be outdone, flattened his tail-post. Both carried out their mission with resolution. Between 11.30 a.m. and 1.40 p.m. three covering missions were sent out. Above Eidtkounen, in East Prussia, the patrols came across fifteen Ju-87s protected by twelve Fw-190s. A battle ensued with the Fw-190s; Mourier shot one down, Laurent fired but saw no result. The Yak-3 worked wonders against the Fw-190s, but jammed guns prevented Major Zamorine from firing. On the return Feldzer was missing; Mourier believed he saw him explode in the air. At 2.45 p.m. nine aircraft of the 1st and six aircraft of the 3rd flew a similar mission. Albert led the squad as far as Goumbinnen, a little Prussian town, whose roofing tiles he made jump with blasts of his heavy 37mm cannon. En route numerous trenches and anti-tank defences seemed deserted.

At 6.15 p.m., on a covering mission over sector Chirvind–Chtaloupienen–Kibartai, the 4th, 3rd, and 2nd Escadrilles put up four aircraft each, commanded by Capitaine Challe. The weather turned bad, anti-aircraft fire was very active, and the patrol had difficulty keeping close together. Le Martelot and Lorillon noticed a Ju-87; they attacked it and set it ablaze while the others attacked Goumbinnen. Meanwhile, Aspirant Pinon disengaged and flew into a cloud, after which there was no news of him. The Regiment would learn that Aspirant Roger Pinon had been attacked by enemy fighters and sustained damage to his aircraft severe enough to prevent him from making it back across the lines. Although not wounded he had no option but to make a forced landing; he belly crashed in a cloud of dust and debris close to enemy positions. Dazed and still suffering from the heavy impact, he was struggling to release himself from the cockpit when a German officer came running towards the aircraft, climbed up on the damaged Yak and shot Pinon in the back of the head. This violation of all laws of war was carried out directly because of Keitel's infamous order of May 1943: 'Aviators of the Squadron Normandie shall be executed on capture.' This particular violation of the Geneva Convention was to form part of the evidence at the Nuremberg trials that would lead to the death penalty being passed on Field Marshal Keitel.

The previous day a salute for the offensive on the 3rd Belorussian Front took place in Moscow. Mariampol was captured, making a breach in the enemy lines 200km wide by 50km deep. Colonel Pouyade and the pilots of Normandie were cited honourably in the 3rd Belorussian Army communiqué.

Monier, unbreakable and waterproof, returned. Attacked by a Bf-109 that set his aircraft on fire, he jumped by parachute and landed 50m in front of the Soviet line. The Soviet troops, under fire, went out to fetch him in. He was taken to the HQ of the 3rd Army and very well received. There he saw three German prisoners telling their story to the captors. They told how they had been pressed into a battle-front battalion just as they were passing through Koenigsberg on a leave train from Finland. This incident had happened on the morning of Chernyakhovsky's attack, 13 January 1945. The leave train, bound for Berlin, was passing through Koenigsberg when it was halted in the station by a large group of Wehrmacht Feldgendarmerie. These military police could instantly be recognised by the large chain-slung metal gorget hung from their neck and resting on their chests; the soldiers used to refer to these hated military police as 'chain-hounds'. The Feldgendarmerie's gorget was in the form of a flat crescent-shaped metal plate, with the title 'Feldgendarmerie' below an army eagle. After the train halted, the police shouted harshly from the platform, ordering all soldiers belonging to divisions whose numbers they were about to call out to leave the train immediately and form up. Many of the soldiers had waited over two years for their leave, so that morning there were many heavy hearts on the platform.

GROUPE CITATION FOR THE BATTLE TO CROSS
THE NIEMEN

The troops of the 3rd Belorussian Front had forced their way across the River Niemen. It was here that Soviet troops ran into a powerful line of defence on the west bank. After three days of brutal fighting and constant sorties by Normandie, the Soviets finally penetrated 50km beyond the enemy lines, enlarging the front up to 230km. During this offensive Soviet troops liberated the town and railway station of Mariampol and the important communication links of Pilvitchki, Ghostakov and Sene. In this advance the Red Army also occupied more than 1,500 other smaller positions.

ORDER of the Day to the troops of the 3rd Belorussian Front

In the battle for the passage of the Niemen and the rupture of the German defences, the pilots of Colonel-General Khrioukine and of Colonel Pouyade distinguished themselves. To celebrate the victory, the units which were most distinguished in the passage of the Niemen and the rupture of the German lines of defences, are recommended for decorations and will bear the honour title 'Niemen'. Today, 21 July 1944 at 24.00, Moscow, capital of our country, will salute in its name our brilliant troops of the 3rd Belorussian front who have forced their way across the Niemen and broken the enemy defences; 20 salvos of artillery from 224 guns were fired. For this wonderful warlike action, I express my gratitude to the troops under your command.

Signed J. Stalin

On 2 August the 2nd Escadrille was on standby. Three patrols were sent on covering missions to different sectors. At 5 p.m. the colonel and Albert, while hunting at the front, came up against eight Fw-190s. The surprise was so complete on both sides that nobody fired. At 7.30 p.m. Commandant Delfino, Major Zamorine and six aircraft of the 3rd covered bridges on the Chechoupe to the south of Mariampol. For the first time since its arrival in the Soviet Union, Normandie had its landing strip bombed, probably by several He-126s. Amarger's aircraft blazed, as did two La-5s. The courage of the pilots was put to the test. However, certain people took advantage of the disarray caused by the situation to reassure and give excessive comfort to some of the feminine operatives on base! The following day the 3rd was on standby. Since nighttime, Commandant Delfino and Bertrand had protected the base. At 9 p.m. the Groupe personnel met to say farewell to Kapitans Kounine and Chourakov. Chourakov was decorated with the Croix de Guerre. Both of them were with Normandie for a long time and had served the cause well. The canteen had been supplied with wines and spirits – a bottle for each pilot – white wines, ports, champagne most satisfactory. The 2nd Escadrille chaps let themselves go in noisy horseplay; the rest joined them in letting off steam. Magnificent loud salutes with pistol shots ended the evening.

The Yak-6 departed with Kounine and Chourakov in fine weather on 4 August. The 3rd was on standby. From 8.30 a.m. to 1.30 p.m. fifteen patrols on missions covering the front were carried out without incident. At 3 p.m. a Pe-2 photographing the East Prussian front was accompanied by two patrols of the 3rd Escadrille. Two Fw-190s which tried to attack the Pe-2 were chased off by two La-5s. From 5.35 p.m. until nightfall four covering patrols went up. Danilenko, engineer of the 3rd, departed. He had been with Normandie for nineteen months and was well liked and respected. The following day at 10 a.m. four patrols protected two Pe-2s on reconnaissance in the Souvalki region. At nightfall two aircraft of the 3rd protected the landing strip.

On 6 August missions at 9.30 a.m. and 4.45 p.m. accompanied Pe-2s photographing in the Tilsitt–Insterburg sector. The patrol commanded by Lieutenant Sauvage on a sortie flying east spotted for the first time the Baltic Sea: this was Normandie's first sighting of the Baltic coast. This reaffirmed the great distance the Regiment had travelled fighting the enemy; as the Germans retreated further west so the expectation of the enemy's final defeat grew along with Normandie's return to France. At dusk two aircraft of the 1st covered the strip. The following day at 2.30 p.m. and 2.45 p.m. protection was provided for a Pe-2 aircraft photographing on the East Prussian front above the Niemen as far as Tilsitt. At an altitude of 5,500m, the Yaks banked 15km from the Baltic coast.

At 5.45 p.m. on 8 August two patrols of the 3rd provided a covering mission over the sector of Souvalki, reinforced 30 minutes later by another two patrols. On landing Le Martelot went too far and crashed into an aircraft of the 4th at the end of the runway. It was noted that the civilian population was returning slowly to the town. It was said that they all had such dreadful memories of the battle in June 1941, when the base had been so badly bombed, that this time at the first sound of gunfire they went into the woods and lived there for a month, probably waiting to see what would happen once the Soviet Army arrived. They were aware of what the German Army had done to towns and villages in the Soviet Union.

A little drama occurred at 9.30 a.m. which many of the Normandie pilots watched with great interest. An unusual parade took place. The Soviet officers had assembled all Soviet troops on parade. Their adjutant-storekeeper, now a prisoner, was marched out between two very tall guards, and stood to attention before a senior officer ready to hear his punishment. Earlier the adjutant-storekeeper had been convicted of embezzlement and theft of state property. The traditional degrading then took place; the officer struck the man a severe blow on the shoulder with a standard service bayonet, then his epaulettes were ripped from his tunic. A paper was handed to the parade officer, who with a stroke of a pen ordered that the thief be sent to a disciplinary battalion. The event concluded with the prisoner being quick-marched off the parade in front of the assembled troops. This form of bayonet-smiting and rank-stripping punishment dated from Czarist times. The term 'disciplinary battalion' does not really describe or explain the true meaning of the punishment he was to receive. The theft of Red Army war supplies while on active service in a battle area could be punishable by death. Disciplinary battalions were ordered and used in 'forlorn hope' attacks, usually against heavily defended enemy positions, crossing rivers under intense fire or attacking across thickly sewn minefields. The theory was that the offenders could win their freedom from these penal or disciplinary battalions only by glory or death.

At 8 p.m. the Yak-6 returned from Moscow with Castin and Bourveau, who had come to take a breath of good warlike air with the Regiment, far from the stifling miasmas of peace found behind the desks of Moscow. With them came 350kg of cigarettes, tinned fruit, and chocolate. They also brought regimental promotions: Castin and Risso appointed lieutenants, Cuffaut, de Saint-Marceaux and Jeannel appointed capitaines. In addition Commandant Delfino, whose title was temporary, had now been confirmed in that position for the duration of the war. After dinner there were great liquid celebrations for the promoted. In an ambiance rendered magnificent by the liveliness of everyone, aided by the whisky and wines, the pilots of the 2nd Escadrille, soon supported by those of the 1st, indulged in an unfettered saraband. It started in the barracks of the 2nd, continued to the colonel's quarters, then in front of the 1st, moving on to the abodes of the 3rd and 4th, where the horseplay and noise reached its zenith. That was a beautiful and enjoyable evening!

On 9 August a small German counter-attack was encountered to the north of Souvalki. To slow enemy movements all the Stormoviks were sent out; in total about 350, with flights of six every 10 minutes right through the day. At 7.30 a.m. the 1st was summoned to the airstrip; it was a question of obtaining 'mastery of the sky', but as that had already been achieved it did not take off. At 8 a.m. two patrols of the 2nd scrambled but encountered no enemy. At 8.30 a.m. two patrols of the 4th went up on a protection mission covering Pe-2s photographing as far as Tilsitt at an altitude of 5,000m. At the end of the evening the burial took place of an La-5 pilot who served with the 523rd Regiment; he had been been killed the previous day beside the banks of the Niemen. The cortège went from the infirmary to the cemetery. In front a pilot carried on a red cushion the pilot's two Orders of the Red Banner; then came the red-painted coffin, whose upper part was covered in flowers, with the dead man, uncovered, surrounded by flowers. Behind were his comrades of the Regiment. Speeches were made around the grave. The master of ceremonies invited anyone who wanted to say a few words to do so. One of the pilots, his voice interrupted by sobs, spoke of his hatred for the Boche who had taken away his best comrade. The colonel of the Regiment concluded by displaying the dead man's decorations; he recounted why he had deserved them and what an example he had left to the Regiment. Then the coffin was closed and lowered into the grave, and salvos were fired. The machine guns of the aircraft and the airfield anti-aircraft fire intermingled. The noise became thunderous and flashes spread to all parts. An impressive and sombre performance!

A call came through from Division at 6.30 a.m. on 11 August awakening the pilots. Intelligence confirmed that the enemy had 700 aircraft opposite the front line, half fighters, half bombers. It was known they were preparing to attack. Until 8 a.m. all were on 'super-alert'. Then the weather clouded over and the ceiling came down low. The pilots went back to sleep; the 700 German aircraft had been beaten by the cumulus.

At 9 a.m. on 12 August, a day of fine weather, all the pilots were asked to fetch their helmets and map holders, which they kept in their aircraft: the French pilots were handing over the Yak-9s, except for two that would be retained to liaise with Moscow. The Regiment had been using Yak-9s for more than a year; a good aircraft, with easy, reliable, stout and manageable pilotage.

By the end of this first part of the campaign of 1944, the following results had been obtained.

1st Escadrille: two victories ratified: Casaneuve and Iribarne; 261 sorties without loss (discount Amarger aircraft burnt by bombing).

2nd Escadrille: one victory ratified: Mourier; 255 sorties, three pilots lost (de Faletans in an accident in a Yak-7, de Seynes in an accident in a Yak-9,

Feldzer in aerial combat); three aircraft lost: those of de Seynes, Feldzer and
Brihaye, who landed in the country after fuel failure.

3rd Escadrille: four victories ratified and one participation: Challe, Miquel,
André, each an Fw-190, the patrol of Le Martelot–Lorillon one Ju-87,
Monier half a Bf-109 (shared with a pilot of the 4th); plus three probable
victories: Le Martelot one Fw-190, Challe one Ju-87, patrol André–
Penverne one Ju-87; 228 sorties, one pilot lost: Bayssade in aerial combat.

4th Escadrille: five victories ratified: Capitaine Challe one Bf-109, de La Salle,
Querne, Génès, Manceau one Bf-109, Moynet one Fw-190, Taburet one
Fw-190, patrol Pinon–Perrin one Ju-52; 253 sorties, two pilots lost: Gaston
in aerial combat and Pinon during a mission.

In short, the Regiment brought off twelve certain victories and three probables.
It carried out 1,015 combat sorties. It lost six pilots and preserved forty-three
aircraft. The colonel fulfilled ten sorties and Commandant Delfino eighteen.

On 15 August the two Yak-9 aircraft left were on standby. To take
advantage of this rest, a visit was organised to Kaunas. The 3rd and 4th went
on 14 August, the 1st and 2nd had their turn on the 15th. The car that took
the pilots was a beautiful German Mercedes, a war trophy from Stalingrad.
The road was good and pretty, especially where it bordered the River Niemen.
After going over a small bridge, a burnt-out Tiger tank half blocked the road.
On the right bank of the river, the town had a pre-war population of
150,000 inhabitants, mostly Lithuanians and Jews. On the other side of the
river was the ghetto. It was a former workers' quarter constructed by the
Soviets in 1941, with houses in brick and wood. The Germans surrounded it
with barbed wire. Each morning, before going to work, all the Jewish men
were checked; if in the evening any of them were missing their families were
immediately murdered. On 14 July 1944 the population had to stay at home;
the Germans mined the brick houses, then forced some Jewish prisoners to set
fire to the houses and to prime the mines. Whoever tried to flee was machine-
gunned by the SS, who were surrounding the camp.

The pilots of Normandie decided to visit the ghetto to see for themselves
what had happened. In the centre of the town the main thoroughfare was
bordered by the opera house and numerous official buildings. It finished at
one end with a grand rococo-style church and at the other with the market.
The Normandie pilots were quickly surrounded by the curious and friendly
inhabitants. Some had come to throw themselves at the pilots' feet, to kiss

Groupe de Chasse 3, Normandie, the official group photo taken at Rayak air base, Lebanon, October 1942.

The FAFL engagement form signed by Didier Béguin.

FAFL badge produced in London 1940; the reverse of every badge was numbered individually for each volunteer.

Above: Left to right: Préziosi, Tulasne and Albert at the Kazelsk strip, summer 1943.

Left: Soviet ace Boris Safonov. Good detail of Soviet flying equipment and parachute harness.

Préziosi and Castelain holding puppies, July 1943 at Katiounka during the Orel campaign. Both pilots would be dead within the month.

Normandie pilots taking a break during the July 1943 Orel campaign. Tokarev pistols are on the table.

Left to right: Forges, Durand, Préziosi, Bon, Léon, Balcou, Michel and Albert, June 1943.

Béguin against his Yak-9, wearing the Order of the Patriotic War. He is flanked by Soviet mechanics Nazine and Casimir, October 1943.

Capitaine Joseph Risso, wearing the FAFL badge on his Russian fur hat, January 1944.

Igor Eichenbaum rests on a Soviet T-34 tank. Eichenbaum kept the service records for Normandie-Niemen, and his detailed accounts were used for this narrative.

Soviet mechanic Bielozoube. Lieutenant de Seynes died trying to save him in an air crash.

The 'five musketeers'. *Left to right:* Marcel Albert, Roland de La Poype, Didier Béguin, Marcel Lefèvre and Josph Risso. Credited with sixty-eight victories between them.

Lieutenant Lefèvre with Soviet mechanics by his Yak number 14, showing personal emblems including ten victories.

Soviet commemorative postcard celebrating Normandie 'ace' Lefèvre, Hero of the Soviet Union.

The fourteen pilots of Normandie's 3rd Escadrille, summer 1944.

The tragic Nina flanked by Delfino and Pouyade, with Dr Lebiedinsky on the extreme right, Doubrovka, 1944.

Marcel Albert (twenty-three victories) holding his Gold Star Hero document with fellow Gold Star recipient Roland de La Poype. Two Soviets officers look on.

Béguin after returning from the USSR, seen here with RAF officers by a victory, Antwerp, 1 October 1944. Béguin was killed the following month.

Taburet at Le Bourget, June 1945. He is wearing the second-type Normandie badge. The Cross of Lorraine appears above his service badges, and he wears RAF wings. Moynet is on his right.

Senior 'ace' de La Poype, Gold Star, Hero of the Soviet Union. Above his right breast pocket de la Poype wears the French pilot's badge in the form of a circular silver wreath overlaid with a pair of gilt wings topped by a gilt star.

Lieutenant Colonel Pouyade wearing the Cross of Lorraine on badges and Lieutenant Colonel Delfino without this Free French symbol, Le Bourget 1945.

Normandie at Le Bourget on parade, June 1945. Soviet mechanics on the right, and French pilots on the left.

Capitaine Joseph Risso on his return to Le Bourget, 20 June 1945.

Legion of Honour, Knight.

Order of the Liberation, reverse.

Médaille Militaire, obverse.

Gold Star, Hero of the Soviet Union.

Order of the Red Banner.

Order of the Patriotic War.

Normandie badge, first type.

Normandie badge, second type.

Normandie-Niemen badge, third type.

The Order of Alexander Nevsky.

The Yak-3 of Major-General G. N. Zakharov, Commander of 303rd Fighter Aerial Division, parent division of Normandie-Niemen Regiment. The 303rd Division's emblem the white thunderbolt lightning flash is shown along the fuselage. This same symbol was used on the Normandie-Niemen third-type badge. *(ART-TECH)*

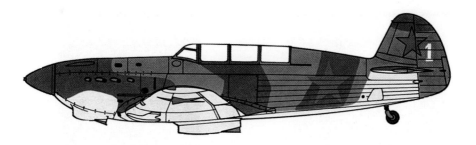

Yak-7V, two-seat trainer, updated from the Yak-1. Although the high fuselage behind the cockpit restricted rear view, in training mode this was acceptable

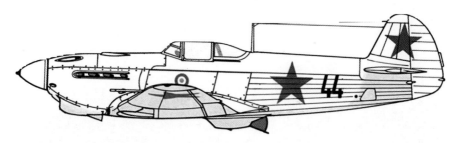

Yak-1M, first operational fighter flown by Normandie in 1943. In winter white with French roundall. The aircraft of Marcel Albert, top-scoring French fighter pilot of the Second World War.

This Normandie Yak-9T was flown by Capitaine René Challe, when based at Doubrovka, June 1944. The main gun centre, the tricolour spinner, is a 37mm cannon.

Yak-3, the nimblest dog-fighter of the Second World War. This aircraft was flown by Hero of the Soviet Union, Sergei Luganskii, who scored thirty-four victories.

A LA MÉMOIRE DES PILOTES FRANÇAIS
DU RÉGIMENT "NORMANDIE - NIEMEN"
TOMBÉS DURANT LA 2ME GUERRE
MONDIALE AUX COTÉS DES
COMBATTANTS DE L'ARMÉE SOVIÉTIQUE

В ПАМЯТЬ ФРАНЦУЗКИХ ЛЕТЧИКОВ
ПОЛКА "НОРМАНДИЯ - НЕМАН"
ПАВШИХ ВО ВРЕМЯ ВТОРОЙ
МИРОВОЙ ВОЙНЫ СРАЖАЯСЬ
БОК О БОК С ВОИНАМИ СОВЕТСКОЙ АРМИИ

BALCOU André ASPIRANT 20-9-43	LARGEAU André ASPIRANT 14-9-43
BARBIER Léo S/LIEUTENANT 15-10-43	LEFEVRE Marcel LIEUTENANT 5-6-44
BERNAVON Adrien S/LIEUTENANT 16-7-43	LEON Gérald LIEUTENANT 4-9-43
BERTRAND Jean LIEUTENANT 26-8-44	LITTOLF Albert CAPITAINE 16-7-43
BIZIEN Yves ASPIRANT 13-4-43	MANCEAU Jean ASPIRANT 2-11-44
BON Maurice ASPIRANT 13-10-43	MENUT Lionel ASPIRANT 29-1-45
BOURDIEU Maurice ASPIRANT 18-3-44	MIQUEL Charles ASPIRANT 18-1-45
CASANEUVE Jacques ASPIRANT 13-10-44	MONGE Maurice ASPIRANT 26-3-45
CASTELAIN Noël S/LIEUTENANT 16-7-43	PENVERNE Roger S/LIEUTENANT 5-2-45
CHALLE Maurice S/LIEUTENANT 27-3-45	PINON Roger ASPIRANT 1-8-44
DENIS Roger LIEUTENANT 13-10-43	PIQUENOT Jean ASPIRANT 17-1-45
DERVILLE Raymond LIEUTENANT 13-4-43	POZNANSKI André LIEUTENANT 13-4-43
DURAND Albert S/LIEUTENANT 1-9-43	PREZIOSI Albert CAPITAINE 28-7-43
DE FALETANS Bruno LIEUTENANT 30-6-44	QUERNE Louis ASPIRANT 25-9-44
DE FORGES Paul CAPITAINE 31-8-43	REY Jean ASPIRANT 28-8-43
FOUCAUD Henri S/LIEUTENANT 21-4-44	DE SEYNES Maurice CAPITAINE 15-7-44
GASTON Jacques ASPIRANT 26-6-44	DE SIBOUR Jean ASPIRANT 31-8-43
GENES Pierre ASPIRANT 18-1-45	DE TEDESCO Jean LIEUTENANT 14-7-43
HENRI Georges ASPIRANT 12-4-45	TULASNE Jean CAPITAINE 17-7-43
IRIBARNE Robert S/LIEUTENANT 11-2-45	VERDIER Marc LIEUTENANT 22-9-44
JOIRE Jules S/LIEUTENANT 18-3-44	VERMEIL Firmin ASPIRANT 17-7-43

Memorial plaque on the wall of the French Military Mission, Moscow, listing the forty-two
Normandie pilots killed during 1943–5.

them and to bless them with signs of the cross while shouting 'Long live France'. Some comrades heard themselves challenged thus: 'Well is it true, old chap that you are from Paname', a slang term for those who hailed from Paris. Others met high-society ladies who offered them cups of tea and conversation. They returned after having made purchases that reminded them that shops and civilians still existed. In this beautiful town the good people charged a mere three roubles for a poor meal, but a roll of photographic film cost an amazing thirty roubles.

NORMANDIE TAKES DELIVERY OF THE NEW YAK-3 FIGHTER

Normandie Regiment received delivery of the new Yak-3s on 17 August 1944. This most manoeuvrable of the Yak series, capable of 450mph, and a ceiling of 35,440ft, was to prove a superior dogfighter to anything the Luftwaffe had available; the Messerschmitt Bf-109G was no match for this nimble racehorse of the sky. The Luftwaffe would suffer increased losses from the pilots who flew the new Yak-3 fighter. The Luftwaffe senior commander in East Prussia found it expedient to issue guidance orders to their pilots to avoid combat with any Yak fighter that did not have an oil cooler below the nose section; the new Yak-3 had had the oil cooler moved back to the wing roots, out of view. As the battle advanced further towards East Prussia, the Yak-3s were continually in action and made a name for themselves as the number of enemy aircraft they destroyed mounted dramatically. Next day the weather was bad, so the mechanics worked on the newly delivered Yak-3s, getting them ready for the expected forthcoming action.

On 19 August was the Festival of Soviet aviation. It began with sporting competitions for the whole Division. Normandie won the volleyball match against the La-5 and Il-2 regiments. André won the long jump (5.35m) and high jump (1.65m) and also the 1,000m. In the afternoon the first flights in the new Yak-3s were made. The pilots were very enthusiastic about its performance; the aircraft was very light and easy to handle, with impressive zooming. Visibility was perfect, especially forward. Only the landing gear, similar to that of the Yak-1M, caused concern. At 10 p.m. the large official meal was well lubricated with vodka. At 11.45 a.m. the next day a patrol from the 3rd Escadrille left to hunt in the sector Goumbinnen–Souvalki and successfully attacked a freight train to the south of Souvalki. From 2.40 to 7.45 p.m. three similar missions were carried out.

At 7, 8, and 9 a.m. on 21 August, patrols from the 2nd carried out hunting missions in the Insterburg–Augustovo region. The 7 a.m. Verdier–Delin patrol attacked a truck, which tumbled into a ditch together with a light vehicle. At 10, 11.15 and 11.30 a.m. different patrols carried out similar missions. At 6 p.m. a mission by Moynet and Castin attacked a stationary train and soldiers in the fields. Hunting sorties continued. The following day the 3rd sent out a patrol at 8.10 a.m., consisting of Challe and Miquel, who strafed a train caught in a station. From 10.25 a.m. to 5.30 p.m. three further patrols went out.

The date of 23 August would be a day for all to remember. The colonel and Albert went out on patrol, and then the 2nd was sent on a patrol with orders to hunt any enemy aircraft or ground targets. The big news then broke: Paris had been liberated! The first to hear the news were the colonel, Mourier, Le Martelot, Bertrand, Carbon, Bagnères and Bourveau, who heard it at 1.30 p.m. on the radio. The last were the doc and Jeannel, who made the trip from Moscow to Alitous without suspecting anything. The joy of all was widely shared by the Soviets, who came to congratulate the Regiment. At nightfall a salute was organised by Kapitan Agavelian, the Soviet chief engineer: five salvos of anti-aircraft fire joined by salvos of guns and pistols and the entire stock of flares. The fireworks were very dramatic and recalled the celebrations taking place in Moscow. All the pilots sang the Marseillaise. At a grand get-together in the mess toasts were proposed to the 'partisans of Paris', to Général de Gaulle, and to the Red Army. The colonel announced that the bells of the city of Manchester rang at full volume for 6 minutes after the announcement of the deliverance of Paris; he asked all to think of the comrades in the French Interior Forces (FFI) who had died for country and liberty. Then thoughts, prayers and finally thanks were given to Général de Gaulle, to whom all owed the day's great joy. The commander at the Divisional HQ then asked the Groupe to take advantage of each mission to annihilate the Germans, whether they were on foot, in cars or flying aircraft; they should be attacked everywhere, and as many as possible of these evil beasts destroyed. After many joyful songs and lively stories, all went to dream of the life that awaited them when they returned to a liberated France.

To celebrate a free Paris, a great banquet was organised in the evening of 24 August. Six musicians, full of gusto, set the tone. It started off with the Marseillaise, sung at full volume by all. The menu was read into rhyme by de Saint-Marceaux. The feast was cooked by Émonet, Carbon, Martin, Charras and Verdier: hors-d'oeuvres with cream, roasted chicken and crème au chocolat, washed down with vodka and wine. The sight of the tables alone, so weighed down, put everyone in a cheerful mood. The joy became total after toasts to the people of Paris, to Général de Gaulle, to Marshal Stalin, to General Zakharov (he was present at the celebration) and to Colonel Pouyade. The noise and disorder reached its highest pitch. Then came the entertainment: Laurent and Delin performed a sentimental duet, followed by Émonet in the 'angler'. Charras performed the 'blind fiddler', a great success. What a great time!

There was one slight mishap at this important celebration meal. It so happened that the five busy pilot 'cooks' had help in the kitchen from a Soviet mechanic who had professed to be acquainted with the culinary skills. Unfortunately the 'crème au chocolat' just like grandma used to make became a victim of the hired help. The mechanic had a problem reading the labels; he opened a packet of salt instead of sugar and proceeded to add the entire contents without restraint. The 'sweet' had reached the guests before the disaster was realised, the Soviet cook was mortified, everyone in the Regiment had gone without sugar for some time to save it for this celebration dinner, as the hosts were looking very despondent. General Zakharov came to the rescue and sent a runner for several bottles of vodka to make amends and pacify the five cooks. All ended in good spirits.

On 26 August the fine weather continued, and four patrols did their usual hunting. At 12.30 p.m. the Bertrand–Marchi patrol reached a point west of Goumbinnen and began a dive from 4,000m. It appears that Bertrand pushed his dive too far. Marchi, feeling the controls grow hard, reduced and slowly stopped the dive; in spite of that, he lost his cockpit cover. Above him he saw Bertrand, who had continued to dive, lose part of his aircraft's wing. The Yak then went into a spin at 1,000m. Marchi returned alone: Bertrand did not come back, and no one held out any hope that he was alive.

The next day the 4th Escadrille sent out six hunting sorties. In the course of these missions, at 1 p.m. the de La Salle–Émonet patrol, returning from Augustovo, arrived over the River Niemen well to the south of Alitous and had to land at Grodno. With orders to send out more hunting missions on 28 August, the Regiment sent five patrols. Cuffaut and Amarger shot up a train standing in a station. The Moynet–Taburet patrol, from the 4th, was transferred to the 1st Escadrille.

The hunting missions no longer formed up for big raids into enemy territory, but for smaller raids aiming at specific points along the front. Some sorties lasted only half an hour. In the course of the day, visibility was very bad and targets were difficult to spot; a mist covered the ground to about 1,000m. Missions of one hour and of half an hour were carried out. In the course of these sorties the Verdier–Delin patrol attacked a horse-drawn convoy and the Pouyade–Casaneuve patrol shot up a column of trucks in the Souvalki region.

On 30 August, with bad visibility, missions were interrupted from midday to 5 p.m. In the morning there were five patrols, in the evening nine. Their aim was to sow disorder and panic in the German transport on roads or railways. They succeeded and were happy to have proved their superiority. The pilots came back from their missions radiant. Just like Jupiter, they had cast their thunderbolts over roads and railways and had seen men adopt odd silhouettes deformed by fear. They were the 'lords of war'.

On 31 August, because of mist the first two patrols returned without having accomplished their task. From 2.10 to 15.05 p.m. the Génès–Manceau patrol in the region of Souvalki attacked light vehicles, then stealthily approached a large farm complex where the pilots noticed German troops feeding and drinking farm produce and looting goods from the farmhouse. The patrol swept in low and strafed the startled Germans. From 2.30 to 4.50 p.m., five patrols went out but all was quiet. From 6.10 to 7.05 p.m. the Lemare–Schoendorff patrol, 40km west of Souvalki, attacked a horse-drawn convoy and some trucks carrying guns. A truck trailing its heavy gun overturned in a ditch beside the road. From 7.45 to 8.25 p.m. the Delfino–Querne patrol hunted for targets. In the evening a meeting of the commanders with the colonel prepared the next day's missions. The Soviets would attack in the morning to the south of the River Niemen, where the front line cut across the river. Along all the fronts only about ten air regiments had the new Yak-3s; they would operate in conjunction with Normandie pilots for the first time on the following day. Missions were planned from dawn over the German lines; other fighters, Yak-9s and La-5s, would cover the interior of the lines. The Soviet command had asked Delfino to act as 'voyeur' over the front; he was to leave that evening with the Russian-speaking Pistrack, their brief to draw tactical lessons from the battle. That night, with the operation in people's minds, the discussions were heated and the plans very fanciful.

On 1 September the pilots were ready to take off from dawn to cover the sector. It went from where the front was bisected by the Niemen as far as 25km to the south, which corresponded approximately to the extent of the Soviet attack. The 1st Escadrille sent up three patrols. Above the lines the Red Air Force was very active, with circles of Stormoviks, Pe-2s, Bostons and accompanying fighters. On the ground many fires could be seen. The squad returned after 30 minutes over the sector. Brihaye, in trouble, landed on an emergency strip with only about 30 litres of fuel left. At 12.35 p.m. the 2nd took off, returning at 1.30 having encountered no enemy aircraft. At 6.30 p.m. Risso left on patrol with General Zakharov and Major Zamorine. They arrived back without having met any Boche. However, enemy fighters were not completely inactive: witness the Stormovik which was forced to land on the strip riddled with holes after its patrol was attacked by eight Fw-190s. In general, the Yak-3 gave a lot of trouble with its undercarriage, which did not always lock up when required; it could also come down of its own accord, at the worst time! Apparently, these aircraft could have been a bad batch from the factory.

PERSONALISED MARKINGS ON AIRCRAFT

With the arrival of new Yak-3 aircraft, the Normandie Soviet groundcrew had the job of painting squadron numbers on the fuselage and other national or personal emblems deemed necessary. It was a tradition dating from the First World War that certain aircraft would be personalised with an emblem or message appropriate to the pilot or crew. The practice was observed in the Second World War. The Yak flown by Lieutenant Marcel Lefèvre, who had achieved a personal victory score of eleven enemy aircraft to his credit, had painted on the fuselage of his Yak the words 'Père Magloire', a play on words that, roughly translated, meant 'My favourite beverage [Normandie calvados], My Glory'. Together with the representation of a Punch-like character wearing a red and white striped stocking hat, this appeared beside emblems of his enemy victories, signified by black crosses painted just below and to the rear of the cockpit, and over the white lightning streak seen on the 303rd Fighter Air Division aircraft. Capitaine Joseph Risso, also with a victory score of eleven enemy aircraft, had the cartoon character Donald Duck painted below his cockpit. Other French Yaks had mythical and heroic characters painted on the fuselage. The Yak-9T flown in 1944 by Capitaine

René Challe had the portrait of Fury on the fuselage below the cockpit, the same portrait that had been used in May 1940 by Groupe de Chasse III/7. The Normandie Yaks from summer 1943 onwards were to be embellished with red, white and blue concentric nose cones; previously they were all white. The French tricolour roundel appeared on the fuselage just below the cockpit and the Cross of Lorraine was painted on the tail fin.

Soviet Major-General G.N. Zakharov, Commander of the 303rd Fighter Air Division, parent Division of the Normandie Regiment, had his personal aircraft, a Yak-3, kept in immaculate condition by his groundcrew, which had painted his insignia directly below the cockpit. This consisted of a large metre-high baroque shield depicting a knight wearing a Soviet officer's uniform mounted on a white charger in the act of lancing a serpent that had the face of the hated Joseph Goebbels. A replica of the Order of the Red Banner and Guards badge was painted in red and white below the exhaust of General Zakharov's aircraft. Along the fuselage was painted the broad white lightning streak used by the 303rd Fighter Air Division. The Soviet red star markings on the fuselage and tail fin were dramatically outlined in white. In all, not a difficult aircraft to notice in any aerial fracas. Zakharov's expertise as a pilot was legendary. On one occasion when local commanders had grounded their squadrons because of atrocious weather, Zakharov arrived at the airfield to enquire about the lack of missions from that strip and was told of the adverse weather and runway conditions. A disgruntled General Zakharov marched to an aircraft and proceeded to give a breath-catching acrobatic display before the assembled pilots. Soon after he landed the Regiment had no alternative but to leave on combat missions.

Lieutenant-Colonel Sergei Dolgushin, recipient of the Gold Star, Hero of the Soviet Union, who was continually in combat over eastern Germany in February 1945, had his La-7 fighter painted in a most distinctive colour scheme. The engine fuselage section was bright red, the main fuselage was dove grey with the underside in sky blue, and the tail fin had horizontal broad red and white stripes. Lieutenant-Colonel Dolgushin's emblems consisted of a representation of his Hero Gold Star on the engine fuselage section, and below the cockpit his combat victories were indicated by seventeen red stars for confirmed kills, while eleven white stars represented shared kills.

It was one of the duties of the ground staff when preparing newly delivered Yaks to paint on them large identification numbers and also personal emblems and entitled victory symbols; each victory symbol denoted an enemy aircraft destroyed. The Soviet emblem for a combat victory took the form of a red or white star on the fuselage, whereas the French pilots used a similar system to the British, which took the form of a German black cross outlined in white, one cross for every aircraft the pilot had shot down.

On one occasion after some new replacement Yaks had been delivered to the base, the groundcrew had instructions to paint up these new aircraft with their identification numbers, then embellish them further with tricoloured spinners and roundels; at the same time any entitled victory symbols would be added to the appropriate aircraft. It was at this stage that a delicate situation arose. A new aircraft allocated to Commandant Louis Delfino was in the process of being painted up. The Soviet painter approached Delfino and respectfully enquired whether he should add to the group of German crosses shown under the cockpit an additional roundel to denote the RAF aircraft the commandant had shot down earlier in the war. The startled reply was an instant 'no'. It would seem that a fellow pilot, one of the early 1940 de Gaulle volunteers, well known as a bit of a wag with a terrible sense of black humour, had contrived the situation with the innocent Russian painter. This leg-pull would fit in well with the friendly rivalry that had existed between the original 1940 escapers and those ex-Vichy pilots who joined Normandie after the Allied liberation of North Africa. Every pilot's logbook showed his flying hours, identified aircraft flown and combat activities and locations, and indicated any confirmed combat 'kills'. In the case of Lieutenant-Colonel Delfino, who had previously served at Dakar in Vichy West Africa, an entry in his pilot's logbook from that period confirmed that on 12 August 1942 he had shot down an RAF twin-engine Vickers Wellington bomber. As this was a confirmed official entry in his pilot's logbook, it would have been noted during counter-signing by the new command.

MORE YAK-3S ARRIVE BUT LITTLE MAIL FOR NORMANDIE

On 2 September the wind was so strong that Cuffaut and de Saint-Phalle, returning from Mikountani in a U-2, took 1 hour 40 minutes to cover 100km. They brought back lots of chickens, which would form the pièce de résistance for the meals of each squadron. The following day five patrols strafed targets on the ground, provoking much anti-aircraft fire. In the evening, on the occasion of the third anniversary of its formation, the 523rd

Guards Air Regiment received the escadrille commanders, who were well 'wined and dined'.

The pilots visited a Tartar village not far from the base on 4 September. The people, with their Mongol faces, were very hospitable. The houses were very clean and well appointed. The population was Muslim, with muezzin chants from the minaret. Some read Arabic in the Koran, but they all spoke Polish or Russian. There were about 6,000 of them in the Vilno region. About 500 years ago a king of Lithuania, lacking soldiers, appealed to a Mongol tribal chief for military assistance. After the victory he ennobled them and gave the Tartars land. They stayed on. The Germans had planned to banish them to the Crimea away from this Baltic country.

Monday was market day at Alitous. Many went there to buy eggs at five roubles each and tomatoes at three roubles each. In the evening the Yak-6 returned from Moscow with little mail. The Regiment was getting hardly any post and no personal packages. The scandalous way in which the mail operated made the chaps extremely dissatisfied. Those who sent parcels to Normandie also despaired.

At Moscow, in the 'gastronomes' (grocery stores) it was quite easy to buy certain products, which the lucky chaps who acted as liaison had brought back to the Regiment. These controlled stores had been set up by the government to combat the free (black) market. Prices were very high: 100g of caviar cost 110 roubles; 100g of ham 80 roubles; 1kg of peaches 150 roubles. Yet all these goods were inferior to those on the local free market. Normandie's food supplies fluctuated from place to place; it was either little or plenty according to the location and the ability of the Supply Battalion, or the clever ones.

In Smolensk the Yak-6 had picked up pilots of the 18th Guards Air Regiment who were ferrying about thirty Yak-3s, ten of which were due for Normandie. They had left the collection point at Saratov about two weeks before and were delayed by the general lack of aviation fuel available at bases behind the front lines. The front was also suffering from fuel shortages. On 10 September, after no flying for six days, the standby patrol by the 4th Escadrille had taken off after two Bf-109s, signalled by the radio control post some 25km away. Few aircraft were available: nineteen Yak-3s and two Yak-9s. It was noticed that the offensive was slowing down. Many lost faith in an end to the war before the dreaded Russian winter; all had hoped the Regiment would return to France before the bad weather closed in. While waiting they all busied themselves with trips to Alitous. Some sat in the town park and tried to engage in polite conversation with the elegant ladies who promenaded at the fashionable time. Others, who were less demanding, enjoyed conversations with little old ladies. It was noted that the names changed as the Regiment moved further west. Formerly one met Galla, Maroussia, Tania; now the names encountered were Albine, Vladi, Broni, Rodia, Auna or even Jenny: obviously Hollywood had influenced the educated Lithuanians. Here pilots learned that gambling with cards could make you a richer or a poorer person!

At 7 p.m. on 11 September a commemoration was held of the death of Guynemer. Capitaine Mourier read the posthumous citation without consulting notes. A minute's silence was observed in memory of the thirty Normandie pilots who had died that year. Guynemer was the French Air Force's First World War 'ace of aces', having been credited with fifty-three enemy aircraft destroyed. His patriotic tenacity and courageous achievements were such that they were held up as an example for all French pilots to follow.

At 7.30 p.m. the colonel returned from Moscow. Helped by a good tail wind, he accomplished the Alitous–Moscow trip in 1 hour 55 minutes. He brought back very little mail. In the few letters, more than two months old, lots of parcels were mentioned which the chaps were still waiting for; causing much dissatisfaction. The nights become cool and the days resembled those of a very advanced French autumn. A memo came from the Division ordering four patrols to carry out hunting missions. The 18th Guards Air Regiment had a similar order. The colonel procured permission for ten patrols, which involved all the aircraft available to carry out these missions. The working sector was limited to the north by the River Niemen, to the south by the parallel of Mariampol, to the west by the vertical of Tilsitt. The sorties were not to last more than 55 minutes. Having indicated the extent of regular German air activity, the Chief of Staff outlined the principal objectives: the boats on the Niemen, cars, trucks and railways. He also indicated approximate locations of the anti-aircraft positions and informed the Regiment that on the German airstrips of the sector and surroundings there were about 200 enemy aircraft of which about 130 were fighters. Thus prepared, the patrols fulfilled their missions to the best of their ability.

On 14 September the following missions were carried out. From 7.45 to 8.40 a.m., the Génès–Manceau patrol strafed a train on the line north-west of Pilkallen. From 9.20 to 10.20 a.m., the Challe–Querne patrol strafed a train and a station, on the line from Pilkallen to Nanenungen. From 3.40 to 4.45 p.m. the Matras–Sauvage patrol was active. Just as Matras was going to retract the undercarriage, Capitaine Challe, who found himself at the radio post on the ground, signalled that a Boche, probably an Me-110, was flying above the runway. Matras set off in hot pursuit and, well directed by Challe, caught up with him at 6,500m near Chaki. Unfortunately during combat the guns jammed and made his firing ineffective; to add to his frustration he had to abandon the pursuit due to lack of fuel. As he landed on the opposite runway with the engine overheated and seized up, his face told all around him how he felt. From 4.35 to 5.30 p.m. the Le Martelot–Monier patrol strafed a column of enemy trucks to the north of Goumbinnen. On his return Monier was forced to land at Kaunas to take on fuel. Others scrambled on an alert – de La Salle, alone, at 11.40 a.m. and the Charras–Castin patrol at 2.45 p.m. – after information about an Me-110 spotted above Krasnoie, which made off before he could be caught. Once again Cuffaut and de Saint-Phalle came back from Mikountani, the U-2 filled with chickens, eggs and Samagonka (self-distilled hooch). As a result, a magnificent meal was served by the 2nd Escadrille, whose choice dish was a superb scented aioli.

On 15 September sorties were carried out from 9.15 to 10.05 a.m. by an Albert–de La Poype patrol. From 11.00 to 11.50 a.m. a Delfino–André patrol at the end of the mission attacked a staff car near Goumbinnen. Commandant Delfino scored a bull's-eye but, on regaining height, the patrol passed above a small wood hiding vicious anti-aircraft fire. Delfino's aircraft was hit by a shell behind the pilot's seat; the water radiator was punctured, the control functions were partially severed, but he made it back. From 11.30 a.m. to 12.30 p.m. a Pouyade–Cuffaut patrol neutralised the anti-aircraft position recently located. At 1 p.m. a Mertzisen–Douarre patrol scrambled but nothing was located. At the end of the day came the order to prepare for departure to a new airstrip at 9 a.m. the next morning. The last patrol of the day by de La Poype–Fauroux carried out a strafing sortie.

MOVE TO ANTONOVO

At 9 a.m. on 16 September the weather was fine but the order to move arrived at only 1 p.m. and was then cancelled immediately; the La-7s on the runway had not moved. However, in the afternoon about ten pilots, without aircraft, left for the strip by truck. The colonel and Albert went in a Yak to the new airstrip. On their flight they did a tour of the front and were violently taken to task by enemy flak to the north of Goumbinnen. The following day after lunch seven pilots went to ferry Yak-9s (formerly Normandie's) of the 523rd Air Regiment. The aircraft were taken to the strip at Sassnava, then the pilots were driven by truck to Antonovo, about 20km away. At 4 p.m. the 1st departed for Antonovo. The La-7 fighters had left the shared landing ground and all their groundcrew were leaving for Romania. They had done exceptionally well and achieved thirty-five victories in a month. From 10 a.m. on 18 September the last departures for Antonovo were made. This strip was not far from Pilvitchki, a railway station on the Kaunas–Koenigsberg line; the Chechoupe river, a tributary of the Niemen, ran by not far from the runway, which was very sandy and had been farm fields. The countryside was rich and heavily populated, with small farms scattered to the four corners of the base. It was here that the Regiment was to be stationed. It rediscovered one of the Regiment's old Supply Battalions from the previous year. The last mission carried out at Alitous was by Perrin. He scrambled at the sight of a twin-engine enemy machine that was trailing condensation but could not catch up with it. The first two operations at Antonovo were covering missions protecting the radio control of the 1st Air Corps at Sassnava, to the east of the runway. This same control centre was attacked the day before by a group of Fw-190s.

From 11.30 a.m. to 2.15 p.m. on 19 September four hunting missions went out. In the course of an attack on the station at Nanenungen some train carriages were destroyed. Another mission was in pursuit of a tug and a barge sailing on the Niemen. Mourier and Menut patrolled from 17.15 to 18.05 p.m. Menut's engine sounded very rough and vibrated to such an extent that he had to turn back. Mourier continued alone and, to the south-east of Tilsitt, surprised a pack of Fw-190s going towards the east. Closing to less than 100m and with the sun in his back, Mourier moved behind the patrol leader and shot him down before he noticed anything. Then he attacked the rest of the group, but his guns jammed and he returned. The last mission, at 6.55 p.m., went off without incident.

General Zakharov had come to lunch with the Regiment. At 4 p.m. he held a meeting with all the pilots and explained the Division's mission. The principal mission was to prevent enemy aircraft flying over the Division's territory, that is, between the Niemen to the north and the Insterburg–Kaunas railway line to the south. The two covering radar stations would provide location plotting of the enemy's position within a series of numbered 20km squares; they had issued pilots with cards identifying the individual position of each 20km square. They would then transmit, on the wavelength used by the Yak aircraft, details of the numbered square in which the enemy had been located. The transmitter on the ground would act as interpreter. However, with the translation prolonging transmission delays, this standby mission would fall not to Normandie but to the 18th Guards Air Regiment. French Yaks would have a standby of four aircraft of which two would be on full alert. Normandie's main mission would be to make incursions into enemy territory and to attack objectives on the ground and in the air. Between Tilsitt and Insterburg many enemy aircraft were in circulation. As a result, the general advised passing over the lines at 6,000m then arriving over the Tilsitt area at 3,500m. If no enemy were encountered in the air, objectives should be sought on the railway lines, roads or the River Niemen. He also advised pilots to avoid the front line and towns stuffed with anti-aircraft fire; instead they should search for the enemy's secondary bases and log their activities. Information coming from intelligence regiments would be communicated to the control post. Strafing missions on precise objectives may be demanded of the Regiment. The general concluded by making all ashamed of the ease with which enemy aircraft were flying with impunity over Normandie's territory; a great effort would have to be made to forbid them airspace. The Regiment's missions against the enemy must always be successful, nobody must return without having at least fired a machine gun. He invited the pilots to ask him questions about life on the base; Carbon asked for the vodka ration to be restored. The general added that cinema and theatre performances and trips to Kaunas would be organised. The upshot was that the escadrilles would continue to fly and perform tasks for which the Yak, so manageable and so fast but relatively poorly armed, was ill-suited. If only the Luftwaffe would come out and show itself. Whereas in the same period of the previous year Soviet communiqués daily reported nearly 100 enemy aircraft shot down, in 1944 they were mentioning only about 15 destroyed daily. This was what was distressing a lot of those who had come to feast on Boche and cover themselves in glory and decorations.

On 20 September the following hunting sorties went out: from 7.00 to 8.05 a.m. an Albert–Marchi patrol was attacked by anti-aircraft fire. Marchi returned with a small shell in the engine. From 8.15 to 9 a.m., a Challe–Miquel patrol between Tilsitt and Gillen attacked two trains travelling in opposite directions just as they were about to pass each other. From 10.15 to 11.10 a.m. a Cuffaut–Amarger patrol left on a mission to attack trains, and obtained positive results with locomotives smoking from all parts and carriages on fire. However, a Mertzisen–Douarre patrol and de La Salle–Manceau patrol, which took off at 11.20 a.m. to strafe locomotives, found nothing but some carriages in Gillen and a locomotive in reserve to the north of the station, which were strafed by Mertzisen. From 9.05 a.m. to 5.15 p.m. three missions went out. The last mission attacked a column of vehicles. During the day there were two scrambles. The first was at 10.15 a.m. to chase a Ju-88, which climbed towards Kaunas, then two Fw-190s were located going to land at Kaunas. The Fw-190s were piloted by two pro-Nazi Czechs displeased at finding that Kaunas and its landing strip were no longer in German hands but recently captured by Soviet troops. The second take-off was at midday.

General Zakharov sent a generous telegram to Mourier on his recent successes.

On 21 September seven hunting missions set off between 8.50 a.m. and 4 p.m. They all succeeded in attacking various means of transport: train carriages, locomotives, convoys of cars, motorbikes, and, on the Niemen, barges and canal-boats. In the course of the day enemy aircraft crossed the sky several times; the Soviet detector did not once succeed in spotting them in time. Fortunately, they betrayed themselves with magnificent trails of condensation. The following took off on sightings: at 10.50 a.m. a de Saint-Marceaux–Brihaye patrol looked for an He-111. At 12.40 p.m. Mourier–Menut patrol went off in pursuit of an He-111 above Tilsitt without being able to reach it; the aircraft climbed to 7,000m. Mourier, who was able to open his oxygen bottle only belatedly, came back very weary. At 1.40 Carbon took off without Lebras, whose aircraft – the one in which Mourier had just flown – was not ready. Carbon caught an He-111; some well-aimed shots stopped one of its engines. At the very moment when he went in to take out the other engine, he noticed four Fw-190s, which bolted for him. He called for reinforcements by radio, but no more aircraft were left in the standby escadrille; only Lebras took off but, unable to retract his undercarriage, had to land. Carbon, after having circled a few times with the Fw-190s, headed into the clouds and returned. At 2.35 p.m. he took off again, still on his own for lack of available aircraft, in pursuit of an Me-110. But the enemy escaped by going into a vertical dive. That day standby missions could not be carried out due to lack of aircraft, also the base was without bottled oxygen and no replacements were available. At dinner in the mess a good Burgundy was served; it had been liberated from German supplies. With the help of five energetic musicians, the wine created an ambiance very like Sheherazade.

From 7.05 to 8.05 a.m. on 22 September, a Verdier–Delin patrol was up. After having reconnoitred the area, Verdier decided to attack a locomotive on the Tilsitt–Insterburg railway line. He began to dive towards the line in perpendicular fashion. Delin banked to place himself in the axis of the line; he rectified his dive, pulled up at tree level, zoomed to 2,000m but could no longer see Verdier. He had probably struck the ground after the dive and there was little hope of seeing him return. Verdier was much liked, always in good humour and an excellent comrade. From 8.35 to 9.25 a.m., an André–Penverne patrol attacked two goods trains 4km north of Gillen and wrecked them. From 9.30 to 10.35 a.m., a Dechanet–de Saint-Phalle patrol, having reconnoitred behind the German lines, shot up a vehicle near Nasdenien and fortifications under construction close to the front in the north of the sector. From 10.50 to 11.40 a.m. a Martin–Versini patrol attacked a vehicle near Donden. From noon to 12.45 p.m. a Le Martelot–Schick patrol was ordered to go on reconnaissance, but the mission was cancelled as an La-5 had been brought down by flak the previous day in the same region. The patrol found a vehicle to strafe near Zadenelt. The standby patrol took off twice in the morning without any engagements. From 2 p.m. all flights were cancelled because of poor visibility. In the evening it was pleasing to watch the arrival of ten new Yak-3s.

In the morning six patrols went hunting. From 3.50 to 4.35 p.m. the Cuffaut–Amarger patrol was on a mission to strafe the station at Goumbinnen, where reconnaissance had spotted goods trains. On arrival over the station the patrol came up against a Fieseler Storch. Cuffaut put some lead into the wing and the Fiesler Storch disappeared into a small wood. Amarger machine-gunned the remains. But on arrival over the station the patrol was welcomed by fierce anti-aircraft fire, so sustained that after several unfortunate attempts the patrol had to return without having carried out its mission. On that day, of the seven hunting missions three had been for reconnaissance and one for strafing, all ordered by the Division. The flak was always precise and many aircraft returned having been hit by it. At the end of the afternoon a Douglas DC-3 came to pick-up the Yak-3s' ferry pilots. Albert, de La Poype, Laurent, Cuffaut and Amarger joined the ferry pilots and flew to

Saratov to return in Yak-3s. Fauroux went on leave to Moscow. Thus the 1st was now only a shadow of the escadrille originally commanded by Moynet.

In the morning of 24 September there were five strafing missions. From 2 to 2.55 p.m. the Matras–de Geoffre patrol shot up a train to the south of Tilsitt. Having fuel problems, de Geoffre landed in a field, ended up in a wood and escaped unscathed. From 4.50 to 5.30 p.m. the Challe–Miquel patrol attacked a train to the north of Gillen. The 1st standby patrol took off at 11.30 a.m. without results. Several patrols flying over the region where Verdier was lost were attacked by anti-aircraft fire, the guns camouflaged in a small wood that was apparently where Verdier went down the day before. Perhaps he was hit by flak and had to land behind German lines. If Delin did not see any flak, it is probably because he rectified his dive by skirting the little wood instead of flying over it. On Sunday twenty pilots spent a pleasant day in Kaunas, being very well received by the Lithuanian ladies.

In the morning of 25 September there were three strafing missions, during which Schoendorff had to land at Kaunas. From 10 a.m. to 12.25 p.m. the Le Martelot–Monier patrol went above the clouds, headed west, then crossed once again the cloudy strata. Le Martelot began a spiralling descent; Monier did not follow him and emerged over the Baltic. He then headed to the east and landed after a flight of 1 hour and 20 minutes. His aircraft looked a real mess: battered by the branches he grazed in his hedge-hopping, pierced at the base of the wing by a bird, with the petrol reserves near empty, it told the story of his epic journey. But Le Martelot was missing. At midday the Perrin–Querne patrol departed between two banks of cloud. Then Perrin looked for the ground and found it a little before Tilsitt. At that moment he lost Querne. He returned at once and landed at Kaunas, thinking to find him; but Querne was not there. At the end of the morning, of six patrols that left three aircraft landed at Kaunas and Le Martelot and Querne were missing. The three aircraft returned from Kaunas in the afternoon. At 2 p.m. the missions were interrupted and the standby abandoned.

The following day the Regiment was on call for an important covering mission. The Military Command had organised an attack in the Souvalki region to seize a military observation post situated on top of a hill. An infantry division took part in the operation on a front stretching from 3km to 5km. Fifteen squads, each of four Stormoviks, supported the infantry; tanks were not used. At dawn four patrols were ready to ensure cover over the sector to be attacked. The assault began at 2 p.m. German artillery and air power did not react and the hill was taken by the end of the evening. It was defended by fifty-six German soldiers. The officer in command, a lieutenant of 21 years, gave himself up out of fear that, had he retreated, he would have been shot by his own side; he had received orders to hold out whatever the cost. He was a former fanatical Nazi supporter, wearing an Iron Cross together with two Eastern Front assault award badges pinned on his tunic. His morale was at an all-time low, as was that of his comrades. He added, 'We lack munitions: the rear is at breaking-point; 50g of meat per week per soldier.' Soviet losses were insignificant. With some disappointment, Normandie pilots taxied the aircraft back to their standing areas without having taken off. At 6 p.m. the prodigals returned. Albert, de La Poype, and the others who left to pick up new aircraft near Moscow, after collecting their Yak-3s from the ferry park, were told to turn round immediately and head back to the front; they could not visit the aircraft factories of Saratov or sample the delights of Moscow. During dinner the news arrived that Le Martelot has been found to the south of Riga, 180km to the north of the base, wounded and with his uniform in tatters; poor dear 'Mimile'. The news gave all great joy. After dinner a grand concert was organised by the troops of the First Aerial Army, with choruses and dances of a very Russian nature. But all had eyes for only one of the performers, Marta Ivanovna, a very Slavic beauty. From 2.15 to 3 p.m. the Sauvage–Pierrot patrol hunted over East Prussia, locating and strafing a barge and tug on the River Niemen.

In the morning of 27 September four patrols undertook sorties like those of the previous day. Pistrack returned at 10 a.m. from the front and reported that the attack of the previous evening had been successfully completed. There were no missions during the day owing to lack of fuel. In the afternoon a hospital U-2 brought Le Martelot back. He remembered nothing of what happened to him other than that he turned over on the ground. The doc feared concussion. Albert returned with astounding news from the Moscow Mission: he informed the Regiment that the departure of the senior veterans had been decided. These eighteen happy people now made plans for travel and celebration. The rest of the chaps looked anything but pleased at the prospect of wintering there without them. The following morning from 10 a.m. to 2.15 p.m. four hunting missions went out to strafe trucks and trains. The colonel had been called to Division in the morning to discuss details about a possible departure for another front. But the command remained discreet and information was scarce.

On 29 September there were hunting missions from 11.05 a.m. to noon. At the moment the Dechanet–de Saint-Phalle patrol attacked a canal-boat and coal-barge lighter, Dechanet's engine stalled. Expecting to be obliged to land close to the Germans they were due to hit, he ordered de Saint-Phalle not to machine-gun them, doubtless to please those on the ground among whom he expected to land by parachute. Then at 20m, fortunately, the engine restarted and Dechanet was still flying, the Germans having escaped punishment. In the afternoon seven missions went up. Capitaine Challe attacked an Fw-190, which took refuge in the clouds. The next day, with fine weather, strong condensation trails allowed watchers to detect enemy aircraft at altitude. Soviet detection was still just as bad. The standby patrol of the 4th took off on a sighting at 10.45 a.m., soon supported by the Delin–Jeannel patrol, which also went hunting. The Génès–Manceau patrol of the 4th climbed to 8,000m and noticed directly in front at the same height a diving Ju-88. They tried but failed to catch up with it. Pilots of Normandie had previously noted that one of the tactics adopted by the experienced Ju-88 pilot, when hard pressed by the faster Yak, would be to nose dive in a vertical spiral for some 2,000m; if that had not thrown off the pursuing Yak the Ju-88 pilot would repeat the vertical dive for another 2,000m, and the procedure continued until he ran out of altitude, escaped or was ultimately shot down.

At 11.30 a.m. the Cuffaut–Bagnères patrol was sent up towards two condensation trails and at 6,000m recognised a Pe-2. At 7,000m Cuffaut spotted two Bf-109s under him and to his left. He dived on them. Bagnères followed him but spotted an Me-110, which was looking to attack. He banked over it, crossed and lost it. Cuffaut attacked the two Bf-109s on his own. One of them exploded; the other started to bank and then, seeing that Cuffaut was catching him up, turned round to leave and dived towards the clouds. At that moment Cuffaut fired and hit him in the tail. The Bf-109 disappeared in the clouds. For Cuffaut one sure victory and one probable. From 12.25 to 4.40 p.m. there were four hunting missions. In the evening, with the help of none too wonderful Lithuanian alcohol, the 2nd and 4th Escadrilles celebrated success.

On 1 October Normandie was without any fuel reserves, so saw little activity. In the course of the day only three patrols took off, and reported nothing. In the morning the standby patrol by the 3rd took off to catch up with Pe-2s and protect them during a mission over the front line.

On 6 October, the departure for the new base at Stredniki had been delayed by four days due to bad weather: 100m ceiling and rain. For the same reason the offensive on the front was postponed to a later date. Since it was a clear period that day, orders to transfer to Stredniki were given at 10 a.m. Those pilots without aircraft made the trip in the Yak-6. The pilots took with them only what was strictly necessary for the two or three days to be spent at Stredniki. Those remaining at Antonovo included Le Martelot, who was wounded, and Eichenbaum, the Regiment's organiser. At 2 p.m., shortly after arrival at Stredniki, a protecting mission was required to cover for bombing. Bostons and Pe-2 bombers passed above the strip, and the Yaks quickly caught up with them. All four escadrilles took off; 1st, 3rd, and 4th sent up two patrols and the 2nd three. The bombing took place all along the front. Anti-aircraft fire was forceful but the Luftwaffe non-existent. The mission lasted in total 15 minutes. On 7 October there was only one patrol over the front, by Carbon and Lebras.

The new airstrip was set in a vast belt of fields to the east of Stredniki, positioned on the right bank of the Niemen. The Regiment was staying in an agricultural college at the edge of the river; the trees in the park were beautiful and the view over the Niemen charming. It was to be the prettiest billet so far. The control HQ was at the far end of the runway and the aircraft were on all sides. On 8 October the weather was bad; but at the end of the evening, taking advantage of a break in the clouds, several patrols went out to strafe trains. Two Fw-190s were spotted and pursued but without a result. At 6 p.m. the Yak-6 departed for Moscow taking Schick, Risso and Le Martelot: two on leave, one, wounded, to the hospital.

On 9 October the weather improved. The offensive, which had been going well, now accelerated. Pilots took part in the battle by covering the front and going hunting behind German lines. After the André–Penverne patrol had tested the weather, the Moynet–Bagnères patrol took off. Moynet's aircraft was hit on the left wing by flak. From 4 p.m. the Regiment ensured permanent cover over the front in the Taouraguie region. The first mission was covered by two patrols of the 3rd Squadron, whose leader was Matras. Arriving over the lines at 3,000m, he found intense Soviet aerial activity with Airacobras, Stormoviks, Yaks and La-5s. Taouraguie was burning under great bursts of artillery. Matras attacked some dubious aircraft. In the disengagement he lost his comrade de Geoffre, but Douarre joined him. Matras then spotted a Bf-109 and surprised it at 100m. He fired, the Bf-109 acknowledged the hits, and made a very brutal turn and then a vertical dive. At that moment Douarre fired at it, as did Matras once again, and the Bf-109 went into the clouds. Matras extricated himself at more than 800kph. The Division reported the fall of this Bf-109 near Taouraguie. However, de Geoffre was attacked on his own by two Fw-190s and was relieved just in time by Mertzisen. At 16.30, two patrols of the 1st returned without having encountered the enemy. At 17.30, two patrols of the 2nd and one patrol of the 3rd, commanded by Martin, met a number of Soviet aircraft and turned with them. While banking Miquel lost contact. He returned alone having expended his ammunition. At 6 p.m. two patrols commanded by Delfino, consisting of a patrol of the 3rd and a patrol of the 1st, encountered eight Bf-109s and four Fw-190s. The patrols circled them without a result. However, André fired at an Fw-190 and damaged it.

On 10 October, despite bad weather, the patrols worked in shifts to ensure coverage of the Taouraguie sector, and attacked trains and other objectives. The bridge at Taouraguie was burning and subsided into the river in a red cone of fire. At 11 a.m. two patrols of the 2nd accompanied an Il-2 photographing, and also covered some Stormoviks that were flying at 300m; the covering Yak flew at 800m. The front was smothered in smoke; an enormous tangle of trenches stretched across 15km but there were no signs of troop activity on the ground. From noon to 1.30 p.m. three hunting missions took place, but the weather was so bad that the squad was broken up. Challe–Castin, having strafed a factory near Insterburg, attacked an Fw-190 and succeeded in shooting it down in flames. At 3 p.m. all the missions were cancelled. At the end of the day, all returned to Antonovo, some by aircraft, others by truck.

On 11 October there was good news for the seniors. Meanwhile, operations continued; the Martin–Versini patrol, testing the weather, went as far as the front and ran into heavy anti-aircraft fire. The Yak-6 returned from Moscow bringing the news that a Douglas DC-3 had been given for the use of those time-expired veterans travelling to Moscow; from there it would be reassigned to service in other theatres. This movement order became the great business of the day for those leaving: Colonel Pouyade, de Pange, the doctor, Albert, de La Poype, Risso, Moynet, Mourier, Jeannel, Laurent, Sauvage, Monier and de Saint-Phalle. They were woken at 7 a.m. by the announcement that a Douglas DC-3 was waiting for them at Kaunas to travel to Moscow. They packed their cases, gave their watches and belongings to their mechanics and shook numerous hands. At 8.30 a.m. it was announced that departure had been delayed until the next morning in order to sort out all the administrative matters. Good, reliable Eichenbaum, who was really indispensable to the Regiment, agreed not to leave for Moscow. At 7 p.m. the colonel and those leaving said their official farewells to the Russians. At 8 p.m. a great banquet was prepared in the mess, which was decorated with placards reading 'Indefectible attachment to Colonel Pouyade and Glory to the veterans'. But the colonel did not make the expected farewell speech; instead he announced that the Soviet Army senior commandant had warned Normandie of an imminent offensive on the front, and the colonel had agreed, in the name of all those who were going to leave for Moscow, to remain to take part in the coming struggle. Admirable veterans! They abandoned without a thought all their magnificent plans; farewell Tehran, Cairo, family and pretty girls.

On 13 October the skies were clear and condensation trails visible at altitude. During the day the Regiment carried out many hunting missions; two strafing sorties on the station at Chtaloupienen; and numerous missions to protect, reconnoitre and cover the sector. Protective missions accompanied bombing and reconnaissance aircraft, in the course of which a wood containing gun emplacements was strafed and an enemy aircraft pursued but not caught. On return, two Yaks, having used up their fuel, were forced to land a few kilometres from the base. During all these missions, enemy anti-aircraft fire was very active and accurate. Casaneuve was missing and several aircraft were damaged by flak. Three scrambles were followed by covering missions over the front line. In the course of one of the sorties a Ju-88, intercepted by the André–Penverne patrol, was shot down in flames. For the Regiment the day had been one of the most active of the period: sixty-six sorties, one victory, six strafings; but unfortunately Casaneuve was missing and three aircraft were damaged by enemy flak. It was a day full of emotion for those who were watching from the airstrip. At 3 p.m., almost vertically above the runway, a German twin-engine machine was set on fire by two hunters who were unfortunately not from Normandie. The machine exploded in the air. Shortly afterwards four parachutes were spotted descending towards the strip; one landed at Pilvitchki. Only a few minutes later a Stormovik crashed near the strip; then Iribarne and Commandant Delfino had an accident. And finally de La Salle, very worried, called to report that ordnance staff of the 4th, being stuffed full of caviar and intoxicated on vodka, were crashing all over the beds in the quarters.

In the morning of 14 October there were two covering missions, then continuous activity until 2 p.m. At 12.25 p.m. the de La Poype–Taburet, Sauvage–Bagnères squad surprised over the enemy landing strip at Ragnite some Fw-190s and Bf-109s, which took off, some loaded with bombs, others acting as fighter protection. At the first passage de La Poype shot down a Bf-109, Sauvage destroyed an Fw-190, and then had to disengage. Taburet fired at an Fw-190 and then attacked another. Bagnères assaulted a Bf-109 and damaged it. It was a fine spectacle for those on the runway to see comrades return one after the other and do a slow 'victory' roll. In addition, four aircraft of the 1st protected a Stormovik on a photo mission. And six aircraft of the 2nd Escadrille covered and protected the Pe-2, which had been sent to accomplish and finish the previous day's mission, from which neither Casaneuve nor the Pe-2 that he was accompanying returned. Dear 'Cassepipe' (Casaneuve), so discreet, so well brought-up, such a charming comrade: there was little chance of seeing him return. At 1.30 p.m. a patrol composed of the duos Matras–de Geoffre and Mertzisen–Douarre, while covering the front, intercepted a Ju-88. Having received a blast from each of them, the Ju-88 crashed to the ground. The 1st standby patrol had taken off twice without any encounters. A good day for Normandie: three victories without loss. General Zakharov sent a telegram of thanks for the work carried out the previous day, and ratified the Bf-109 fired on by Matras on 9 October.

On 15 October, while hunting, the Lemare–Charras–Castin squad strafed a village near Chtaloupienen. Missions were then halted for work on the aircraft. The tricolour rosettes and regimental numbers were painted on the fuselage and the spinners beautifully painted in concentric stripes of red, white and blue. The 2nd standby escadrille took off three times after Bf-109s; the Yaks took the opportunity to make some cone of fire adjustments to their guns and tested them. At 7 p.m. the colonel assembled all the pilots at the canteen and announced that the offensive would start the following day; it would take the Red Army to Koenigsberg in four days and soon after to the end of the war. He asked all to give of their utmost and to adopt an attitude that was resolutely on the offensive, never losing the opportunity to hit the Germans: 'Strafe military objectives on the road, in the fields, factories, farms. Have your revenge on the Boches!'

NORMANDIE'S TWENTY-NINE VICTORIES IN A SINGLE DAY

The offensive against East Prussia began at 10.30 a.m. on 16 October with a great artillery barrage. From 11 a.m. to 7 p.m. the activity of bombers and Stormoviks did not stop. The combat zone was on fire; the fires seemed to have spread to the west, which was a good sign! Normandie carried out two types of missions: protecting the bombers and covering the ground offensive, especially in the Vilkavitchki sector. Operations in the air and search for the enemy were greatly helped by the radio voice of Pistrack, who guided the patrols to the enemy from the radio position at the front. During the morning two squads went on a mission to protect some bombers. During these missions there was serious confusion in the attempt to locate the bombers, which were not where control expected them to be. In the last mission, Aspirant Challe came across a Bf-109 in the act of firing on a Boston. He closed quickly on the enemy and hit the Bf-109, which exploded and came down in many pieces. During the day ten missions covering the offensive in the Vilkavitchki region were accomplished. At 12.45 p.m. a squad with Delfino–Perrin and Challe–Émonet attacked some Fw-190s. Perrin shot down one Fw-190, which crashed at Chtaloupienen, and Capitaine Challe shot down another Fw-190 at Chirvind. Commandant Delfino probably shot down an Fw-190 at Chtaloupienen. At 1.10 p.m. a squad with Matras–de Geoffre and André–Penverne swung into action. Matras and de Geoffre attacked some Fw-190s. In the region of Chtaloupienen Matras shot down an Fw-190, which he saw crash into the ground and de Geoffre damaged another. André shot down an Fw-190 in the Goumbinnen region. At 1.30 p.m. a squad of the 1st Escadrille encountered eight Ju-87s without protection. Albert, Taburet, Marchi, de La Poype, and Sauvage cut out and killed a Ju-87, which crashed in flames in Chtaloupienen. Then Albert–Sauvage fired on one, which went into a spiral and crashed to the ground. Marchi shot down a Ju-87; likewise, de La Poype and Taburet each destroyed a Ju-87. The battle took place 100m from the ground. At 2 p.m. the Carbon–Lebras and Martin–Versini squad attacked Bf-109s. Carbon shot down two Bf-109s at Chtaloupienen, while Lebras shot down an Fw-190 in flames in the same region.

At 2.45 p.m. a squad commanded by Colonel Pouyade and composed of four aircraft of the 2nd, two aircraft of the 1st and four aircraft of the 4th, protected four groups of bombers. In the course of this mission, the colonel shot down one Fw-190 at Vilkavitchki, and Perrin attacked an Fw-190 to the east of Chtaloupienen, which also went down in flames. Amarger fired at an Fw-190 at Cheirgallen; it crashed in a cloud of smoke as it hit the ground. Cuffaut hit one Fw-190, whose pilot parachuted down in the Goumbinnen region; Castin probably finished another Fw-190; de La Salle got an Fw-190, which went down belching smoke and flames. Charras destroyed an Fw-190 at Chtaloupienen. At the same time important missions covering the offensive in the Vilkavitchki were being carried out successfully. At 3.50 p.m. the Delfino–Laurent, de Saint-Marceaux–Brihaye squad was in action. Delfino pursued a Bf-109 along the ground and shot it down. Laurent pursued an Fw-190 and destroyed it. Brihaye circled with six Bf-109s, damaged one and managed to escape with difficulty. De Saint-Marceaux scuffled with two Fw-190s without a result. At 4.15 p.m. the Challe–Schoendorff, Génès–Manceau and Matras–de Geoffre patrols went into action. Challe shot down a Bf-109 in flames at Goumbinnen. Génès and Manceau pursued and attacked a Bf-109, which crashed to the south-east of Insterburg. At 5 p.m. a squad composed of four aircraft of the 2nd and four of the 1st shot down an Fw-190 15km south-east of Chtaloupienen. Carbon–Émonet scuffled with some Fw-190s without a result, as did Cuffaut–Amarger.

At 6 p.m. a squad made up of three aircraft of the 3rd and four of 1st attacked some Fw-190s and Bf-109s. Mertzisen and Aspirant Challe shot down a Bf-109 in flames 5km east of Chtaloupienen. Albert shot down a Bf-109, which was seen to crash to the ground. De La Poype and Marchi together shot down two Bf-109s; one crashed to the ground, the other was left diving in flames. During the day the Regiment made a total of 100 sorties, protected 126 Soviet bombers, Bostons and Pe-2s, and shot down 29 enemy aircraft: 16 Fw-190s, 8 Bf-109s, 5 Ju-87s, plus 2 probable Fw-190s and 2 Bf-109s. Normandie suffered no losses. A truly memorable day for the Regiment.

On the morning of 17 October many pilots felt a glow of achievement after the previous day's multitude of victories, many of which were now confirmed as aces. The Regiment again carried out missions to accompany bombers and hunting missions covering the front. At 9.20 a.m. a squad composed of eight aircraft of the 4th with Commandant Delfino and commanded by Colonel Pouyade protected three groups of Pe-2s. Several aircraft in these groups were attacked by enemy fighters and were shot down. The colonel fired on an Fw-190 and probably shot it down. Schoendorff saw a Bf-109 that had just set a Pe-2 bomber on fire; he pursued the fighter and attacked it, leaving it in flames. The Charras–Castin patrol shot down an Fw-190 10km south-west of Chtaloupienen; the pilot jumped by parachute. Capitaine Challe saw his comrade Émonet with his wing on fire: 'Émonet does not return but could have jumped by parachute', he declared on his arrival back. At 12.30 p.m. six aircraft of the 3rd Escadrille commanded by Capitaine Matras went up. Patrol Challe–Miquel attacked a patrol of Bf-109s and shot down two in the Goumbinnen region. At 12.30 p.m. eight aircraft of the 1st Escadrille, commanded by Albert, encountered about thirty Fw-190s, which were dive-bombing; they were protected by many Bf-109s. Dechanet shot down an Fw-190 in flames, and the pilot parachuted out. De Saint-Phalle shot down another, which crashed to the ground; it was his first victory. Aspirants Sauvage and Cuffaut probably shot down one, then another in collaboration; they saw the pilot leave by parachute. Marchi shot another down, de La Poype and de Saint-Phalle each damaged one. All the battles took place in the Chtaloupienen region. At 2 p.m. the Pouyade–Perrin patrol and four aircraft of the 3rd came across about twenty-five Fw-190 bombers; they let the majority pass, then mounted towards the sun and dived down in a classic attack mode on the last group. Twelve patrols were involved; Perrin shot down an Fw-190, which landed belly up; Lorillon shot one, which struck the ground; he then fired on another head-on, tearing off the left part of the enemy's tailplane. Monier shot down one that he watched as it turned and hit the ground. The Sauvage–Pierrot patrol, which had remained above as cover, attacked another formation of eight Fw-190s, and Pierrot probably shot one down. Lieutenant Sauvage was within 10m behind an Fw-190 when his guns jammed. The colonel, circling in battle with some Fw-190s, was attacked by four other enemy aircraft; he broke away with such a brutal turn that he went into a tail-spin and could rectify the situation only near the ground. Between 3.25 and 4 p.m. three missions went up without result, in spite of two scuffles.

During the day the Regiment made 109 sorties and shot down twelve aircraft – nine Fw-190s and three Bf-109s – and probably shot down four more Fw-190s and damaged a futher two; all this as they flew in action against approximately ninety-nine enemy bombers. Normandie suffered one loss, poor Émonet, with two aircraft damaged (Lorillon and Taburet). In the evening a Douglas DC-3 arrived from Moscow with Eichenbaum, Risso, Schick and Fauroux. As well, seven new trainee pilots arrived: Guido, Ougloff,

Henri, Reverchon, Bleton, Piquenot and Monge. With them came warm things for winter service and lots of very welcome supplies.

UNUSUAL DEATH OF NORMANDIE'S SOVIET SECRETARY

In the afternoon of 17 October 1944, Nina, the Regiment's secretary for eighteen months, committed suicide. The pilots of Normandie were absolutely shattered when they heard the news; everyone was at a loss to explain her tragic action. She was only 21 years old. This sad event left everyone mystified at the time and caused great sadness for everyone, especially as she was so young and had been so full of life before the tragedy. With all the hectic combat activity and recent Regiment casualties, little blonde Nina had to be considered just another victim of the cruel war. Some years later, on a visit to the Soviet Union for an anniversary reunion, a discussion took place with one of the Regiment's lady parachute packers named Zoe, a great character and well liked at the time by all the Normandie pilots. The unresolved subject of Nina's death came up. Zoe, who had been a close friend of Nina, unfolded the full sad story of her friend's death. Nina served as secretary on the staff of the Russian technical officer Kapitan Agavelian. During her regimental office duties she was brought into close contact with all the French pilots; she had formed a fond attachment to one of the senior Normandie pilots, which had been brought to the attention of the original base NKVD commissar officer, Kapitan Kounine. He had looked into the matter and, considering it a light affair, took no action. A little later Kounine was replaced by a very active NKVD officer, Kapitan Vdovine. When he discovered her attachment to one of the French aces, he threatened Nina with severe and drastic consequences if the liaison was not immediately terminated. At this juncture the pilot involved in the affair was warned of the impending serious nature of the situation for Nina. The officer, much concerned and fully understanding the unfolding problem for the girl, not least the political repercussions, was left with no alternative but to finish the liaison. The combination of both events must have been too much for Nina to stand. She took Agavelian's pistol from his office holster and shot herself in the head. The shot was heard by Commandant Pouyade, who came running to find Nina already beyond help; he was so very distressed and it was said he had tears in his eyes on seeing the poor girl's limp body. General Zaharov, informed of the happening, had to write an official report; he put the suicide down to 'battle fatigue and depression'. The matter was closed and a veil of silence descended.

Kounine, the original commissar, was officially listed as the Soviet liaison officer to Normandie; he was an easy chap to get on with. His duties as an NKVD officer often meant he accompanied the Regiment's officers on various official trips to Moscow as a sort of watchdog. These political police had authority far beyond their rank. A story is told of a Russian battlefront general who was with his staff in a front-line bunker. Just before the advance, suddenly two unknown NCOs entered the bunker wearing green trimmings on their uniforms. When they approached the general he was near to collapse with fearful apprehension before he realised they were MVD frontier troops sent to guide his men through the lines. The NKVD had similar green trimmings on their uniforms.

On 18 October, the Regiment made fourteen missions to cover the sector in the Chtaloupienen region. The following morning two squads of six aircraft each took off and returned without encountering any enemy aircraft. At 11 a.m. a squad composed of seven aircraft of the 4th led by Commandant Delfino attacked a group of Fw-190 bombers, fully loaded and ready to attack targets. Delfino shot down one of them and probably another. Castin fired at one, which crashed to the ground with a massive explosion. Capitaine Challe fired at one, which also exploded as it hit the ground. Manceau shot down an Fw-190 that was firing at patrol leader Génès. From 11.25 a.m. to 12.05 p.m. there were two squads in the air, without any action. Martin found himself alone above six Fw-190s in a defensive circle, while Risso–Laurent fell upon some foolishly unprotected He-129s. Risso shot down one of them. At 12.45 p.m. a squad composed of six aircraft of the 1st and two aircraft of the 3rd, led by Albert, were directed towards a group of He-129s and shot down four of them: Albert–Amarger one; Fauroux–Albert–Cuffaut one; de La Poype–Marchi one; and de Geoffre–Cuffaut–Amarger one. After this mission the colonel performed barrel rolls above the landing strip to announce the multiple victories. At 1.20 p.m. four aircraft of the 4th led by Génès took off. At 2 p.m. a squad of five aircraft of the 2nd was led by Delfino; the Delfino–Jeannel patrol pursued one Fw-190. While diving Commandant Delfino's engine misfired and the pursuit was broken off. At 2.10 p.m. eight aircraft of the 1st led by Albert–Amarger shot down an Fw-190, which hit the ground, breaking into many pieces. Marchi, who got into a good firing position, suffered weapon failure and had to withdraw. At 3.10 p.m. four aircraft of the 4th led by Génès–Charras fired on an Fw-190 and Schoendorff fired on another without result. At 3.35 p.m. a squad of eight aircraft took off without encountering any enemy. At 4.35 p.m. a squad of six aircraft of the 1st led by Dechanet encountered some Fw-190s. Dechanet shot down one; the others 'battle circled' with the Fw-190s without result. Bagnères had engine problems and landed at Kaunas. At 5.20 p.m. a squad of four aircraft of the 4th and two aircraft of the 3rd, commanded by Capitaine Challe, met a dozen Bf-109s and circled with them. Challe fired at one of them, as did Perrin, whose right wing was hit by a cannon shell. At 5.55 p.m. a squad of six aircraft of the 2nd led by Carbon took off but returned without any encounters.

During the day the Regiment made eighty-eight sorties and shot down seven Fw-190s (and probably two others) and five He-129s. It suffered no losses, but the aircraft were now showing signs of much use and were very tired. At midday, for example, only one aircraft was available for the 3rd. Compressors frequently broke down and took a long time to repair. In the evening a Yak-9B bomber landed at the base, lost; four bombs of 100k were noted in place vertically behind the pilot. On the fuselage an inscription indicated that the aircraft was a present 'From the Little Theatre of Moscow to the Front'. The offensive had made good progress in the previous three days to the north and south of Chtaloupienen but had not yet cleared all the enemy defences, with the result that the advance was behind the estimated timetable. The Chtaloupienen region was nothing but an immense blaze, and the cloud of smoke that had risen to 1,000m was very opaque. Another productive day for Normandie with twelve-plus enemy aircraft destroyed.

After a day's rest because of constant rain, missions restarted at 10.30 a.m. on 20 October. The Regiment was still covering the offensive, which was approaching Goumbinnen. At 1 p.m. the weather cleared a little; Pistrack signalled by radio from the front that German aerial activity was increasing. A squad of six aircraft led by Cuffaut took off. Taburet returned to land with a fuel breakdown. The squad attacked some Fw-190 bombers. Lemare and Castin, positioned some 15km to the west of Chtaloupienen, opened fire on an Fw-190; the pilot jumped in his parachute, his aircraft in flames. Moynet, Cuffaut and Amarger fired on a Bf-109 which was seen to hit the ground; then Cuffaut attacked an Fw-190, set it alight, and pursued it until it crashed in flames. Cuffaut, Amarger and Moynet as a team attacked an Fw-190, which dived smoking and disappeared into a bank of cloud. From 1.40 to 3.20 p.m., three missions took off but found nothing to attack. At 4.15 p.m. eight aircraft of the 2nd Escadrille took off in two squads; one working to the south of the Chtaloupienen–Goumbinnen road and led by Risso, the other working to the north of the road, led by Carbon. Halfway through the mission two groups of Pe-2s arrived, which were taken to task by Bf-109s and Fw-190s. Risso–Laurent came to the aid of the Pe-2; Laurent probably shot down one. Aspirant Alexandre Laurent was Commandant Risso's wing-man; his job was to protect and keep watch on Risso's tail during combat sorties. Laurent was dedicated to his task, a responsibility that he carried out religiously, so much so that he was given the Regiment's nickname 'semelle' (sole), meaning that no matter what took place he would always stick to Commandant Risso.

At the end of the mission Carbon, directed from the radio post by Pistrack, intercepted about eight Ju-87s protected by about twelve Fw-190s. 'Each his own', he commanded his team over the radio. He damaged one of them, then pursued an Fw-190 and shot it down to the south-west of Goumbinnen. Delin shot a Ju-87, which hit the ground. Jeannel, after having fired on a Ju-87, pursued and fired on an Fw-190, which shattered on the ground. Martin, who had remained at altitude, circled with the Fw-190s without a result. On return Lebras was absent; Carbon had seen him being pursued by two Fw-190s. At 5 p.m. eight aircraft of the 3rd, led by Matras, encountered at 1,500m two enemy groups; they were separated, with six in one group and eight in the other. They were Fw-190s, probably protecting Stukas (Ju-87s). The upper part of the squad kept an eye on the eight Fw-190s while the lower part attacked the other six. Challe–Miquel set one on fire. André and Penverne each shot one down. The entire battle took place to the south-east of Goumbinnen. From 5.10 to 5.50 p.m. three missions took off; they returned without encountering the enemy. The Regiment made seventy-one sorties in the day, shot down eight Fw-190s, one Bf-109, and two Ju-87s, damaged one Ju-87 and probably shot down two Fw-190s. Normandie's aircraft situation was still showing a deficit, especially with the 3rd Escadrille, which was restocked with two aircraft from the 4th and one from the 2nd. This same day a regiment of Stormoviks landed at the base. The runway became very busy and congested.

NORMANDIE ACHIEVE THIRTEEN VICTORIES
IN THREE HOURS

On 21 October the weather ceiling was at 100m. From 5.15 to 5.40 p.m. three missions were accomplished, two without result; the 3rd Escadrille shot down a Bf-109. During working hours, as aircraft came and went, great excitement on and around the landing strip was caused by the dedicated Stormovik crews, who turned out to be really excitable and noisy in everything they did.

On 22 October there was fog on the ground until midday. Pilots took off for missions and landed at Sterki or Didvigie, the new airstrips. The Regiment continued to cover the front. At 1.50 p.m. a squad composed of six aircraft of the 4th commanded by Capitaine Challe encountered some fully loaded Fw-190 bombers protected by Bf-109 fighters. Challe shot down a Bf-109, which exploded on the ground while trying to land on its belly. Castin shot down an Fw-190, which was hit while hedge-hopping; the German tried to bank and then hit the ground. This happened so many times that there seemed to be a problem with the Fw-190 whenever it banked at low altitude. Lemare and Manceau fired on one whose pilot left it by parachute. Lemare and Castin shot one that exploded as it dived into the ground; the pilot had escaped by parachute. Génès shot down a Bf-109. At 1.15 p.m. a squad composed of seven aircraft of the 2nd, commanded by Delfino, pursued a solitary Fw-190 which was returning to its base in an erratic and almost drunken fashion. It was shot down in a joint action by Delfino, Carbon and Menut. From 3.05 p.m. to 12.30, three missions were undertaken without any engagements. At 2.30 p.m. four aircraft from the 3rd led by André went up. Challe shot down an Fw-190 north-east of Insterburg and Miquel another in the same region. At 4.40 p.m. six aircraft of the 3rd led by Mertzisen went hunting, André and Mertzisen pursued two Fw-190s and each shot one down. André saw the pilot jump by parachute but the parachute did not open. At 4.30 p.m. one patrol went out without encountering any enemy. At 5.15 p.m. a squad of six aircraft of the 2nd, led by Carbon, encountered a dozen Fw-190s, still laden with their bombs. Versini fired at one of them and hit its load, causing it to explode in the air, sending a thousand pieces into a brilliant arc of orange fire. Saint-Marceaux fired at another and had to abandon his attack as it passed close to a group of Stormoviks. Delin then pursued it at speed, fired and saw it crash to the ground. However, Carbon spotted an Fw-190, the cunning one of the group, which was playing hide-and-seek in the clouds. He surprised it and fired; the pilot jumped by parachute. Then Carbon fired at another Fw-190 and damaged it. At 5.50 p.m. there were two missions without action.

At the end of the day the Regiment had made fifty-six aggressive sorties, shot down thirteen Fw-190s, damaged another, and shot down one Bf-109. Lemare and Manceau, returning from a mission by hedge-hopping, experienced violent anti-aircraft fire; Manceau, his aircraft riddled with bullets, had to land on his belly not far from the front, but was unhurt. The previous day Lebras had returned having spent the night in Semno. In his battle on 20 October he had shot down an Fw-190, having pursued it over a great distance. On his way back, battered and short of fuel, he landed at Semno. In the evening all the Regiment assembled at the strip at Sterki, a long, sandy, well-flattened stretch. The Regiment was well housed on wealthy farms, with farm buildings positioned at the four corners of what was now Normandie's landing strip. The pilots noted that the countryside was rich and well cultivated.

From 11 a.m. to 4 p.m. on 23 October, the Regiment provided un-interrupted coverage of the skies over Goumbinnen. Albert–Marchi attacked a Bf-109 about 8km to the south of Chtaloupienen. The Bf-109 crashed to the ground in flames. At 1.45 p.m. six aircraft of the 2nd went up, led by Risso. Risso–Laurent pursued a patrol of Fw-190s that were on their way home. Risso probably shot one of them down. At 2.20 p.m. a squad of six aircraft of the 1st led by Cuffaut attacked some Fw-190 bombers and massacred them in the Goumbinnen region. Iribarne fired at one, which crashed to the ground. Cuffaut and Taburet attacked another, which crashed amid much black smoke and sparks; then a second Fw-190 was hit and burst into flames. Amarger hit one; the pilot jumped by parachute. De La Poype fired at two of them; one was in flames, the other probably shot down. Moynet shot down one whose pilot left by parachute, another which was in flames, and a third probable. At 3.30 p.m. three aircraft of the 3rd went up, led by Lieutenant Sauvage. André and Penverne pursued an Fw-190 at 100m; it started to bank then crashed to the ground. The Fw-190 was not stable at low altitude. Miquel pursued another, which he hit and watched as it crashed. From 4 to 5.20 p.m. four further missions were flown. In the course of the day the Regiment had made fifty-six aggressive sorties, shot down eight Fw-190s and one Bf-190, and probably shot down three Fw-190s and damaged another.

The availability of aircraft was very bad; many were out of action with broken compressors or with the upper fairing on the wings having come adrift. The seriously ill Mourier departed for a Moscow hospital.

On 24 October news came that the Regiment was mentioned in Marshal Stalin's Order of the Day, announcing that an amazing breach 140km wide and 30km deep had been opened in the German defences in East Prussia. From 8 a.m. to 4 p.m. Normandie filled the skies over Goumbinnen, carrying out thirteen patrols. The 2nd, hampered by thick fog, could not find the landing strip on its return. It landed on a strip used by the Stormoviks, where it received a warm welcome. The 4th encountered two groups of eight Fw-190s. The usual team of Risso and Laurent pursued them and each shot down an Fw-190, to the south-west of Goldap. The last two missions were lively and resulted in more fruitful hunting: Lemare at his first burst of gunfire shot down a patrol leader whose aircraft was set on fire. De La Salle hedge-hopped while pursuing a Bf-109, which crashed to the ground. And to bring the day to a noble conclusion, the last patrol carried out a similarly successful deed. The Regiment made sixty-five aggressive sorties that day, shooting down four Bf-109s and three Fw-190s. Some Yaks suffered slight damage but there were no casualties. The fires now extended beyond the town of Goumbinnen to the south but neither Chtaloupienen nor Goumbinnen had fallen. The village of Sterki was situated in the enclave of Souvalki, which the Germans had preserved as Polish territory. The church where snipers were hidden had its steeple reduced by gunfire; it was noted that the graves in the cemetery all bore epitaphs in Polish. None of the population remained; it had been completely evacuated by the Soviets before the offensive.

COMMAND ORDER of General Chernyakhovsky

The troops of the 3rd Belorussian Front going on the offensive with the massive support of aircraft and artillery have broken the defences which were spread out and covered the frontiers of East Prussia and have made a breach 30km deep and 140km wide into East Prussian territory. In the course of the offensive our troops have seized support points in our opponent's defences at Kibartai, Dydjounen. Chtaloupienen and have also occupied 900 other localities of which 400 are in Prussia. During these struggles the following have distinguished themselves: the pilots of Lieutenant-General of the Air Force Khrioukine, and those of Lieutenant-Colonel Pouyade. Today, 23 October, at 23.00, the capital of our country,

Moscow, will salute our brilliant troops of the 3rd Belorussian Front who have penetrated East Prussia, with 20 artillery salvos by 224 guns. Eternal glory to the heroes who have fallen in the struggle for liberty and independence of our Country! Death to the German invaders!

Commander-in-Chief, Marshal of the Soviet Union, J. Stalin.

23 October 1944

From 10.30 a.m. on 25 October, two missions were flown without results. Missions started again at 5 p.m., but the weather was so overcast that only two aircraft from the 3rd made it as far as the front lines. Eichenbaum and Schick were back from Kaunas, where they went to fetch some 'samagonka', a potent home brew that was some 90 per cent alcohol. They also brought back the good news that Émonet, wounded in the thigh, was being cared for in a hospital in the region. He arrived there after a long epic flight of which the details were not yet known. Good old Émonet, always in such a good mood! What a pleasure it was for the chaps to find him again!

A window in the clouds was announced on the radio by the young interpreter Bondariev, who on 26 October found himself at the front to guide the aircraft. At 10.25 a.m., when the sky was clearer, covering missions began over Goumbinnen and lasted until evening. At 11.35 a.m. four aircraft of the 1st went up, led by Albert. Albert and Iribarne pursued a Bf-109 as far as Chtaloupienen and shot it down. A further two missions returned without any enemy contact. At 1.35 p.m. five aircraft of the 3rd, led by Matras, scuffled with some Fw-190s, without success. On their arrival back three aircraft could not find the airstrip, which was now covered with 'scum'; they had to land at another landing strip, and returned shortly afterwards. At 2.10 p.m. four aircraft of the 1st, led by Cuffaut, pursued some Fw-190s. Cuffaut and Amarger on patrol together fired on a group of Fw-190s at low altitude; each of them shot down an Fw-190. Moynet battled with several others and probably downed one. On his return Cuffaut miscounted and did two victory rolls instead of one over the runway! These mistakes of accounting proved a great joy to those fellow pilots who had a wicked sense of humour. From 2.50 to 5.30 p.m. five missions were undertaken without incident, except for that led by Commandant Delfino, who with de La Salle pursued a Bf-109 and shot it down in flames. During the day the Regiment made fifty aggressive sorties, shot down two Bf-109s and two Fw-190s, and probably shot down another Fw-190.

On 27 October the strip was covered by clouds but the weather was clear over the front at Goumbinnen, only 50km away. The first mission took place at 1 p.m. on the orders of Division. It was cold, scarcely 1 degree, and the wind was strong, making life on the runway very difficult. The aircraft situation was bad, only sixteen were at the disposal of the entire Regiment. In the course of missions pilots often had to abandon their patrols to return to base, either because the engine was spluttering or because the landing gear did not want to retract. At 1 p.m. four aircraft of the 2nd took off, led by Carbon. From 1 until 5.30 p.m. there were nine missions, of which three were particularly happy. In the course of one of them the squad was attacked by two Bf-109s; Risso diverted their attack by a clever manoeuvre and Lemare was able to shoot down one of the enemy, 'servie chaude'. Good work, for which all the pilots covered Risso with praise. During another patrol four aircraft found and attacked four Fw-190s. Sauvage shot down one in flames then pursued the other three with Pierrot and Penverne, while Miquel dragged in his wake six keen Bf-109s that had come to the rescue of the Fw-190s; he probably shot down one of them. Finally, at 5.10 p.m. a reduced patrol was attacked by Bf-109s and Fw-190s. Cuffaut's aircraft was hit and caught fire, but Cuffaut was able to get out of the cockpit and jump by parachute. In the night it was learned that he had arrived safe and sound inside Soviet lines; soldiers had been sent out to guide him to safety. The Regiment made thirty-two aggressive sorties, shot down one Bf-109 and one Fw-190, and one probable Bf-109. It lost the colonel's aircraft, the one containing Cuffaut, which had been set on fire.

The following morning the strip was covered in cloud, but the weather over the front was again fine. The temperature was 2 degrees plus, with strong winds. Staying on the runway was difficult. The offensive had almost come to a complete halt, troop activity on the ground was zero; in the air there were few aircraft, only some hunters or photographic aircraft. From 8.25 a.m. to 4.35 p.m. there were nine missions in succession, but no enemy was encountered. The aircraft situation was still bad. Only the 2nd proudly displayed eight aircraft on the perimeter; often it had to lend aircraft to those escadrilles in deficit.

Decree of 26 October 1944, decorating a specified number of
Normandie pilots.

DECREE of the President of the Supreme Soviet of the USSR, relating to the award of Soviet decorations to officers of the Normandie Regiment of Free

Fighting France, for the exemplary execution of combat missions carried out on the front. In the struggle against the German invader, for their courage and fearlessness, the following are decorated:

Order of the Red Banner: Lieutenant Marcel Albert. Capitaine Yves Mourier. Lieutenant-Colonel Pierre Pouyade. Lieutenant Joseph Risso. Capitaine René Challe.

Order of the Great Patriotic War 1st class: Aspirant Jacques André. Lieutenant Roland de La Poype. Lieutenant Jean-Emile Le Martelot. Aspirant Maurice Challe.

Order of the Great Patriotic War 2nd class: Lieutenant Maurice de Seynes. Lieutenant Bruno de Faletans. Aspirant Alexandre Laurent. Aspirant Charles Monier. Lieutenant André Moynet. Aspirant Roger Pinon. Aspirant Yves Fauroux.

Order of the Red Star: Capitaine Jean de Pange. Aspirants Jacques de Saint-Phalle, Pierre Génès, Jacques Casaneuve, Charles Miquel, Marcel Perrin, Gaël Taburet. Sous-Lieutenant Michel Schick.

The President of the Presidium of the Supreme Soviet of the USSR, M. Kalinin
The Secretary of the Presidium, A. Gorkin.
Moscow, The Kremlin, 26 October 1944

On 29 October the easterly wind was strong and cold. Several missions were carried out in the afternoon. Many took advantage of the slowing down of the number of flights to go for walks in the countryside and went as far as the first front lines to look for souvenirs. In the evening Manceau and Perrin found themselves in front of the former German lines when Manceau stepped on a German landmine, which tore off his foot; when he fell another exploded and took off his left arm. Transported immediately by Perrin and two comrades who heard his cries, he was taken in an ambulance to hospital. The whole Regiment was upset by this tragic accident, all the more so because it could have happened to any of them. In the evening Pistrack returned. He had been at the front since the start of the offensive; he had radioed the aircraft in the air with information about enemy aerial activity. Always regular, always calm, his voice was appreciated by all, especially in moments of confusion, when it inspired confidence with its steadiness.

Pistrack was welcomed by hurrahs and the Croix de Guerre by order of the Regiment, a rare distinction awarded to few, for it necessitated the recognition of all in the Regiment. He was serving under the senior Red Air Force liaison officer, General Zakharov, stationed at a post to the north of Kibartai, then later with the HQ of the nearby fighter group.

After three days of the offensive, the 18th Guards Air Regiment were entrusted with protecting Pe-2s, while Normandie had covering duties. The first day of the attack started with artillery fire for two solid hours; amazingly there was a gun every 2m along the front. The barrage preceded the ground force attack, then the T-34 tanks went in together with infantry, which broke through the German defences to the north of Lake Olvita. At this point the line was 10km wide and 8km deep, and to the south 15km wide. The infantry reached Eidtkounen. The battles were hard; the German infantry gave up only step by step, retreating during the night. In the evening of 29 October the tanks of the corps, some 200 T-34s, and an infantry brigade (with which Pistrack was in liaison) attacked to the south of the Chtaloupienen–Goumbinnen road, and stormed over the River Pissa to the south of Goumbinnen. The next day the Germans counter-attacked with two of their crack divisions; they attacked the flanks of the pocket with tanks of the Hermann Goering Division from Chtaloupienen, and then the Grossdeutschland Division attacked towards Goldap. The German counter-attack was successful; it encircled the Soviet corps of about 20,000 men. General Chernyakhovsky gave the order for the tanks to withdraw. Thanks to the Stormoviks attacking any Germans on the move, the Soviets freed themselves with some considerable loss and withdrew, but the offensive was halted. The tank corps lost about two-thirds of its armour and half its personnel in the whole operation. Finally, the Germans counter-attacked and recaptured Goldap. There was intense Soviet artillery fire against enemy positions.

During these days of aerial combat it could be said that the German Air Force had been clearly outclassed by that of the Soviets. The Soviet bombers, Pe-2s or Bostons, had operated only to the immediate rear of the front, probably because the Soviet command, hoping for a more rapid advance, did not want to destroy the lines of communication and the enemy aerodromes. No patrols had encountered any German bombers on the front and had not heard of any. Earlier on 18 October, pilots from the 1st and 2nd Escadrilles intercepted some He-129s, rather slow aircraft without any protection, and massacred them. The Germans sometimes brought out Ju-87s, of which several had been shot down; they were the same old models as used in 1940. They had often employed their Fw-190s as dive-bombers. The pilots of these

Fw-190s were probably former pilots of Ju-87s as they knew only how to dive; when encountered they proceeded with speed to the west by hedge-hopping. Soviet hunters were composed of several La-5s or La-7s, employed especially as protection for Il-2s, four fighters to a squad of five or six Il-2s. But the Soviets employed above all the Yak-3, with which Normandie was endowed; marvellous machines, surpassing, up to 4,000m, the Fw-190As and the Bf-109Gs in banking, climbing, horizontal flight, and diving. Its piloting was simple and without fault. It allowed banking close to the ground, something the Fw-190 could not do without crashing. Above 4,000m its performance fell away and the Bf-109 became spiteful. Above 6,000m one had to be careful. In the early days of the campaign the Germans threw into combat major aerial forces which acted without much judgement and skill; a pilot was always less competent when he had an aircraft which banked 'like a bistro table'. Normandie's victorious days dated from then. As a result German aircraft were staying closer together in serried ranks.

NKVD HAVE A DOSSIER ON NORMANDIE'S DOCTOR

At 5 p.m. on 30 October, the Yak-6 departed for Vilno, now the terminal for aircraft going on to Moscow. On board were Schick, who was on his second leave, Bagnères, returning to France for retraining, and the doctor, Lebiedinsky, recalled to Moscow by top-level orders.

Georges Lebiedinsky was of recent Russian extraction; like many exiled Russian families he had taken refuge in France. He of course spoke perfect Russian, which made it much easier to gain a full understanding of the medical condition and treatment when wounded or sick pilots were transferred to military hospitals and medical establishments. The new, diligent NKVD officer (Commissar) Vdovine unfortunately discovered that a cousin of Lebiedinsky had been arrested during the 1936 Stalin purges and shot. In the political mind this made him, his family and all associates a political threat to the state, and the Soviet authorities declared Lebiedinsky persona non grata. In the circumstances something had to be done to keep things running smoothly with the Soviet authorities. The French Military Mission ordered Lebiedinsky to Moscow for a posting out of the country to another theatre of war. He was an excellent doctor who had served Normandie extremely well; it just so happened he had the wrong name and family connection. Once the

NKVD had made an investigation and turned up the connection with a purged individual, there was nothing anyone could do to stop the process of retribution from rolling forward. The NKVD had the ultimate power over all politically suspect individuals. When investigating officers visited any unit, large or small, to collect suspects, their arrest warrants would have to be complied with, even at the highest command levels. The only recorded case where they returned without collecting their prisoner happened in Berlin during 1946. At that time Marshal Georgi Zhukov was the commander of all Soviet forces in Germany. A trio of senior NKVD officers arrived unannounced at Zhukov's Berlin headquarters and demanded that two colonels serving on the Marshal's HQ staff be handed over to them to be taken to Moscow for interrogation and trial. Zhukov, who had known the two colonels during the long campaign to capture Berlin, refused point-blank to comply with their orders, and would not even consider handing over these two highly decorated officers. The NKVD senior officer standing directly in front of the great man then dared to challenge his decision. Zhukov, who had a terrible temper, flew into a violent rage, mouthing the most earthy soldier language; he had the three immediately arrested by his guard, who then forcibly deposited the startled NKVD trio on a train bound for Moscow, with dire threats of what would happen if they ever dared to return to his command.

On 2 November the weather cleared at midday. At 11.45 a.m. four aircraft of the 3rd Escadrille climbed towards the front lines. Aspirant Challe returned shortly afterwards; the engine of his Yak was running badly. On his arrival Miquel announced by radio that his engine had packed up and that he would have to land on another strip. At the end of the evening they were without news of him. A few hours later they heard the sad news that at 2 a.m. dear Manceau had died; the gangrene had reached his wounds sustained when he was blown up by German landmines. Cuffaut was to leave the Regiment on 31 October for health reasons, along with Schick, Lebiedinsky and Bagnères. This was again a rather strange affair; Léon Cuffaut, who was of an aggressive and determined nature, had a burning desire to get involved in any aerial battle. Cuffaut's overwhelming motivation was to increase his mounting personal tally of enemy aircraft destroyed; it was said he wanted to emulate Albert's score. He was prepared to do almost anything to achieve this, no matter the cost or situation; his actions during one mission were watched from the ground. It had so upset the parent Soviet Divisional Command that it made strong representations to the commandant of Normandie. It was then felt a posting back to the Moscow Mission ready for transfer to operations in the Middle East would ease a difficult situation.

On 3 November Manceau was buried in the village cemetery near the landing strip. In pouring rain the colonel read the service and recalled his good Parisian humour, his true camaraderie, his qualities as a fighter pilot. Capitaine Challe read out his citations and listed his six combat victories.

On 4 November the cold set in. Miquel returned in the U-2; he had stayed for two days with the regiment of Stormoviks, where he received a warm welcome. The senior pilots of the Regiment had a meeting to respond to a certain number of questions concerning the use of the Yak-3 fighter in combat, including improvements that could be made and details of winning manoeuvres and techniques used in combat. The Soviet commander asked all these questions, which were also being asked of all Soviet fighter units at the front. Missions had been stopped for two days to allow the much-needed overhaul of the engines. The results of these questions and the answers provided by experienced combat pilots were later collated and formed the basis for a Soviet combat tactic manual that was produced as a guide for all Soviet fighter air regiments.

On 5 November the day started with mist covering the ground. After six hours in an open truck, in biting cold, twenty-five pilots had gone on this Sunday to Kaunas. They went on a walk lasting three hours through the streets of Kaunas. During their time in the town they were able to admire the spectacle of a column of camels pulling pole carts ('telegues') along the road to Mariampol. Visits among escadrilles were the main activity on days without flying. It was said that on a visit, after paying one's respects to the colonel, who was billeted on the same farm, one could sip an excellent drinking chocolate just like at Bebattet's or Rumpelmeyer's. At Mikountani they cooked. At Alitous they courted girls. Here, the chaps led a society life; 'crapette', puzzles, and conversation. The colonel had received the good news that Émonet was in hospital in Moscow and not seriously wounded; he was making a good recovery.

On 7 November it was the 27th anniversary of the October Revolution. In the morning wind and rain did not interfere with the proceedings of the anniversary or the investiture. Awards of Soviet decorations and medals were bestowed upon the mechanics. At dinner in the mess, all the pilots and Soviet officers gathered together. Menu: zakouski (potato salad, tinned crab and vodka), roast pork and mashed potatoes, and sponge cake or mille-feuilles.

Speeches were copious. Twice the Chief of Staff rose to thank Normandie for the work accomplished and to exhort all to continue the struggle against the Fascist barbarians. He did not say a word about the anniversary that was being celebrated. Colonel Pouyade recalled that since the summer campaign this anniversary was the third that the Regiment had celebrated. 'More than the 14th July or the 24th August, we ought to celebrate this one with joy and pride, which we give to the work accomplished. However, we must not forget that all our successes are due for the most part to the wonderful qualities of the Yak-3. Let us thank the Soviet command for having given us this excellent machine.' After dinner, there was dancing and a wrestling match between Eichenbaum and Schoendorff; Eichenbaum unfortunately withdrew from the contest with a sprained foot. The following day the weather was dismal; the first winter snow had fallen.

On 11 November the Yak-6 was meant to depart for Moscow taking the colonel, Bourveau, Brihaye and Jeannel. The weather was so bad that the departure was cancelled. Also, the colonel decided the eight 'veterans' of the Regiment, Bourveau and he himself would reach Vilno by plane and travel from there to Moscow by rail. The authorisation, requested from General Zakharov, then from the Army Chief, was for some reason refused. Finally the colonel left with Bourveau for Moscow; the weather being very bad, the colonel reached Vilno by jeep.

The previous two days had been very cold, the night temperature minus 7 degrees. On 15 November the Division asked for two hunting missions, each with four aircraft, over Insterburg–Tilsitt; if necessary strafing was to be carried out. But Normandie was forbidden to attack the farms because the 'casseroles' (tricoloured nose spinners) were easily recognised. It would seem the Division wished to keep secret from the enemy the fact that Normandie had moved into this combat area. A weather check by two aircraft of the 1st Escadrille showed that it was raining in East Prussia. However, at 4 p.m. four aircraft of the 3rd, led by Matras, left on a sortie, made less efficient by intermittent banks of cloud at 300m, 1,000m and 1,500m.

On 17 November two hunting missions into enemy territory left in the afternoon, returning without any encounters. At 3 p.m. four aircraft of the 4th led by Génès undertook a covering mission of Goumbinnen; again, no enemy was encountered. The 303rd Fighter Air Division was decorated with the Red Banner. A banquet took place at Divisional HQ on this auspicious occasion. Commandant Delfino, together with the Commanders, de La Poype and Risso, took part. General Khrioukine, also present, said that the Division was one of the best provided for because it was almost entirely supplied with modern equipment. Then he announced that the Soviets would soon be in Berlin and perhaps the Division would be there. Over the radio the pilots learned that Général de Gaulle had been invited to Moscow. It was everyone's hope that he would visit the Regiment. The new day opened with fine but cold weather. On all these 'flyable' days training continued. Preparing for the change of airstrips, Delfino and Risso went to see the intended base situated near Goldap in East Prussia.

On 19 November the ceiling was at 1,200m and dropping slowly. Snow was falling in the Goldap region. In the afternoon flights were halted because of hoar frost. The adjutant to the head of the Soviet General Staff informed the colonel that the offensive would be launched as soon as the Masurian Lakes were frozen solid. The Germans were now reinforced and stronger than on 16 October: they could count on about 126,000 men together with 440 tanks, 2,000 guns and 400 aircraft, of which 150 were fighters. To cross the three lines of fortifications around the River Haguerrape, which had still to be breached, the Soviets estimated that there would have to be three times as many Red Army men than Germans. In this pre-offensive period the Regiment would carry out hunting missions in the sector between Lake Vichtitiere, the location of the next airstrip, and Treuburg. Soviet reconnaissance indicated intense activity on the rail network in this sector. Normandie had been entrusted with restricting this by attacking along this rail link. In the Stalovaia a celebration dinner was held for the artillery feast-day, 100g of vodka per head. Philippov, the Regiment's armourer, explained the purpose of this feast-day and the role played by the artillery in this war. However, Commandant Delfino, the squadron commander and some 'veterans' who had gone to dine at the 523rd Regiment's mess had an accident in a vehicle and returned to base after four hours' uncertain navigation on smashed-up and cratered Lithuanian roads.

On 20 November there was much feverish activity on the base as the Regiment was to be filmed. Preparations were being made to shoot a film which would spread to the four corners of the globe the image of the Regiment's monastic life. The Stalovaia acted as the setting. The 'Sunlights' (the artistic film crew) accentuated the fullness of the sucking-pigs cooked for this special occasion. Several songs were recorded!

There was very little aerial activity the following day. The movie people filmed several scenes, but then rain put an end to all activity. On 22 November the weather cleared and the Regiment carried out some hunting and strafing missions with sorties of four aircraft from each escadrille. Miquel landed on the future strip with engine problems. Lieutenant Risso went to Minsk, from where he was to guide back the aerial flotilla of brand-new Yak-3s due for the airstrip. They arrived towards 6 p.m. and were immediately allocated by engineer Agavelian. The following day, despite the first snows, two patrols did some timid training with the new aircraft. On 24 November they were delighted to learn over the radio of the liberation of Mulhouse, Metz, Belfort and part of Strasbourg. The next day the weather was still bad. Whispers abounded that Général de Gaulle would visit the Regiment. After dinner the mechanics put on a show. The performance was indeed mediocre but the intention was very touching.

Orders came to report to the new landing strip on 27 November. Capitaine Brihaye and Ougloff left as the advance party and the Regiment followed at 3 p.m. The weather ceiling was 150m and the ground soft, but all went well but for one incident: Monge broke half his undercarriage on landing. For the first time the Regiment was treading on captured East Prussian soil, the first Western allies to do so. Quarters were in the village of Gross-Kalvaitchen near Lake Vustitersee, which marked the Lithuanian–Prussian border. The population had abandoned the place and a house was found in a satisfactory condition. The Regiment was in company it knew very well, for the 117th Regiment of Stormoviks now occupied part of the strip. It was moving on shortly, and the Supply Battalion was one known from the past at Doubrovka and Alitous.

SEVEN

HONOUR TITLE: 'NORMANDIE-NIEMEN'

On 28 November the visit by Général de Gaulle seemed to be confirmed and the Supply Battalion had undertaken massive works to prepare for this eventuality. A telegram received in the morning informed the commandant that Lieutenants Albert and de La Poype had both been awarded the highest Soviet decoration of valour, the Gold Star Medal, 'Title' Hero of the Soviet Union. In addition 'Normandie Regiment' was to receive, on Marshal Stalin's direct orders, the battle honour title of 'Regiment of the Niemen', from that day on they would be known as the 'Normandie-Niemen Regiment'.

At 9 p.m. a meeting at the mess added an official character to the honour. The impromptu speakers overpowered Normandie with speeches, sometimes clumsy, but touching, all with much feeling.

The weather was still overcast on 2 December. For some days aerial activity had been non-existent. It was two years since Normandie had received its first war plane. Commandant Delfino was counting on making the celebration of this anniversary coincide with the arrival of Général de Gaulle. It was decided to accompany the dinner with the usual vodka and beer and to reserve the better wines for the important projected visit! On 3 December Radio-Paris confirmed that Général de Gaulle was to pay Normandie a visit, but all wondered if the weather would allow him to fly in. The Supply Battalion was still working steadily towards the arrangements for this important visit. On 4 December the ceiling had risen to 1,000m. The Regiment made the most of it by carrying out training exercises under the eye of the commandant; flights in the shape of the Croix de Lorraine were intended to display the patriotic fervour of the Regiment. These flights were swiftly interrupted by an abundant snowfall. The 117th Regiment of Stormoviks issued an invitation to some of the pilots on the occasion of the anniversary of the 'Stalinist constitution'. Commandant Delfino, the commanders and some 'veterans' went to the neighbouring base where they attended a very good performance. All awoke on 5 December to more bad weather; it seemed to have arrived for good. The visit by Général de Gaulle seemed distant. Normandie celebrated the Stalinist constitution with an artistic evening in which everyone took part.

EAST PRUSSIA MARKS THE END OF THE CAMPAIGN IN RUSSIA

The Normandie-Niemen pilots were the first Western allied fighting force to capture and occupy German territory during the Second World War.

On 6 December, despite the bad weather, the Regiment was informed that Général de Gaulle would arrive in the middle of the day. Nothing was ready. Wines, poultry, and so on had been neither purchased nor plucked. The quarters were inspected by General Zakharov, then by the area commander. Some pilots had gone to hunt in the woods for game; as well, Lieutenants Albert and de La Poype had left at 5 a.m. accompanied by Capitaine Brihaye for Moscow, where the two lieutenants were to receive their Soviet Gold Star decorations. Could they be stopped at Kaunas and made to return in time for the visit? In the midst of all this turmoil, suddenly at 3 p.m. Delfino assembled the commanders to pass on a monumental counter-order. All the Regiment, including some Soviet officers and mechanics, were to go to Moscow to be presented to Général de Gaulle. A special train would be waiting for the group at Kaunas, from where it was to depart at 5 a.m. Everyone packed quickly and piled into Studebaker trucks at 10 p.m. The trip to Kaunas lacked in comfort and the chaps were dazed by intermittent sleep and cold when they finally came to a halt in the station square at 4 a.m.

Arriving on 7 December, the travellers were welcomed by a heated waiting room close to the station. There they learned that the train would not depart until noon; consequently, they were asked to get into the trucks again to go to local quarters for what was left of the night. They arrived at an extremely modern military hospital where the staff, clad in white, gave every care. The wake-up call was at 10 a.m., followed by showers and so forth; then one of the doctors invited them to go to the canteen. They were amazed at the menu: fresh caviar, various hams and sausages, fried eggs, cutlets, sauté potatoes, cakes, chocolate with whipped cream, not to mention vodka and local wines. General Zakharov presided over the banquet where the gaiety became somewhat noisy. To the sound of an accordion played with virtuosity, a ball was soon improvised with the nurses as partners; the 'special train' was completely forgotten. However, the Soviet officers who were organising the move came at 3 p.m. to remind everyone of the train departure time.

They made their way to the station, where they met up with Capitaine Brihaye and Lieutenants Albert and de La Poype. Delfino inspected the train and allocated personnel to various carriages. The 'special train' was magnificent. General Zakharov's carriage consisted of a suite with dressing room, a vast salon with large windows and furnished with very comfortable couches and armchairs, and two compartments of sleepers. General Zakharov, Commandant Delfino, Capitaine Brihaye, Major Vdovine (NKVD) and Lieutenants Albert and de La Poype would travel in one of them. The veteran officers and aspirants were installed in the other carriage. Then came several less comfortable coaches where mattresses and blankets alleviated the hardness of the wooden benches. Finally there was a wagon fitted out as a restaurant car. General Khrioukine, Commander of the Air Force, accompanied the group to the platform. The train left Kaunas at 3.30 p.m. From the start the trip was joyful. Vodka flowed, caviar abounded, and at each station teams told about the group's passage brought plentiful and varied refreshments to the travellers. Thus it was with optimistic thoughts that each fell asleep to wake in the morning with anticipation.

On 8 December they reached Smolensk station, where the train arrived at 11 a.m. All could observe the many ruins which bore witness to the violence of the battle more than a year beforehand. The famous Wall of Tatars and the cathedral seemed not to have suffered too much. They set off again at midday, expecting to arrive in Moscow at the end of the night.

GÉNÉRAL DE GAULLE IN MOSCOW

Normandie-Niemen and retinue arrived in Moscow Central on 9 December at 3 a.m. The Soviet officers who had organised the stay in the capital took the pilots to the House of the Red Army (Moscow No. 1 Barracks), where rooms had been prepared. After some hours of sleep, the chaps assembled in the lobby, where Commandant Delfino gave the orders of the day. At 11.30 a.m. Lieutenants Albert and de La Poype, along with some other pilots, made their way to Marshal Novikoff's reception, from whose hands they would receive their decorations. The setting of the reception was luxurious. According to

Soviet military custom, the two Heroes of the Soviet Union were expected to say a few words of thanks, in Russian. They then rejoined the rest of the Regiment at the French Embassy, where they found Colonel Pouyade on arrival at the reception; he recounted the adventures of his recent journey. Several Soviet personalities were introduced to the Normandie personnel as well as the staff of the embassy and the Military Mission. Representatives of the press and the film crew cluttered up the rooms. For the awarding of decorations, the recipients were placed in four rows: first row the Legion of Honour; second row Order of the Liberation; third row Médaille Militaire; fourth row Croix de Guerre.

Général de Gaulle made his grand entrance, followed by Général Juin, Général Petit and Colonel de Rancourt. The investiture began; the 'cravate' Commander of the Legion of Honour was bestowed upon a Soviet Marshal who was specially invited to the ceremony. The next bestowal was on Colonel Delfino, and several Soviet generals and senior officers in this group were confirmed as Officers of the Legion of Honour.

Major Vdovine, Kapitan Agavelian and most of the French officers of the Regiment were decorated as 'Chevaliers' – Knights of the Legion of Honour. Then Général de Gaulle pinned the Order of the Liberation on the Colour Standard of the Regiment de Chasse 'Normandie', with the words: 'We recognise you as our Companion for the Liberation of France, in Honour and for Victory.' Colonel Pouyade and Lieutenants Albert, de La Poype and Risso also received the Order of the Liberation. Finally, the Médaille Militaire was conferred on the most distinguished aspirants, and the Croix de Guerre rewarded the less dazzling but just as courageous work of the other pilots. On that day all the members of the Regiment, without exception, had been honoured – quite rightly so, as all had played their part, large or small, in the glory of the Normandie-Niemen Regiment.

Général de Gaulle proclaimed the glory of Normandie-Niemen with a citation in Moscow that read: 'On the martyrized soil of France, like Russian soil, Normandie my Companion, supports, demonstrates and increases the glory of France.'

After the investiture ceremony Général de Gaulle described life in France; he talked of villages destroyed or spared by the war, of material life, of battles fought on the Rhine. Then the Normandie pilots returned to the House of the Red Army. Each one organised his evening as he wished. Colonel Pouyade was invited to the Kremlin with Général de Gaulle and his entourage; and while the diplomats organised, on paper, the future of the world, the colonel drank champagne with the 'Little Father' (Stalin) to the health of the victorious military. After the feverish and intoxicating activity of the investiture, the following day seemed calm. Nevertheless, a dinner brought all together at the Moskva restaurant, where they had invited their mechanics who had travelled with them.

Capitaine Risso, on this short official visit to Moscow, would soon leave, but his much-lamented comrade Marcel Lefèvre would now remain permanently in Moscow, buried in the hero soldiers' memorial area in central Moscow at the foot of the 1812 monument.

RETURN TO EAST PRUSSIA

On 12 December General Zakharov announced Normandie's return to East Prussia. The train would leave at 8 p.m. The veterans of the Regiment in Moscow would depart for France to spend some leave. Other pilots would benefit from some extra days' leave; it was intended that they would stay in Moscow until the 18th and then rejoin the Regiment.

At 11 a.m. Général Petit gave the pilots assembled at the Military Mission a 'vin d'honneur', a drink to celebrate the important honours recently bestowed. At 6.30 p.m. the pilots of the Regiment said their goodbyes to the veterans, whom they would not see for several months. They then made their way to the station, where Colonel Pouyade accompanied the group. It had been decided that the Regiment would be reduced to three escadrilles. At 8 p.m. all left Moscow feeling a little fed up but hoping to rediscover under Prussian skies the fruits of victory that the previous autumn campaign had brought. Rohmer and de Friede arrived at the front. On 14 December, after having spent all day on the special train, they reached Kaunas at 6 p.m. to learn that the new aircraft were now with the 18th Guards Air Regiment on their airstrip. Accordingly the trucks that came to collect the pilots at Kaunas went to Sterki, not to Gross-Kalvaitchen. The accidental nature of the transport prolonged the journey so much that the travellers arrived stiff and cold at 2 minutes after midnight on the 15th.

PART FOUR

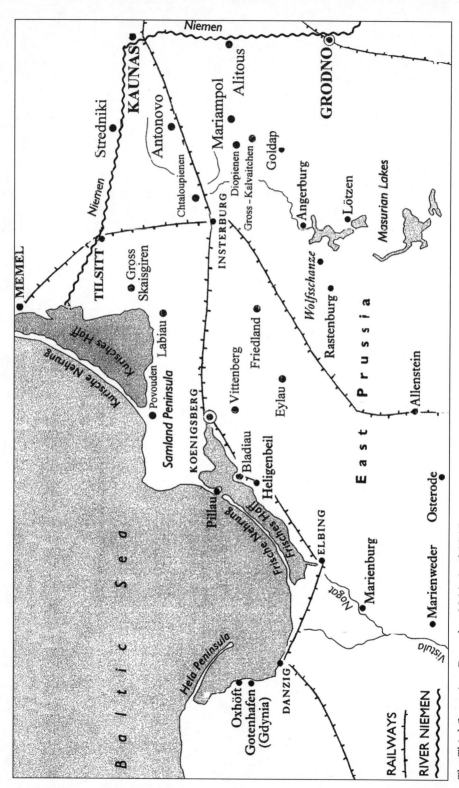

The Third Campaign, December 1944–April 1945.

EIGHT

THIRD CAMPAIGN,
EAST PRUSSIA,
DECEMBER 1944–APRIL 1945

The Supply Battalion of the 18th Guards Air Regiment hastily improvised the quarters and served an excellent dinner, despite the late hour. The pilots woke at 9.30 a.m. and proceeded to breakfast. They went to the strip where each collected his allotted aircraft, and took off in the direction of Gross-Kalvaitchen. On landing Guido broke half his undercarriage; this particular once-perfect aircraft had been allocated to Capitaine Brihaye! On 16 December the pilots settled in. The quarters were improved by the fact that there were fewer pilots.

With reduced personnel, the escadrilles were revised and re-formed, as follows:

1st Escadrille: Commander: Capitaine Challe, Lieutenants Charras and Sauvage, Aspirants Génès, Marchi, Iribarne, Perrin, Piquenot, Reverchon, Schoendorff, Taburet and Ougloff.
2nd Escadrille: Commander: Capitaine de Saint-Marceaux, Lieutenant de La Salle, Aspirants Dechanet, Lemare, Martin, Delin, Henri, Guido, Versini, Menut and Monge.
3rd Escadrille: Commander: Capitaine Matras, Lieutenants Douarre and Castin, Aspirants Mertzisen, Challe, Pierrot, Penverne, de Geoffre, Miquel, Lorillon and Bleton.

On 18 December a patrol carried out coverage of Goldap without incident. The following day they awoke to bad weather. Some training flights took place. Two days later the weather improved and training and aggressive patrols commenced. The Matras–de Geoffre patrol was scrambled on an alert, and some hunting and strafing missions were carried out. In the course of the mission Aspirant Guido was forced to return; his aircraft was hit by flak and lost a great deal of fuel. Partly blinded by this leakage, Guido succeeded in reaching the strip of the 117th Regiment of Stormoviks but, forced to land with the wind behind him, he overshot the end of the runway and the aircraft broke against a tree. Guido extracted himself without harm and returned to base the same evening. As well as undertaking several training flights, the Perrin–Piquenot patrol took off on an alert, the Génès–Reverchon patrol carried out a review of the sector, and Commandant Delfino carried out some hunting with Aspirant Dechanet.

On 22 December the 2nd Escadrille was on standby in severe cold ready to take off at the sight of the trails of condensation that streaked the sky. Unfortunately, the German aircraft were moving at altitudes which guaranteed them too great a lead, and pursuit was fruitless. The bitterness was heightened by the two La-5s which brought down a Ju-88 less than 2km from the strip, just when Lieutenant de La Salle got into an attacking position. The Ju-88 was shot down in flames and the crew perished except for the machine-gunner at the rear, who managed to parachute down. He was taken prisoner and brought to the strip, where Commandant Delfino interrogated him with Schoendorff as go-between. Some other missions were equally fruitless. The next day the fine weather continued. A regrettable accident happened: Bleton, taking off in too much haste, and hampered by the dust on the runway, hit Taburet's aircraft at full throttle. Miraculously, both pilots were unhurt, but the two new aircraft were badly damaged. As often happened, General Zakharov, escorted by Commandant Zamorine, landed at this exact moment. After drawing attention to the need to avoid such accidents, they took off again to make a tour of the German lines accompanied by Commandant Delfino and Aspirant Dechanet.

On 24 December the weather worsened. However, some training flights took place. In the evening the chaps organised a dinner to which some officers of the 117th Regiment of Stormoviks were invited. In the course of the dinner they learned that Major Pilchikoff of the 523rd Regiment had been brought down behind German lines. Everyone was very moved by the loss of this excellent comrade and friend of the Normandie Regiment. Towards midnight heavy snow fell. It was still snowing on Christmas Day, which they spent in their quarters. The bad weather continued right through 26 December. Capitaine de Saint-Marceaux took advantage of this to give a course on the use of electromagnetic detection. This really got the pilots into the Christmas spirit.

At 3 p.m. on 27 December the sky abruptly cleared, ready for flying, but plans were dashed by the mechanics who were working on the aircraft, ready for a technical review. A nearby landing strip was attacked by twenty-five Fw-190s, after which General Zakharov sent a telegram to the Regiment warning of similar attacks and instructing it to increase the standby squads and to dig trenches and shelters, which would be necessary for the protection of the staff. On 28 December some training flights took place in the morning. At 4 p.m. all made their way to the gas testing chambers for an exercise trying out the issue gas masks.

The following morning brought uncertain weather. The sky was blue but there was thick fog at ground level, which prevented take-off. It finally dissipated and allowed some flights. The patrols of Aspirant Génès and Aspirant Reverchon, Lieutenant Charras and Aspirant Piquenot, and Aspirant Dechanet and Aspirant Menut carried out these missions. A certain wobble in transmissions and a false interpretation of the Regiment's available aircraft led Division to ask Normandie for more sorties than could be managed. General Zakharov made known his concern about the Regiment's reduced activities. That evening Commandant Delfino gathered together the escadrille commanders to discuss in the presence of Major Vdovine (the NKVD political ears of the Division) the questions and problems caused by this misunderstanding and to find a solution with the few aircraft available.

On 30 December the weather was excellent. Flights began at dawn with numerous covering missions. Many patrols covered the sector in the Chtaloupienen–Goumbinnen region. Hunting missions in the Goldap–Darkiemen sector were carried out as well as numerous scrambles. In an unfortunate incident, after the patrol of Aspirants Challe and de Geoffre had engaged two Bf-109s, de Geoffre did not return and Challe could give the Regiment no information about him. However, the chaps were not too anxious, for de Geoffre was famous for his disappearances followed by reappearances, and for this reason they remained hopeful.

On the last day of 1944 the weather deteriorated and prevented any flying. At 3 p.m. those on leave in Moscow returned, bringing with them some provisions, mail and news. Général Petit was due to visit the Regiment towards 15 January, and Capitaine Brihaye was returning to France. At

7 p.m. decorations were presented in the mess to selected Soviet mechanics serving with Normandie. Then all went to Commandant Delfino's quarters to empty some bottles of champagne sent by Mme Adle. Colonel Piltchouk, representing General Zakharov, participated in the imbibing. Earlier a small entertainment had preceded this get-together. At 11.30 p.m. they returned to the mess, where dinner had been prepared. Numerous toasts to the New Year rapidly warmed up the ambience, and soon all the pilots deserted the table to dance with the unit's 'office' staff.

NORMANDIE STARTS 1945 WITH 201 COMBAT VICTORIES

New Year's Day brought fog and snow. At 5 p.m. Mme Adle's champagne was finished off at a get-together at the Stalovaia. Some cigars perfumed the atmosphere. The following day the weather was still bad; some training flights took place. At 7 p.m. Commandant Delfino gathered everyone together to specify the conditions for the confirmation of victories. In this connection, a Soviet colonel witnessed a battle engaged by Marchi on 30 December and saw two Fw-190s brought down. The Regiment was thus officially at its 201st victory. Aspirant de Geoffre, who, as usual, had resurfaced, on the same day pursued a BF-109 and shot it down in enemy territory. He was therefore given it as a probable. On 4 January, in spite of the overcast weather, a scramble took place at 3.30 p.m. without any engagement. At 5 p.m. there was panic; everyone returned swiftly to the ground as the result of a telephone call from Division. Without knowing the cause of the panic, they all waited patiently for orders, but in vain: after three-quarters of an hour they returned to quarters in biting snow.

On 5 January the weather had improved. Consequently, training flights continued and a few missions took place without incident. Aspirant Guido, having left in a U-2 for a meeting at Division situated at Kaunas and Alitous, landed with fuel problems on this latter airstrip, from where he was to pick up the Regiment's tailor, who had taken a few days' leave. Bad weather continued.

The next day the patrol of Aspirants Challe and Miquel won a bottle of Martell cognac in an inter-escadrille pistol-shooting contest. The bad weather, which had kept all inactive for four days, persisted. But the evening was enlivened by a jazz concert given by an excellent orchestra which recalled the rhythm of pure 'swing' that most had rather forgotten.

In the course of a technical presentation by Kapitan Agavelian on 11 January, the commander gathered together the escadrille commanders to pass on great news: the long-awaited offensive would take place the following day. Normandie was to move to the landing strip at Diopienen as soon as covering missions over the front were required. Missions would begin 20 minutes before zero hour. Aspirant Eichenbaum left for Division's advance HQ, from where under the call sign 'Michel' he was to communicate by radio urgent orders to the patrol while it was in the air. All baggage was to be packed and pilots were to be on the runway at dawn.

On 12 January the weather was absolutely magnificent, and missions began towards 10 a.m. Numerous patrols took to the skies, without success. Between times crews carried on with the important running-in of the many new engines which had just been installed in the aircraft. However, the day passed without the zero hour being signalled, and so the pilots spent another night at Gross-Kalvaitchen. In the morning Aspirant Guido, who had left some days previously in a U-2 for Kaunas and Alitous, finally reappeared with his passenger: the absent tailor.

The pilots got their flying equipment together and went to the airstrip at dawn the next day. The offensive was officially announced for 11 a.m. and indeed, at 8 a.m. the rumbling of the artillery preparations could be heard. At 10.15 a.m. a squad of the 3rd took off to cover the lines, but the sky clouded over abruptly, forcing it to turn back. In 10 minutes an extremely dense fog covered the whole region, with the result that the pilots passed the remains of the day waiting for news of the attack. There was talk of the capture of the station at Trakenen and of a general advance of 3–4km along the whole front. An incident occurred in the morning: after taxiing, aircraft No. 19, piloted by Aspirant Dechanet, collapsed on a wing after breaking half the undercarriage. Those problem undercarriages!

Towards 1 p.m. on 14 January the weather improved and the 1st inaugurated the missions. North of Goumbinnen the patrol led by Aspirant Dechanet engaged in combat with two Bf-109s, which tried to break away by turning. The pursuit began. Martin fired on one of them, which caught fire and broke up in the air; then he fired on the second, which turned away by hedge-hopping but then came into the line of fire of Dechanet and Menut, who opened up with their guns and scored many terminal hits. They watched as the Bf-109 dived into the ground. After reassembling, the patrol engaged in a turning battle with three new Bf-109s over the railway to

Chtaloupienen–Goumbinnen. One of them broke away from the circle and was pursued by Martin, who fired and scored some hits but could not observe the results as he was obliged to disengage under pressure from the two remaining Bf-109s. However, one of them, having broken away to climb, was pursued by Versini, who fired on it and found himself similarly forced to disengage before he could observe the outcome. The result was two Bf-109s shot down and two other probables.

The 3rd patrolled on a hunting mission and found a group of enemy fighters who were heading west at speed. The patrol followed them for some distance but was forced to abandon the long pursuit when the enemy tried to draw it too far into German-held territory. The result was one probable in collaboration. Aspirant Mertzisen, Lieutenants Douarre and Castin, and Aspirant Bleton then took off; within minutes they were listening for radio information. 'Michel' from the radio post sent them to the Insterburg region. They noticed four Bf-109s but in the course of the attack, the patrol lost Mertzisen in the smoke. He pursued two of the four Bf-109s, which had become separated, and got in close; having taken them by complete surprise he fired at one of them point-blank. The Bf-109 caught fire immediately and was finished. However, Lieutenants Castin and Douarre and Aspirant Bleton encountered to the north of Goumbinnen fifteen Fw-190s, which they attacked. Castin fired at one of them, which crashed to the ground (seen by Douarre), then fired at another, whose fate remained uncertain. Bleton fired at a third, which crashed. The result was one Bf-109 and two Fw-190s certain, plus one Fw-190 damaged.

The Regiment's strip at Diopienen was about 8km south of Chtaloupienen. From here the pilots could easily hear and see artillery fire on the front. The move, with all the practical difficulties involved, had slowed down the rhythm of missions. Nevertheless, some take-offs had been accomplished. In the course of a patrol, Capitaine Matras and Aspirants Challe and Miquel encountered two Bf-109s 5km south-west of Goumbinnen. Challe and Miquel attacked; one Bf-109 crashed and another was damaged but succeeded in fleeing. The day would have been perfect if Aspirant Miquel, after the emotions of his victorious battle, had not forgotten to lower his undercarriage before landing. He made a dramatic pancake which alarmed all those who witnessed this drama. At 6 p.m. they made their way to the respective billets, which turned out to be satisfactory although less comfortable than those at Gross-Kalvaitchen. Normandie rediscovered the Supply Battalion which it had known the previous October in Stredniki. In the evening 100g of vodka and a drop of red wine enlivened dinner. However, some German aircraft came to roam in the locality and launched some illuminating flare devices and bombs, whose explosions were noticed amid the din of the anti-aircraft fire.

On 15 January it was snowing, when Aspirants Martin, Menut and Pistrack left to try to discover any traces of the enemy aircraft counted as probable kills from the previous day's battles. Their expedition was crowned with success and confirmation of the last two victories. The adjutant to the Chief of Staff of the 55th Guards Infantry Division gave these victories to Martin and Versini. At 2 p.m. the weather cleared, allowing missions to be carried out. Aspirant Dechanet survived a confrontation with a large formation of twenty Bf-109s and disengaged. The following morning the 3rd Escadrille was on standby and took off at 9.45 a.m. The patrol Aspirants André, de Geoffre, Penverne and Lorillon spotted to the south-west of Kussen two waves of Fw-190 bombers, and attacked them. Aspirant Penverne hit and exploded one in flight; Lorillon fired on another, which spiralled down and crashed. De Geoffre, getting up close at about 50m, fired at the third, which burst into flames; the fire and smoke seemed to envelope his Yak. Having broken away, he fired at another; he observed hits but then had to break off the battle. André fired and scored some good hits but had to disengage. He climbed towards the sun, attacked an Fw-190 which had been in the protecting group, pursued it hedge-hopping and saw it crash. The result was four definite and two probable.

Then the 1st, Aspirants Sauvage and Ougloff, Lieutenant Charras, Aspirants Piquenot, Perrin and Taburet, also had a fruitful sortie. They spotted to the north of Goumbinnen twelve Fw-190s in a defensive circle. Sauvage and Ougloff attacked two of them. Ougloff fired on an Fw-190, which threw up showers of metal pieces that seemed to form an arc over its fuselage. Sauvage fired at close range and the Fw-190 crashed to the ground. Then he fired at a second, which at 100m altitude dived towards the ground. Ougloff fired at another Fw-190, destroying it. Lieutenant Charras fired on an Fw-190 at close range but could not observe the results. He then returned to the rallying point and saw some Pe-2s protected by American-built P-39s. The Pe-2s were attacked by Bf-109s; Charras shot down one of them jointly with the pilot of the P-39. Just as they were about to begin a pursuit, in which Martin and Henri were already engaged, Lemare, Guido and Capitaine de Saint-Marceaux banked on four Fw-190s protecting the first ones. Lemare shot at one of them, whose pilot jumped immediately by parachute, while Capitaine de Saint-Marceaux pursued two others without catching them. On rejoining the squad Henri encountered the comrade of Lemare's victim and shot him down in flames. Commandant Delfino then left, taking with him Aspirants Miquel, André, Lorillon, Lieutenant Castin and Aspirant Bleton. After two pursuits without result on the Bf-109s, the squad regrouped over Chtaloupienen. But Miquel did not rejoin; Delfino had seen him heading east emitting lots of white smoke. The squad then surprised a large formation of Fw-190s hedge-hopping. Commandant Delfino fired at one of them, bits of the Fw-190 flew everywhere, some of the debris colliding with the left wing of Delfino's aircraft; the remainder of the German aircraft then crashed to the west of Kussen and the actual location was confirmed by Castin. Lieutenant Castin fired at two of them, which crashed, as did the Fw-190s attacked by Lorillon and André. During this engagement André fired at one Fw-190, which burst into a ball of fire directly in front of him. The result was six confirmed. Lieutenant Castin landed on another strip and returned only in the evening.

The patrol consisting of Aspirants Mertzisen, Challe, André and Bleton spotted to the west of Goumbinnen about twenty Fw-190 bombers and attacked them. André fired close range at one, the Fw-190 dropped its bombs and dived towards the ground, where it crashed. Bleton, who was following André, fired at another enemy aircraft, which smoked profusely and finally hit the ground on fire. Bleton then disengaged. André, who was threatened by an Fw-190, was saved by Bleton, who quickly moved into position and shot it down in flames.

The evening at the Stalovaia was lively with celebrations by the victors. General Zakharov sent a telegram of congratulations, and some bottles of champagne were uncorked in their honour. The Regiment had invited to this modest feast a Soviet pilot who parachuted down near the strip, his aircraft having caught fire spontaneously in the air. During conversation in the mess it was learned from the pilot that the second line of German defences had been pierced and the offensive in the sector seemed to have started in earnest.

On 17 January the 1st Escadrille, which was on standby, took off in two patrols of four aircraft. North-east of Goumbinnen the first patrol engaged in battle twelve Fw-190s that were strafing the Soviet ground positions. Capitaine Challe shot down an Fw-190 that he saw go into the ground, but he was attacked in his turn and seriously wounded on the left arm; he succeeded nevertheless in returning to the strip. Aspirant Marchi fired at an Fw-190, which went down in flames, and Aspirant Iribarne fired at two others, one of which he saw strike the ground and break into pieces. The second patrol surprised Fw-190 bombers just as they were diving on their targets. Aspirant Sauvage fired at one of them. The pilot jumped by parachute north-west of Chtaloupienen. The patrol regrouped and was joined by two Soviet fighters, which remained with the squad to share the action. They encountered a large number of Bf-109s and, while the rest of the squad formed a defensive circle, Lieutenant Charras and Aspirant Piquenot engaged in an unequal battle. During this action Piquenot was shot down in flames. Lieutenant Charras did not return. The last three patrols took off, but broke off their missions as the weather worsened abruptly, and Capitaine de Saint-Marceaux landed on the airstrip of the 18th Guards Air Regiment. Capitaine de La Salle took command of the 1st in view of the morning's events. Capitaine Challe was sent to the dressing station and then to the hospital. The rest of the day passed with a violent snowstorm.

On 18 January fog delayed the first mission until midday. The lead patrol, having become separated from the rest, spotted to the south-west of Kussen at 1,500m four Fw-190s in a column. Capitaine Matras fired at the last one, which smoked at once and hit the ground after a second burst of gunfire. The result was observed by Aspirant de Geoffre, who fired at a second Fw-190 and attained identical results. Another patrol encountered two Fw-190s to the north of Goumbinnen. Aspirants Génès, Taburet and Capitaine de La Salle attacked one of them, which dived to the north. Taburet fired at it from 100m and observed the impact but, overshooting at great speed, he broke off the pursuit, as did Capitaine de La Salle, for fear of loosening the 'extrados' (fairing), but Génès continued the pursuit. Reverchon fired at the second without result. After regrouping over Chtaloupienen the patrol Aspirants Génès, Reverchon and Perrin met a formation of ten Fw-190s north of Goumbinnen. A circling battle took place. Two Fw-190s broke away by diving to the west, pursued by Perrin; he fired on one of them, which crashed to the west of Goumbinnen. Then he hit the second, but was obliged to disengage as others were attacking him. Génès did not return. The patrol Commandant Delfino, Aspirants Penverne, Lieutenant Douarre, Aspirants Mertzisen and Bleton attacked a group of twenty Fw-190 bombers, which dived on emerging from the clouds. But another twenty Fw-190s fighters on protection duty intervened and forced the patrol to disengage. However, Lieutenant

Douarre pursued one of the Fw-190 bombers and probably shot it down 5km to the north-west of Insterburg.

Lieutenant Charras suddenly made an appearance on the strip. Engaged in combat the previous day against twenty Bf-109s, he succeeded in escaping from them by heading into the clouds, after which he surprised a single Bf-109 that he noticed at the last moment. The German pilot disengaged by hedge-hopping. Charras pursued it and, just as he was about to fire at it, the Bf-109 struck a tree with the tip of its wing and crashed. How many times the Yak pilots had seen these Bf-109s crash during manoeuvres at very low altitude! The patrol Aspirants André, Challe, Lieutenant Castin, and Aspirant Bleton encountered a group of Fw-190s to the west of Kussen. Aspirant Challe damaged one of them; part of his fairing became detached. Aspirant Bleton, after pursuing two Fw-190s, shot down one, which struck the ground; then he shot and damaged the second. André pursued two Fw-190s. Just as he was about to fire on the nearer of the two, to his surprise he saw the first German open fire on the other Fw-190 and shoot it down in flames. Having confirmed again that was indeed an Fw-190, he fired at the second German. The Fw-190 emitted thick smoke but André had to break off pursuit without observing the results. Castin did not return; the Regiment heard in the evening that he had landed on his belly in the area north of Naumestis.

On 19 January visibility was poor; nevertheless there were numerous missions. A patrol of the 1st Escadrille spotted in the region of Gillen twenty fully laden Fw-190 bombers with ten protecting Fw-190 fighters. At that moment Schoendorff, with engine problems, left the squad heading north-west. André's patrol went into defensive mode and circled for 15 minutes. The Fw-190s remained above without daring to begin to dive. Finally, three of them disengaged. André fired at one of them, which crashed south-west of Gillen; this was seen by Sauvage. The other two were taken to task by Sauvage and Lieutenant Charras. One of them burst into flames and the other crashed to the ground. After reassembling, André, Challe and Bleton noticed three He-129s hedge-hopping about 10km north-west of Goumbinnen. They attacked them as a patrol. One landed on its belly in flames and another crashed 5km west of Insterburg. The result was two He-129s jointly and three Fw-190s certain.

To everyone's joy Lieutenant Castin returned by car with the Soviet political adjutant of the Division. During the battle of the previous day, he had brought down an Fw-190, which he saw crash. After disengaging he noticed a Stormovik being attacked by an Fw-190. He intervened, which allowed the Stormovik to disengage. Castin was immediately hit by a second Fw-190, which he had not seen; the severe damage sustained had forced him to land on his belly. At 8km west of Gillen a patrol attacked nine Fw-190s. Aspirant Sauvage fired at one of them from 50–100m, saw the impact and was obliged to disengage. Then Sauvage fired at another, assisted by Iribarne, who also entered the fray; the enemy aircraft was set alight and went into the ground. Marchi fired at one, which burnt and dived in flames, hitting the ground. Aspirants Perrin and Taburet fired at a fourth, which they saw crash, and finally Perrin fired at one that seemed to have been hit already and crashed on fire. Reverchon, having fired without result at an Fw-190, got lost and landed on a strip in the Vilkavitchki region. He took off again and, getting lost once more, made a tourist visit to Goumbinnen, where he was greeted by lively German anti-aircraft fire. His aircraft was badly hit and he made a late half-turn to land on his belly a few kilometres from Normandie's strip. The absence of Génès deprived the 1st of one of its squad leaders. Aspirant Lemare was moved from the 2nd to the 1st; conversely, Perrin was moved to the 2nd. After two unsuccessful patrols a large squad left to blockade the Luftwaffe strips at Insterburg. During this blockade Pe-2s would carry out bombing missions in the sector. Although the weather did not permit the intended mission, the Pe-2s made their sorties without being troubled by enemy fighters, and the squad returned without incident. In the evening the commandant learned that the Regiment had been cited in an Order of the Day from Marshal Stalin on the occasion of the breakthrough in East Prussia.

On 20 January the weather was bad to begin with but cleared later. A mission to protect Pe-2 bombers in the Insterburg region was carried out; the pilots witnessed during their mission, which lasted half an hour, four successive bombardments of Insterburg. This squad was relieved by another, which likewise protected further Pe-2s. After a break of two hours a new mission was asked to blockade the Luftwaffe landing strips at Gerdaquen, 50km south-west of Insterburg. Then eight aircraft took off to cover Goumbinnen. During the day convoys left to pick up the Regiment's aircraft, which had remained for a month on the airstrip of the 18th Guards Air Regiment. Towards 7 p.m. a German aircraft passed vertically over the landing strip at 1,000m. The anti-aircraft batteries opened up but missed the intruder. During dinner the pilots read in the newspaper, *Pravda*, of

15 January 1945, the text of a speech by their old commandant, Lieutenant-Colonel Pouyade:

Ex-Commandant of Normandie, Lieutenant-Colonel Pouyade. Paris, 14 January 1945. Having arrived in Paris, the Commander of Normandie, Lieutenant-Colonel Pouyade, gave a talk over the radio and recounted the battles of his escadrilles, which are fighting against the Germans on the Soviet-German front. A transcript of that speech reads:

For more than two years, said Lieutenant-Colonel Pouyade, the Regiment Normandie has taken its place on the Soviet–German front, shoulder to shoulder with the brave aviators of the Red Army. We knew how to hold high and firm the tricolour flag and maintain the prestige of French aviation. What a road we have travelled in two years! Then it was Stalingrad, the hardest days of the war. Today we are on the edge of the Baltic Sea. Our comrades who remain at the front are no longer fighting in the skies of friendly countries but above enemy territory. The enemy is losing one position after another and falls back, approaching the final rampart. Towards the end of 1943, Normandie had shot down 77 enemy aircraft, 9 probables and 16 damaged. Now, to the account of the Regiment there were 199 shot down, 26 probables, 28 damaged. For some particularly successful battles they have received the recognition of the Soviet Command. On 22 September 1943, taking advantage of a surprise tactic in a battle of 10 minutes, 10 Normandie fighters shot down 9 enemy aircraft without suffering any losses. Battles of a particularly desperate nature took place on 16 October 1944 at the start of the offensive in East Prussia. In one single day the Regiment shot down 29 enemy aircraft, having carried out 120 missions. Our aircraft were in the air for seven hours. We think, concluded Lieutenant-Colonel Pouyade, that 1945 will be the year of victory. The Normandie-Niemen Regiment will continue to carry out its duty until the end of the war on the Germano-Soviet fronts, raising the prestige of French aviation and reinforcing in this way the affection of France in the USSR.

On 21 January it was snowing. There was talk about the grandiose military events of recent days. Pilots were glued to the radio. The Soviets had penetrated Silesia, and now Breslau was only 50km from the front. During

the day the Division communicated to Normandie the most welcome text of a
telegram from the 1st Corps, Guards Tank Regiment:

> The Tankistes [tank crews] of Tatsinsky send cordial congratulations to the
> glorious pilots of the Smolensk Division who contributed to the success of
> our Army Corps.
>
> *Signed: Bourdieny, Tchernikoff, Karavanoff*

These congratulations affected every pilot, especially because Normandie's
covering of the front took place over the axis of the attack by this heroic tank
corps. The flyers had watched this important battle with great interest and
had given constant air cover to the advancing division. Normandie was once
again cited by Marshal Stalin in the Order of the Day for the capture of
Goumbinnen. At midnight the glorious news came over the radio that the
Red Army had entered Tannenberg.

On 22 January, with snow falling, the Regiment was informed that
Aspirant Schoendorff had been picked up safely. Having suffered a fuel
problem, he succeeded in reaching the right bank of the River Niemen and
landed belly-up in open country. At 5 p.m. Aspirant Pierrot arrived from
Moscow, where he had stayed for treatment. He brought with him some
official mail in which the pilots learned of Adjutant Guido's promotion to the
grade of sous-lieutenant. This happy news was cause for another celebration,
washed down with some bottles of excellent champagne.

The following day the weather improved. Aspirant Schoendorff rejoined the
Regiment. During the evening news came that the Regiment would change
airstrips in the morning. The new strip was 4km south of Gross Skaisgiren
and about 50km north-west of Insterburg. Most pilots spent the evening
glued to the radio, which gave excellent news of the advancing Red Army.
The Normandie-Niemen Regiment had been mentioned once again in the
Order of the Day by Marshal Stalin.

On 24 January fog prevented the relocation. However, most of the baggage
left by lorry with Aspirant Rohmer. Aspirants Marchi and Pistrack attempted
a connection to the new strip in the U-2, but visibility of less than 500m
forced them to turn back. The next day the weather again prevented the
move. However, the liaison U-2 went ahead as normal and Aspirant Pistrack
described the general look of the quarters, which appeared comfortable. The
German population near the strip was limited to one sick old man; the rest

had been evacuated. This confirmed the rumours at the start of the October offensive about the evacuation of East Prussia. The mass evacuation of the civilian population was caused in part by the fear spread by the propaganda of Joseph Goebbels. With his broadcasts of horror stories about the Red Army, he had intended to galvanise the citizens of the Reich to fight to the last man and woman, but instead they fled west. Towards 3.30 p.m. an imminent departure seemed on the cards, but it was immediately countermanded and the take-off was once again scheduled for the following day.

MOVE TO GROSS SKAISGIREN

The Regiment received orders on 26 January to move to Gross Skaisgiren. As usual this relocation in the bitter cold was to be accompanied by a covering mission over the lines. The 1st Escadrille took off at noon and the 2nd at 1 p.m.; neither reported any incidents. As the weather deteriorated the 3rd carried out the move without doing any covering. The other pilots of the Regiment carried out the move without incident, although some noses were frozen during liaison trips in the open cockpit of the U-2. In an adventure which could have turned out badly, Lieutenant Charras, in the U-2 with the faithful Pistrack as passenger, lost his way on account of bad visibility, and crossed without realising it the frozen and snow-covered Niemen. Noting a large town, he headed for it in the hope of finding his bearings. The town turned out to be Memel, where the Germans had been blockaded for three months. Genuinely surprised by the visit, they organised a warm if not heated reception with anti-aircraft fire, which managed to persuade the errant navigators that they had lost their way. Retracing their steps, they finally landed at Gross Skaisgiren, where they recounted their tale of woe to the amused listeners.

Lunch was served very late in a luxurious Stalovaia with a very refined menu. The quarters delighted the pilots less because five 'polks' (Soviet flights) were at the strip at the same time, making all somewhat tightly squeezed. Another inconvenience caused by the crowding was that dinner was served at 1 a.m. From the start the strip proved to be impractical. The Supply Battalion was unable to cope with the technical demands of the officer mechanics of the Regiment, who had ended up in this corner of East Prussia. No aircraft were ready and at 2 p.m., when the order to move to the strip at Eichenwald was confirmed, they witnessed a curious fly-past of Yak-3s, with undercarriage half-retracted, making their way to the new destination. The 18th Guards Air Regiment also shared this strip. Quarters at Eichenwald were comfortable but not spacious, and the Supply Battalion, as at Gross Skaisgiren, appeared overwhelmed by events. Aspirant Perrin and Sous-lieutenant Guido, having left in a Douglas DC-3 to act as ferry pilots for the surplus Yak-3s, returned empty-handed at 3 a.m. Guido had the misfortune to injure his eye during this failed supply attempt, but it was not serious enough to ground him.

On 28 January the weather cleared in the early afternoon. At once some hunting missions were carried out in the Koenigsberg region. The first patrol spotted two Fw-190s at 15km north of Koenigsberg. The patrol banked to take up its position. The Fw-190s fled hedge-hopping. Capitaine Matras and Aspirant de Geoffre fired at one of the group, which hit the ground brutally and slid 200m on its belly. However, Aspirant Challe and Pierrot, both victims of mechanical faults, could not continue the battle. The second patrol, encountering three Fw-190s north of Koenigsberg, attacked two of them, but the third, which had broken away by climbing, forced them to break off the pursuit. This last one was attacked by Aspirant Ougloff, who fired at it but unfortunately missed. The third patrol encountered a single Fw-190 some 10km north-west of Koenigsberg. Battle was engaged immediately, but the Fw-190 manoeuvred fiercely and at a vertical level under a ceiling of 500m. After several attempts it was hit by bursts of gunfire from each of the three pilots; it finally emitted a lot of black smoke. Then it began to turn after having been fired on one last time by Aspirant Henri, and disappeared into a bank of cloud at 200m. Finally night arrived, interrupting the last missions.

At about 10.30 a.m. on 29 January snow stopped falling. Visibility was poor, but even so several patrols took off to hunt. Three patrols returned without incident; the fourth patrol encountered very thick fog on the return from its mission and just managed to make the strip, after a delicate session flying blind. But Aspirant Menut did not return. Some pilots who had gone to visit what remained of the town of Labiau encountered a group of French prisoners liberated by the Soviet advance. The conversation jogged along and the pilots received from them some information about 'French pilots' who came down in the region. Notes were made of this in spite of the lack of detail. One of the prisoners was said to have met, on 29 October, an aviator staying with a Polish family. He was thought to have come down by parachute about two weeks previously in the Insterburg region. The prisoner did not remember the name of the French pilot, but information seemed to indicate that it could be Aspirant Cazaneuve, attacked on 13 October by Bf-109s in the same region. This information accorded quite well with that of two other prisoners: they were said to have witnessed in the same area an aerial battle taking place at very high altitude, from which an aviator was seen to have jumped by parachute. Another prisoner was said to have seen, towards the end of September, an aircraft losing a wing while strafing the Gillen–Insterburg railway line, in the course of which it had crashed to the ground. The papers found on the pilot were said to be in the name of 'Jean Renaud', born in Paris. This name did not ring any bells with the pilots as a nickname or even a false identity of any of their lost comrades; but they thought it could possibly be Lieutenant Verdier, who disappeared on 22 September while strafing this railway line. In any event, Commandant Delfino and some other pilots of the Regiment took provisions and cigarettes to the prisoners, gifts that were very welcome. It was very unlikely that a French Normandie pilot had carried a false identity card, although unofficial papers could be considered most appropriate under the circumstances; certainly it would have helped if he had been captured by Nazi elements. It was known that, when Aspirant Bayssade was captured in July 1944, he gave the false name and identity of an Algerian wine salesman by the name of 'Jean Verdunois', although he had no papers to back this up. In all, eight Normandie pilots assumed false identities but they never had official cards to confirm them.

When Keitel signed a formal agreement with the Vichy government in May 1943, he insisted that any captured Normandie French pilot who had been flying with the Red Air Force should be executed on capture and the family of the pilot back in France punished by being deported to a concentration camp. It is not known how many French pilots were executed on capture, but fourteen Normandie pilots could not be traced after they parachuted or crashed behind enemy lines. What can be confirmed is that, within weeks after Aspirant Yves Bizien was captured on 13 April 1943, his family was arrested by Vichy police officials and subsequently deported to a concentration camp. The same treatment was meted out to the family of Lieutenant Raymond Derville, also captured on 13 April 1943. Only four captured pilots survived the war.

A senior officer from the Normandie-Niemen Regiment was asked whether false identity cards were carried or used by his pilots. His answer was a most definite 'no'; only genuine Soviet cards were carried. He then confirmed that all members of the Regiment carried correct Red Air Force identity cards, issued with the French pilot's correct name and sealed by the Soviet unit stamp. One is left to speculate whether the pilot concerned carried spurious papers in the name of 'Jean Renaud'. Were the prisoners wrong in their assumption? It must be remembered that these deported French prisoners were forced to work for the Nazi war machine, which would have made them feel uncomfortable once the Germans had retreated and the Red Army arrived; some would naturally wish to appear helpful to their liberators, and this type of information would be just what the Normandie personnel required. The deported French workers from the Koenigsberg slave camp could certainly thank Général de Gaulle for his alliance and agreements with the Soviets, since otherwise their returning to France on being released would not have been a speedy matter.

On 31 January it snowed. At 4 p.m. the weather cleared a little but visibility remained poor. Two Bf-109s made two successive passages above the strip and were greeted by anti-aircraft fire. Their behaviour led the watchers to believe that they were lost. The 3rd, which was on standby, received the order to reconnoitre and strafe the landing strip at Gross Kubuiken at the far end of the Koenigsberg peninsula. The mission was carried out by the patrols of Capitaine Matras, Aspirants Bleton, André and Pierrot, who strafed and set on fire a Ju-52. Capitaine Matras only just made his way back to the strip, his aircraft having been badly hit by anti-aircraft fire. On the return journey the André–Pierrot patrol noticed another airfield in the region of Routou and carried out a second strafing of a Ju-52, confirming the aircraft's destruction. Patrols carried out two further missions without incident. At 7 p.m. Aspirant Eichenbaum appeared and recounted his impressions of the forward lines. The services that he rendered to the Regiment during the offensive and the risks that he ran to complete his mission made him worthy of being proposed for the Croix de Guerre. He also met French prisoners and obtained information from them. He heard in particular about two French pilots of unknown identity, one said to be a native of Lyon and the other of Paris, who were thought to be buried between Insterburg and Vielau. Towards 11 p.m. Aspirant Pistrack left for duty with the radio communication post at the front.

The weather was dreadful on 1 February. It thawed and rained, turning the countryside into a mud-bath. The pilots spent the day in their quarters. In the morning, in spite of poor visibility, the Division requested several reconnaissance missions over the Koenigsberg peninsula. Two patrols carried out the missions, without incident. The third and last patrol strafed some trucks circling around the shoreline of the Kurisches Haff on the Baltic. Aspirant Perrin took off to return two Soviet pilots of the 523rd Air Regiment. They left in the U-2 but they could not find their regiment on the landing strip where they left it, and returned in the U-2 to Labiau.

Two days later a break in the clouds allowed the Regiment to carry out several missions in the course of which two aircraft were hit by enemy flak. During the strafing of a landing strip at Gross Kubuiken, a hanger exploded, enveloping the four attacking Yaks with fire and debris. Anti-aircraft fire opened up and three Yaks sustained damage. In another patrol Aspirant Ougloff, having lost contact with the squad due to engine problems, found himself near two Yak-9s and followed them, hoping to find a landing strip, but suffered fuel breakdown 2km from the landing strip where the 117th Regiment of Stormoviks was based, and landed on his belly. Two other hunting missions took place without incident. The day finished with a reconnaissance mission toward Koenigsberg and over the port of Pillau on the Frisches Haff, a stretch of water that lay along the edge of the Baltic.

On 4 February the standby patrol took off to reconnoitre the visibility over the lines. But drizzle kept the rest on the ground. A German twin-engine machine, probably a Ju-88, went past hedge-hoping and disappeared into the fog after suffering blasts from the surprised Soviet anti-aircraft gunners. Leaving for Moscow were Lieutenants Castin and Eichenbaum. On 5 February four missions took place during the early hours over the Koenigsberg area. Towards 10 a.m. the Division ordered the Regiment to move immediately to Povouden, 20km north of Koenigsberg. During this move the 1st Escadrille carried out an important mission strafing the airfield at Heligenbeil. The assault squad hedge-hopped while firing at an Fw-190 vertically above the strip. Aspirant Lemare and Marchi fired at a Fiesler Storch but very intense German anti-aircraft fire prevented them from pursuing the battle and observing the results. Other missions took place. But Aspirants Martin and Versini had to turn back as a result of mechanical problems. Shortly afterwards André and Penverne had a serious encounter with twelve Fw-190s. Aspirant André succeeded in disengaging and returned to base, but Penverne did not come back. Towards 6.30 p.m. everyone went to the billet, which proved to be comfortable. Good news: the billet would shortly have electricity.

The weather was so bad on 6 February that the chaps explored the immediate surroundings of the billet. Quite a number of German prisoners were still there, and they were seen marching past on the roads. Many were confined by the Red Army in a prisoner of war camp which the Germans were made to construct. One of them had the nerve to complain to a Normandie pilot that war was heart-breaking business and that he had already walked more than 10km. They did not seem to realise what they had made others endure. While waiting, some specimens of the 'master' race were asked to sweep the quarters. Lunch was at 3 p.m. in the sumptuous Stalovaia. The Soviet lieutenant who organised these arrangements spoke with emotion of the time when he was a cook in a restaurant in Leningrad. At 9 p.m. a group went to visit some recently liberated French prisoners.

On 10 February, after days of bad weather, it cleared. At 11 a.m. covering and hunting missions resumed. The first patrol to take off noticed in the Wolihuick region six Fw-190s, which it attacked while descending from the sun. Capitaine Matras fired on the last one, which began to smoke; it was also fired on by Aspriants de Geoffre and Lorillon, who really set it ablaze. Aspirants Dechanet, Henri, Perrin, Sous-lieutenant Guido and Aspirant Martin, while hunting, encountered two Bf-109s heading for Heligenbeil. The Germans tried to escape by diving, but the squad pursued them. Aspirant Dechanet, then Aspirants Perrin, Henri and Sous-lieutenant Guido fired at one of the group, which crashed to the ground. All the squad then fired at the patrol leader, which crashed on its belly. Later, a patrol took off to give protective cover to two Stormoviks that were on a photographic mission. The Yaks accompanied them as far as Koenigsberg, then resumed coverage of the sector, during which time they noticed four Bf-109s north of Bladiau. They engaged in a circling battle at the same ceiling height. Aspirant Sauvage and Taburet fired and hit one Bf-109, which disappeared into the clouds. Lieutenant Charras fired at another, which he hit on the left wing, but he was obliged to disengage. Aspirants Sauvage and Marchi pursued the second one, which dived in the direction of Pillau. This latter aircraft was then brought down by Marchi, who saw it crash. Three other patrols went out on a hunting sortie but encountered no enemy aircraft.

The next day the weather cleared towards 3 p.m. The patrol Aspirants Sauvage, Ougloff, Capitaine de La Salle, and Aspirant Iribarne went hunting and spotted three Fw-190s 5km east of Bladiau. The Fw-190s turned back and were pursued by Aspirant Iribarne and Capitaine de La Salle. Iribarne, caught between the first and second enemy aircraft, could not disengage and Aspirant Sauvage saw him go into a steep dive. Iribarne did not come back from the mission. The second patrol noticed, 15km west of Eylau, a battle between quite a large number of Yaks and Bf-109s. The squad approached this mêlée, from which four Bf-109s detached themselves. A circling battle took place almost immediately. Commandant Delfino fired at a Bf-109, which was crippled and finished off by Sous-lieutenant Guido. Aspirant Martin fired at another in a light banking manoeuvre. The Bf-109 pilot pulled on the joystick and dived down. After two more bursts of gunfire the Bf-109 crashed to the ground. Aspirant Versini fired at a third, without success. However, Aspirant Perrin, no longer seeing his comrade Monge, engaged in a battle with two Bf-109s, one of which was shot down in flames. After this first engagement Commandant Delfino and Sous-lieutenant Guido pursued a Bf-109 but were attacked by two other Bf-109s. While the commander continued pursuit as far as the ground, where he circled with his adversary for more than 5 minutes, Sous-lieutenant Guido stayed in contact with the two Bf-109s, which were joined by a third. Having fired three bursts of gunfire in quite a good position for strikes, he succeeded in breaking away without being able to observe the result. Aspirant Monge did not return. Another patrol engaged some Bf-109s and Fw-190s, without a result.

At 5 p.m. Normandie received orders to move to the landing strip at Vittenberg, but because of actions only the 1st was able to make the move. The weather was still bad, and despite numerous attempts, the move could not be made. Aspirant Martin gave half an hour of emotion to the watchers on the strip by struggling with a recalcitrant undercarriage which refused to come down out of its housing, but he finally won the tussle and landed without incident.

On 14 February the weather was good. The transfer finally took place. The aerodrome at Vittenberg had been a Luftwaffe air base before the war, with hangers, stone buildings, cement runways and even pathways. The buildings were now destroyed and booby-trapped by the Germans before they retreated; teams of Soviet sappers working without rest were worn out clearing and lifting the mines. The noise accompanying this dangerous work was exceptional, as some mines had to be blown up *in situ* as they were in a dangerous state.

Missions started at 11 a.m on 15 February. The first three patrols took off but returned without incident. A fourth patrol spotted in the Heligenbeil area twelve Fw-190s, which were on the point of attacking some Stormoviks. The squad took them by surprise. Lemare shot one down immediately; the pilot jumped in his parachute. Lemare then fired on a second and scored hits on the left wing, but could not continue his attack. Sauvage and Schoendorff fired at another Fw-190 whose left wing burst into flames; it then descended in a spiral. Aspirants Marchi and Ougloff fired at another Fw-190, which belched black smoke. Then four further patrols returned with nothing to report. During the day the Yak-6, of which there had been no news for more than two months, arrived with a Soviet pilot assigned specifically to this aircraft.

The next day the weather was uncertain. A patrol of the 3rd took off. Having made a tour of the sector at 300m, it was recalled to base because the weather was worsening and snow was beginning to fall. The following morning it was snowing, several missions took place from 9.30 a.m. at a ceiling of 300m. One of the missions did not encounter anything but was fired on by anti-aircraft fire that hit one Yak on the right wing. At midday a patrol attempted a reconnaissance of enemy activity on the Frisches Haff, but bad weather obstructed the route between Braunsberg and Elbing. A further mission took place with the same results at 2 p.m. Other patrols made fruitless surveys of the sector under a ceiling of 600m.

On 18 February, as a German aircraft had passed near the airstrip the previous day, Division ordered that two aircraft should be permanently on covering duty. A patrol of Aspirants Lemare and Schoendorff carried out this mission, which was cancelled as cover was already ensured by the numerous patrols taking off and landing. Aspirants Martin and Versini pursued two Bf-109s, which escaped by going into the clouds. Aspirants André, de Geoffre, Challe, and Bleton missed a magnificent chance when a Ju-88 or Ju-188 passed over the runway just as they were landing and nobody radioed them; the German got away without having been disturbed. The patrol Aspirants Sauvage, Ougloff, Marchi and Reverchon, who like their earlier comrades were carrying out a covering mission over the lines at a low-altitude ceiling of 500m, were violently fired on by anti-aircraft fire and Sauvage's aircraft was badly hit. He succeeded in returning to the strip accompanied by three Yaks who gave protection during his ordeal. Ougloff landed at the same time as Sauvage, and then Marchi and Reverchon went back over the sector. They were fired on again and Marchi saw Reverchon's aircraft catch fire and crash to the ground. The last two patrols carried out their missions without incident.

The following day, despite poor visibility, a patrol took off to cover the front. Unable to get back to the airstrip, it landed on a strip 40km to the south of Vittenberg. In spite of the improvement in the weather, there were no other missions. Aspirant Pistrack, who had been to collect information about Reverchon's accident, informed the commandant that Reverchon had miraculously escaped death. Despite very serious wounds, amputation of a foot, multiple fractures of the arm, and splinters in the face and neck, the surgeons thought they would be able to get him over it. News of the death of Marshal Chernyakhovsky affected the Regiment, as he was the commander of the 3rd Belorussian Front, under which Normandie served directly. His funeral took place at Vilno.

ORDER of the Commander in Chief to the Commander of troops of the 3rd Belorussian Front

The troops of the 3rd Belorussian Front continue to tighten the ring which encircles the enemy grouping in East Prussia, and have seized the towns of Vormdit and Melzak, important centres of communication, and strong points of support for the German defences. In the battle for the seizure of Vormdit and Melzak the following distinguished themselves: The aviators of General Zakharov and of Commandant Delfino. The units that distinguished themselves will be put forward for decorations. Today, 17 February, at 21.00, the capital of our country, Moscow, will salute with 20 salvos of artillery by 224 guns, the valiant troops of the 3rd Belorussian Front, glory to the heroes who died for the liberty and independence of our country.

17 February 1945. No. 282. J. Stalin

CASUALTIES REDUCE NORMANDIE STRENGTH TO TWENTY-FOUR PILOTS

On 20 February missions followed one another at a good rate; three patrols went hunting and found no enemy. Then in the Pollan region a squad spotted twelve Bf-109s which, while the pilots headed for them, separated into two groups, one of which disengaged by diving. The squad attacked the group that remained at the upper level; but, during the battle the first group, which had broken away, climbed into the sun, forcing the squad to break away in their turn. But Aspirant Bleton, probably with a broken radio, did not follow the rest of the patrol; he was brought down almost immediately and parachuted into the Pillau region, about 5km to the east of the port. Following recent losses the Regiment found itself reduced to twenty-four pilots, including Commandant Delfino. He decided therefore to dissolve one escadrille in order to fill out the other two. The arrival of reinforcements would enable the Regiment to re-create the dissolved escadrille later.

The Normandie personnel were divided up in the following manner:

Commandant Delfino, Regimental Commander.

Capitaine Matras, second in command.

2nd Escadrille: Capitaine de Saint-Marceaux, Lieutenant Douarre, Sous-lieutenant Guido, Aspirants Dechanet, Lemare, Martin, Perrin, Marchi, Versini, Henri and Schoendorff.

3rd Escadrille: Capitaine de La Salle, Lieutenant Charras, Aspirants Mertzisen, Challe, Sauvage, André, Pierrot, Taburet, Ougloff, de Geoffre and Lorillon.

General service personnel: Aspirant Rohmer. Interpreters: Aspirants Eichenbaum, de Friede and Pistrack.

On 21 February, in spite of numerous sorties to cover the lines, no encounters with the enemy took place. At 5 p.m. the Regiment had the happy surprise of seeing Aspirant Monge return; he had been missing since 11 February. Having become lost as a result of the battle against the Bf-109s, he had run out of fuel before being able to locate an airstrip, and was thus forced to land in the country with a belly flop. He related his journey, which was not lacking in the picturesque.

The next day, owing to bad weather, no missions went up. In the evening of 22 February, all celebrated the 27th anniversary of the creation of the Red Army. After the usual speeches and reading of Marshal Stalin's special Order of the Day, numerous toasts were proposed and it was in the warmest ambience that they began to celebrate. In the course of conversation with Soviet comrades the Normandie pilots learned of the exploits of a pilot of the 139th Guards Air Regiment. His comrade having been brought down by flak and forced to land belly-up on the frozen surface of the Frisches Haff, the pilot mounted an aerial guard while calling by radio for reinforcements.

Relieved after some time by the arrival of four other Soviet fighters, he returned to his base landing strip, where he collected a U-2. Returning quickly to the place where his comrade crash-landed, he put the regiment's U-2 down on the ice and picked up the crashed airman and took him back to his base. All this happened inside enemy lines, but under the protection of the other four circling Yaks of the regiment.

At 1 p.m. on 23 February Capitaine Matras made a weather check. Lemare, de Saint-Marceaux and Henri left on a mission. During this patrol Capitaine de Saint-Marceaux announced on the radio that he was making a half-turn, but he did not return to the landing strip. Another four patrols returned without incident. The following day Capitaine de Saint-Marceaux made his appearance. With fuel problems, he had to land at Povouden. Eichenbaum returned from Moscow via Insterburg, where the Yak-6 went to fetch him. He brought mail and the promise of an imminent visit from Général Petit. It was reported that the Normandie-Niemen Regiment would be bestowed with the Order of the Red Banner. The presentation would take place with all the Regiment's personnel on parade. At the same time Soviet decorations would be awarded to selected Soviet mechanics.

On 25 February, despite the weather, it was announced that Normandie was to move to the Friedland airstrip. The patrol of Capitaine de Saint-Marceaux, Lieutenant Douarre, Aspirant Marchi, and Sous-lieutenant Guido attempted a covering mission over the lines but had to abandon it, the ceiling being lower than 200m. At 4 p.m. the move took place. In spite of an extremely bad runway, Normandie landed without incident. The new quarters were 6km south of Friedland on the large estate of a German baron. The Regiment was once again stationed with its good comrades, the 18th Guards Air Regiment.

The next day Commandant Delfino brought the news that the Regiment was to be in a state of 'semi-repos' (temporarily stood down). The shortage of replacements and the lamentable state of the airstrip, with 10–15cm of mud, conditions would probably have prevented any taking off anyway. Before dinner, a troop of performers gave a very pleasant performance of Russian folklore and songs.

At 3 p.m. on 28 February Kapitan Pinchouk of the 18th Guards Air Regiment came to present himself to Commandant Delfino. He deplored the fact that the old friendship of Normandie and the 18th Guards Air Regiment seemed to have 'gone to sleep' and proposed to wake it up by communal reunions. As a result a great dinner, presided over by Lieutenant-Colonel Goloubov, former Commander of the 18th Guards Air Regiment, was organised. The aim of the evening was largely achieved.

In the afternoon of 1 March, Sous-lieutenant Challe and Eichenbaum went to Insterburg to see Capitaine Challe and Aspirant Reverchon. The latter, whose condition was still very serious, had undergone a new amputation of the leg, which was gangrenous. Capitaine Challe had not yet arrived; his brother remained at Insterburg to await him.

On 2 March the Soviet General Staff passed on to Commandant Delfino a copy of the newspaper *Pravda* dated 24 February, where the names of Normandie pilots who had been awarded Soviet decorations were published (see Appendix III).

The next day Major Siberine, Commander of the 18th Guards Air Regiment, invited Commandant Delfino and Capitaine Matras with interpreter Eichenbaum to an intimate dinner on the occasion of the decorations awarded to Normandie. The Division informed the Regiment of the imminent visit of Général Petit and General Levandovitch, who were due on 8 March. At midday on 6 March Commandant Delfino told the pilots that a telegram from Général Petit had brought news of numerous promotions to the grade of Sous-lieutenant; precise details were missing. In the evening Mayor (Major) Profitelouk gave an interesting presentation about the situation on the front, on the ground and in the air. The commandant announced a possible resumption of combat missions.

About 11 a.m. on 7 March, the Soviet General Staff abruptly terminated the temporary stand down by announcing that missions would be carried out during the day. Shovelling the snow away made it possible to take off at 3.30 p.m. The mission to be carried out amazed the Regiment: 'coverage of the front in the Elbing region'. In effect, the 300km return journey would allow the Yaks only a few minutes over the sector. Four patrols accomplished this vast and distant mission without incident. The following day missions continued, but the escadrilles were assigned a somewhat nearer sector. The offensive against the 'pocket' was to be launched and Normandie was to protect the air space above where the Pe-2s were going to bomb. The first two patrols found no enemy. The third patrol, covering in the Braunsberg region, spotted a formation of Pe-2s bombing in the sector; the last group was attacked by a dozen Fw-190s. One of them brought down a Pe-2, but Pierrot, having placed himself behind the German, fired on him. André noticed the Fw-190 in trouble and smoking profusely. The behaviour of the aircraft in its fall led André to believe that the pilot had been killed. Pierrot was attacked in his turn, but André broke away and engaged in battle with eight Fw-190s. He finished by parting company with them and noticed at that moment an Fw-190 on its own, pursued by three Yaks from the squad. Challe fired several times and discovered he had a fuel leak. He had to disengage and Lorillon took over as well as Ougloff. Lorillon re-engaged in his turn and noticed after a first burst of gunfire that he too had a fuel leak. Then the Fw-190 left at very low altitude over the coastal edge of the Frisches Haff. Earlier two other patrols returned without any contact with the enemy. Aspirants Challe and de Friede went in the U-2 to Insterburg to visit Capitaine Challe and Aspirant Reverchon; they were to return the following day. At 7.30 a.m. there was an administration panic: Général Petit's intended visit was announced. Six aircraft were to go to Insterburg to protect his Douglas DC-3; all the Regiment was to be ready for 10 a.m. In addition, the Division demanded an immediate and permanent presence of six aircraft over the 'pocket'. Capitaine Matras also left for Insterburg in order to warn control of the arrival time of the important Douglas DC-3. Missions began during the panic but passed without incident. At 7.30 p.m. Commandant Delfino was informed that the général's plans had fallen through. In the evening, a pleasant concert was given by a troop of performers from Moscow.

On 11 March missions were resumed over the everlasting 'pocket'. Soviet aircraft streaked through the skies and Normandie protected numerous Pe-2s which were going to bomb the most important strategic points. All these missions were made without sight of an enemy aircraft. The next day the weather was poor; a telegram announced that Général Petit still had not left Moscow. In the afternoon a remarkable event happened. Aspirant Pistrack, a non-flyer, was let loose on the U-2. Eichenbaum was mad with jealousy. These two officers were interpreters and their general duties alternated between the radio post at the front and liaison duties for the Regiment. So Pistrack would much appreciate and enjoy a chance to try his hand at aeronautical activities.

On 13 March Colonel Aristov gave a remarkable lecture on the Belorussian offensive of June 1944. The assembled pilots followed the events of this already distant period with mild interest. The Division had been busy doing its paperwork; the results came as a blow when, on 16 March, Commandant

Delfino passed on a note from General Khrioukine, who was 'surprised' that the offensive missions presently under way had been shown to be both less fruitful and more costly than the preceding ones. He felt that the 303rd Division, in which Normandie served, had not recently striven for high achievements.

NORMANDIE-NIEMEN IN COMBAT WITH
THE MOULDERS GROUP

General Khrioukine was chiding the Division, and on this occasion the Normandie-Niemen Regiment, for what he thought was a lack of aggressive spirit. He had studied the combat statistics, which showed a higher loss of Soviet aircraft and fewer victories over the enemy. What General Khrioukine and the Division had underestimated was that in East Prussia, and particularly in the Pillau region, the Normandie pilots had been facing the very experienced cream of German fighter pilots serving in 'Jagdgeschwader' Moulders Group (51st Squadron) that were at one time based at Pillau aerodrome. The Moulders Group was equipped with the latest Bf-109Gs. This elite unit had some notable aces fighting in the skies over East Prussia; neither the Division nor Normandie was aware of how many seasoned aces made up the composition of this German fighter group. Although the German top guns were now fewer in number, they could still send into combat pilots who counted their individual victories in double figures; and their commanding officer, Colonel Brendle, Knight's Cross with Oak Leaves, had an amazing score of 189 victories. Even so, the Moulders Group found the Normandie pilots flying the new Yak-3s to be deadly opponents, so much so that, as already noted, its command had issued instructions to pilots to avoid combat with any Yak fighter without an oil cooler under the nose. This instruction referred to the faster Yak-3, which had the oil cooler moved back to the wing roots, which appeared to hide it.

At this late stage in the war the airfield at Pillau was considered a prime target. It was situated at the tip of the Samland Peninsula, south-west of Koenigsberg. The defending German pilots with their yellow spinners had for some time been quick to identify the attacking French Yak-3s. Although they carried full Soviet markings, on the Normandie-Niemen aircraft an additional tricolour roundel appeared just below the cockpit, and the nose cone spinners were coloured in concentric circles of red, white and blue.

On 17 March Commandant Delfino, Capitaine de Saint-Marceaux and Capitaine de La Salle, assisted by the 'faithful' Pistrack, went to Schipenbeil, where a meeting was held with General Zakharov on his conception of the work of the Division. Little of this theory was new. The Regiment was buzzing with interesting news: a German prisoner, a pilot of the 51st Squadron (Moulders Group) based at Pillau and recently shot down and captured, stated that he had seen a Normandie flyer prisoner at his base, apparently Aspirant Bleton. Towards 7 p.m. on 19 March General Khrioukine came to inspect the billet. Having decided that Normandie were too cramped in their lodgings, the general arranged for supplementary premises to be put at the Regiment's disposition, and the move envisaged earlier was carried out. However, a telegram announced that Général Petit had left Moscow at 1 p.m. and was due to arrive during the evening. Commandant Delfino went to the strip at Schipenbeil where the aircraft was to land; at this time Normandie's runway was unusable. Towards 8 p.m. Général and Mlle Petit arrived, accompanied by General Zakharov. After saying a few words to the pilots, Général Petit went to his lodgings, where dinner was served to a small select gathering. The following day the awarding of gallantry decorations would take place.

At 2 p.m. on 20 March Général Petit presided over a lunch. Generals Zakharov and Levandovitch also attended together with the Normandie pilots. The meal was washed down by excellent French wines recently liberated from the Wehrmacht. At 6 p.m. a parade took place on the landing strip. The French tricolour and the Soviet red hammer and sickle fluttered in front of a row of Yak aircraft. Between the two national flags appeared the colours of the Normandie Regiment borne by Aspirant André and guarded by Aspirants Lemare and Sauvage. On both sides the two escadrilles were lined up. At attention and forming the third side of the 'U' were the Soviet personnel. Commandant Delfino presented Normandie to General Khrioukine, accompanied by Général Petit, General Levandovitch and General Zakharov. General Khrioukine opened the presentation of decorations; his first act was to pin the Red Banner upon the Normandie-Niemen regimental colours. Then he presented to the French recipients the decorations awarded by decree of 23 February. Commandant Delfino then made a brief speech, in which he underlined the symbolic significance of the Normandie regimental colours where the Order of the Red Banner now sat beside the Order of the Liberation, Médaille Militaire and the Croix de Guerre. Général Petit and Commandant Delfino then presented the Croix de

Guerre to a selected number of Soviet military personnel. Among them was Lieutenant Yakoubov, the machine-gunner who saved and defended Émonet on 17 October 1944, when they had both been brought down during an action with the enemy. The ceremony finished with a march past by the Regiment. At 7.30 p.m. a banquet in the Stalovaia brought together the pilots of Normandie, those of the 18th Guards Air Regiment and a number of guests, all presided over by Generals Petit and Khrioukine. Innumerable toasts were proposed, and then, with the help of the various beverages, there was singing and dancing till late.

On 21 March Général Petit brought two items of news of great interest. He confirmed the presence in Tehran of thirteen pilots as reinforcements for Normandie. Then he told the commandant about the putting together of a second Groupe de Chasse, of which seventeen pilots were already in Toula. Capitaine Matras was to take command of this new Groupe; as a result of this appointment he was preparing to leave for Moscow with Général Petit. From there, he would go to Toula to organise the training of the pilots in question.

The following morning Général Petit came to share breakfast with the pilots. As the weather report was unfavourable he did not depart. The movie-makers, who came on account of the parade, took a gathering of pilots to Friedland, where they were shooting some scenes of a touristy nature in the main square of the town. The house where Napoleon stayed in 1807 looked out on this same square. After making a trip to the 'reserved area' where the German population was assembled, the Normandie party returned to its quarters. The rest of the day passed calmly. In the evening Capitaine Matras marked his departure celebration with several bottles shared with his comrades.

At 11 a.m. on 23 March Général Petit departed despite the thick fog. Before leaving he recalled Normandie's mission and declared that he was proud of their work. With him went Capitaine Matras and Aspirant Eichenbaum; but Eichenbaum would return later to the Regiment after his liaison duties in Moscow. All in the Regiment were happy to hear that the authorities had accepted the innovation of routing mail via Warsaw. The bad state of the landing strip prevented flights.

On 25 March the weather was magnificent. The runway improved, although the usable section was quite small. General Zakharov arrived to take note of the possibilities offered by the reduced facilities. As if to prove a point, he then took off in Commandant Delfino's Yak and did a commendable exhibition of barnstorming and zooming above the airstrip – whereupon missions began at once! Two patrols took off to fly protection for Pe-2s above their bombing zone, which was what remained of the enemy pocket. Another patrol carried out a reconnaissance of enemy territory. Then once again a patrol took off to fly protection over the same zone. Lieutenant Douarre's problems with the Yak's fuel supply gave those on the strip a fright on take-off, but he succeeded in landing again without damage. The remainder of the squad flew to the sector where they noticed, after about 25 minutes, three suspicious aircraft heading south-west to the Pillau region. Aspirant André approached and recognised some Fw-190s. Followed by Aspirant Challe, he attacked and brought down one of them, which crashed into the sea about 10km to the south-west of Pillau. Three other patrols found no enemy aerial activity during their sortie; they returned wondering what the next stage of operations would be. Pilots rose at first light; missions to cover over the zone began almost at once. The first patrol returned with nothing to report. Another was attacked by six Fw-190s. Aspirants Perrin and Monge faced up to them and engaged them in combat while turning in circles. Perrin ended up by breaking away. Aspirant Marchi and Sous-lieutenant Guido each took up the fight; Guido succeeded in disrupting the enemy formation. Marchi sustained a battle of 15 minutes, in the course of which he fired at one of the Fw-190s, which unleashed a stream of white smoke. On returning he suffered a fuel breakdown and landed on his belly in a field near the strip. Monge did not come back from this mission. He was seen for the last time during the action a few kilometres to the south-east of Pillau. Three other patrols returned without incident. A fourth patrol arriving at the sector saw a Stormovik attacked by two Bf-109s, which set it alight. The Perrin–Guido patrol broke away and headed for the Bf-109s, which, however, with their greater speed, mounted towards the sun without being disturbed. Perrin and Guido took up the chase and shot at one of them, which was hit and landed on its belly to the south-west of Pillau. Several patrols went out without incident. One patrol, spotting eight Fw-190s over the Frisches Haff to the north of the 'pocket', attacked them; but the Fw-190s went into a defensive circle at 1,000m above their strip at Pillau. Aspirants Sauvage and de Geoffre each fired at an Fw-190 but could observe no results. Aspirants André and Lieutenant Charras then dived on an Fw-190, which made off but surprised them with its excessive speed. It was probably a Bf-109K, a few of which were known to be in East Prussia in early 1945. Charras then fired at the last one, which was hit and immediately started to smoke, but Charras did not observe the final results.

Then an important squad for distant protection of Pe-2s took off. One group of Pe-2s came very late over the strip, arriving after the departure of their protecting Yaks. Major Vdovine, the NKVD political officer, immediately asked for the Regiment's four remaining aircraft; but faced with the uncertain identification of the Pe-2s the commanders awaited confirmation from Division. This first refusal to comply with the commissar's request might well have been a case of Normandie showing its wish to follow correct procedure. Having received a confirmation a patrol took off: Sauvage, de Geoffre, Capitaine de Saint-Marceaux, and Lieutenant Charras. Arriving in the sector, they were attacked by an Fw-190 which, for unknown reasons, did not fire and passed by at great speed. Immediately the four Yaks banked over two Fw-190s about 2,000m above Pillau. One of them broke away but the second, fired on by Sauvage and de Geoffre, fell away in flames and plunged downwards, spiralling to the left and the right. Almost immediately several enemy light patrols were spotted; small battles took place but without any positive results.

Having been deployed on 27 March to hunt the enemy in a designated sector, Commandant Delfino had decided in agreement with Colonel Aristov to make only sorties in strength. Accordingly sixteen aircraft took part in the first mission, which was a distant protection of Pe-2s. As a result of faulty information on the itinerary of the Soviet bombers, the mission ended up covering and giving general protection over the zone rather than flying close protection for the Pe-2s. The squad was composed of two patrols of eight aircraft, one at high altitude and the other low. As soon as they arrived in the Pillau region, the squad made contact with a number of Fw-190s and Bf-109s. A somewhat confused battle took place without an outcome proportionate to the size of the scuffle. Only Aspirant Dechanet, after a brief pursuit, shot down an Fw-190, which crashed into the water of the Frisches Haff. Sous-lieutenant François de Geoffre did not return and no one knew what had happened to him; however, some Red Army soldiers saw a parachute above the lagoon. For the second mission of ten aircraft it was a question of blockading the airstrip at Pillau. As soon as it arrived over the sector the squad spotted about eight enemy aircraft at 4,000m. Opening full throttle, Commandant Delfino attacked one of them while climbing. The

Fw-190, which had been hit, dived and was finished off by Perrin, who saw it crash into the sea. The patrol of Aspirants Lemare and Schoendorff attacked a Bf-109; fired on by Lemare, it crashed along the coastal edge. Several battles took place without a result. Another squad carrying out a similar mission also engaged with numerous enemy fighters but without victory on either side. The experiences of Soviet Air Force and Luftwaffe pilots at this stage of the campaign appeared to be well matched, but the pilots flying the superb Yak-3 made the difference and finally broke the Moulders Group in East Prussia.

Towards 6 p.m. the Division asked for coverage of the sector in the same region. Five aircraft took off for this mission. Sous-lieutenant Guido announced over the radio that he was making a half-circuit, but he did not return to the strip and no one knew what had become of him. Arriving over the sector, Marchi engaged with two Fw-190s. He fired at one of them, which was hit and then finished off by Aspirant Henri after a prolonged pursuit. Aspirant Dechanet initiated a pursuit without result. After regrouping, the patrol now consisted of only three aircraft. Schoendorff was forced to disengage when he had a violent encounter with a substantial number of enemy fighters; much circling but no results. Commandant Delfino instructed a squad of reinforcements to take off; one of its members arrived over the sector and observed a battle between eighteen enemy fighters and Yaks. He moved away to gain range and altitude, and attacked at speed. But the enemy went into a defensive circle, and the manoeuvre succeeded only at the fourth attempt. Sauvage and Ougloff then fired at one of the members of the first enemy patrol. It dived and crashed into the sea while the patrol leader tried to break away by climbing. Sauvage and Ougloff fired shots and observed their impact, but could not follow it in its fall. Meanwhile, Aspirant Challe left in pursuit of an Fw-190 but was attacked by two others. Aspirants Mertzisen and Lorillon attacked a Bf-109 but were threatened in their turn, and while Mertzisen continued the pursuit Lorillon engaged in combat and shot down an Fw-190, which crashed on the coastal shore. Emerging from combat Aspirant André noticed one of the Yaks pursuing a Bf-109 while hedge-hopping and passing over the Pillau airstrip, where it was fired on by anti-aircraft guns. This pilot announced over the radio that he had been hit; André did what he could to give protection to his comrade's retreat. Finally, the squad returned in small groups to the landing strip. But Aspirant Challe did not return. No hope! The last two days had been costly, and the pilots found the strength of Normandie to be dramatically diminished.

On 28 March Aspirant Mertzisen rejoined the Regiment. In pursuit of a Bf-109 in the previous day's battle, he twice overflew the Pillau airstrip at very low altitude. Hit by flack, he reached the outskirts of Vittenberg but was forced to land in the country. More joy: the following day Sous-lieutenant Guido also made an appearance and rejoined the Regiment. With engine trouble and impeded by poor visibility, he could not get back to Friedland and landed out in the country.

Nine

Escapes and Captures

ASPIRANT DE GEOFFRE DITCHES INTO THE SEA

Sous-lieutenant François de Geoffre scored his seventh and final victory on 27 March 1945. Minutes later, as he flew at 3,000ft parallel to the Baltic coast, zigzagging through heavy German flak, his Yak suddenly gave several violent shudders and caught fire. Sous-lieutenant de Geoffre knew instantly he was in dire trouble. The engine stalled, he now had no option but to bale out. His attempt to evacuate the cockpit became difficult because, as he tried to leave the aircraft, the harness caught up his right leg; he was trapped in the burning cockpit and a fight against time started. Eventually his leg cleared the harness strap and became free; he parachuted out knowing he had little altitude left to make a safe landing. In those brief seconds he watched his Yak crash into the sea. Looking up into the grey sky he saw Stormoviks and twin-engine Pe-2s attacking the flames that had been the town of Pillau. Suddenly he hit ice-cold water. Unfastening his parachute straps to free himself he started to swim; although in pain from his leg and feeling very cold, he was elated at the realisation that he was alive. Almost immediately he came upon some heavy timbers floating close by; he struggled onto these planks, which formed a crude raft. Then he surveyed the scene and took stock of his situation. It was late morning and he was some 500m from the bank; but was the shore ours or theirs? The answer came quickly with a burst of automatic gunfire. He slid off the planks and submerged himself briefly; when the firing ceased he climbed back on his raft. The firing continued spasmodically until nightfall. Under cover of darkness he swam to the bank and lay exhausted and cold; he remained silent for a while and then became aware of Russian voices close by. He called out for help; a Soviet infantryman came running and then shouted out 'It is a French comrade.' Others arrived, sprinting towards him; one grinning soldier gave him a swig of vodka from a flask, followed by some tender but rather rudimentary medical attention. Then he was taken to a military hospital at Bartensten for treatment.

Other French pilots who parachuted into enemy territory were not so lucky. Any Soviet or French pilots captured by the Germans were lucky to survive their brutal treatment, which could range from instant execution to a lingering death in a prisoner of war death camp. Of those Normandie pilots missing in action, only four survived capture and the POW camps.

The German treatment of Red Army prisoners was one of the greatest war crimes of the Second World War. Official Russian Federation figures published recently show that over 2.3 million Soviet prisoners died in German captivity. In Stalingrad, with the temperature at minus 30–40 degrees, Soviet prisoners of war were kept in the open day and night within high barbed-wire fences; without any form of shelter or food, they froze to death. After the surrender of Stalingrad by Field Marshal Paulus, commander of the German 6th Army, this cage of death was discovered with just a few frostbitten survivors left alive to tell the harrowing story. The victors' treatment of their German 'Stalingrad' prisoners would reflect in part what they had found in this cage of death.

LIEUTENANT MAHÉ CAPTURED AND LIBERATED

Lieutenant Yves Mahé was detailed out on a mission against enemy aircraft known to be on the Luftwaffe landing strip at Loubinka. Mahé went in at low altitude and successfully attacked the targets, hitting several aircraft. In the course of this mission Mahé's Yak sustained severe damage while hedge-hopping over enemy territory. Mahé indicated to his patrol that he had no option but to attempt a crash landing behind German lines. Although injured in the face and having difficulty seeing, he managed to head for a clearing and braced himself for a crash landing. The aircraft hit the ground hard, the tail was torn off, and the aircraft slid along on its belly in a cloud of dirt and dust, finally coming to a halt in the clearing. Mahé was well belted up in the cockpit, knowing that at the height he was flying there was no chance of using his parachute. As the aircraft came to a halt he immediately released the belt and climbed out. He felt pleasure at surviving but then realised that he was injured, losing blood and partially blinded; worse, he was well inside enemy lines. It was not long before he heard the sound of a vehicle approaching. A group of Luftwaffe personnel arrived and took him prisoner.

He did not appreciate at that time how lucky he was not to have fallen into the hands of one of the SS detachments in the area. The Luftwaffe men seemed most interested in his Yak aircraft, climbing all over it; they would have sat in the cockpit but for the blood he had left splattered about. Mounting a guard on the aircraft, they took him to their base for questioning. He was treated reasonably well and his wounds received some attention. Eventually he was handed over to a regular Wehrmacht unit, which processed him as a Soviet airman. This classification could well have been at the behest of the Luftwaffe officers; whatever the case, it saved his life.

It was not long before he was on a journey to be delivered to a prison camp full of Red Army soldiers. Mahé was instantly taken under the wing of the Soviet soldiers; his wounds were attended to and food was found for him. The care and treatment by his fellow prisoners, who were themselves near starving, reflected the high esteem in which the flyers of the Normandie-Niemen Regiment were held by the Red Army. In this German prison camp the Soviets were in a bad way, many having died; yet his fellow prisoners, with real compassion, made sure he survived. Lieutenant Yves Mahé tried on seven different occasions to escape; each time he was thwarted. When the advancing Red Army recaptured the area and released the Red Army prisoners, those who could carry arms were re-formed for immediate duty at the front. But this particular French pilot was too valuable to be returned to his Regiment: the Soviets wanted him to act as their interpreter. At the end of the war, while all his fellow Normandie flyers were being fêted in Paris and basking in their deserved glory, poor Yves Mahé was still in the Soviet Union being useful to his Soviet allies. It was to be August 1945 before he was eventually returned to France. His long-time comrade and close friend Capitaine Joseph Risso was one of the first to greet him.

BAYSSADE'S STORY OF SURVIVAL IN GERMAN PRISON CAMPS

Aspirant Bayssade had escaped from wartime France via Spain to Casablanca. Members of the resistance who escaped from France had the right to choose their unit of service; Bayssade chose Normandie-Niemen. After a journey via Algiers, Cairo and Tehran, he arrived in the Soviet Union on 8 May 1944, ready to serve with Normandie. On 30 July 1944 he was one of eight pilots of the 3rd Escadrille detailed out on a covering mission that would take them over the River Niemen.

Commandant Pierre Matras led the take-off at 12.30 p.m. Bayssade was partnered with René Challe. It was not long before they noticed a little way off a group of four Fw-190s, which were flying protection for nine Ju-87s. Contact was made and a furious engagement took place, in the course of which Bayssade's Yak was severely hit by enemy fire and Bayssade sustained bullet wounds to his left foot. With the aircraft in flames and breaking up fast, he had no alternative but to try to get out quickly. The aircraft went into a steep dive; he struggled to eject. Suddenly he was out and pulled the parachute cord. Floating down he found that he had landed in a clearing surrounded by German troops. As he lay on the ground one of the soldiers disarmed him and ordered him to stand up, but because of his leg injury he could not do so. His boots were pulled off to reveal his feet and legs swollen and bloody. He was carried to the edge of the wood, where he had his papers checked by a Feldwebel. His pockets were emptied; everything was wrapped up in his handkerchief, which was handed to an officer. He was placed upon his parachute in the back of an open tourer-type car. Everything was happening very quickly. He later learned that had he come down one hour later he would have landed in the middle of the advancing Soviets. As the car sped off, the handkerchief and contents were placed on his chest; he was anxious because the contents included his Soviet identity card, which was in his name. Knowing of the 'Keitel' execution order, he wanted to get rid of the identity card; he crumpled up the sheets, tore them into pieces and threw them and the handkerchief contents out of the car. The officer stopped the vehicle and went back to retrieve what he could find. Bayssade was sure his wounds would heal, so he prepared his story for the expected interrogation. To mask any connection with his family that could cause it to be deported, he would be 'Jean Verdunois' a wine merchant from Algiers.

The Germans drove him to a castle. On arrival the guards used a door as a stretcher and carried him up to a secure room, where he was locked up for two days. Then his temporary cell was unlocked and another painful journey was undertaken, this time to the village, where he was laid in the open upon his parachute. An inquisitive group of German soldiers gathered round him; they could see he was in a bad way, and one gave him refreshments. He was suffering burns from his aircraft which had removed his eyebrows and eyelashes; his eyes were swollen and bloodshot. He was wounded on his chin and the right wrist, and the bullet wounds to his foot were now causing much pain. A nurse came and treated the bullet wound to his left foot, which had become infected. He was taken to the military barracks at Goldap and deposited in a prison cell, given food and water and left on his own, feeling quite depressed. For a month he had been passed from one lot of soldiers to another; he felt he was being hidden and not even interrogated. He recalled the dozen or so Normandie pilots who had crashed behind enemy lines and had not been heard of since. He was aware that Mahé had been taken prisoner, but he was the only one that he knew of.

Bayssade was placed on a lorry together with a fellow prisoner, a Soviet Air Force kapitan whose face was completely covered with a mask of bandages. When Bayssade told him he was from the Normandie Regiment, the kapitan embraced him with joy and would not stop talking. They were put on a train with two guards. The kapitan talked non-stop; he told his story of being shot down in his Stormovik over enemy lines and suffering burns to his face. Then he began to sing and Bayssade joined in when he knew the song. In his euphoria the officer tore off his bandages and threw them out the window. The Soviet kapitan put his fingers in margarine and wiped it over his burnt face. Songs ceased only at nightfall with the arrival of food, but Bayssade declined to put any margarine on his bread!

Next day they arrived in Karlsbad and were taken to a camp of Soviet POWs at Buchau. Bayssade was dumped fully clothed in the shower and undressed afterwards. An hour later, with his clothes dripping wet, he underwent the first interrogation. He told his prepared story and began his life as a Soviet prisoner. He was welcomed warmly by the fellow inmates despite their decrepitude. As he was still a cripple he was given the best pallet. The prisoners asked information about the Soviet battle progress, but unfortunately he could not speak enough Russian to oblige. The rotten bread was weighed on crude scales and the soup was shared religiously, as were vegetable pods or leaves together with a single potato. The 'extra' came sometimes by courtesy of one or two prisoners on fatigue duty who sneaked some carrots or apples despite severe beatings when caught. There were seventeen prisoners in the block and any spoils were divided into seventeen equal parts – even a single apple.

Bayssade was sent to a camp at Lodz, where he underwent further interrogation. The Oberfeldwebel sitting opposite him was a former employee of the National Library in Paris and was very correct. He told Bayssade about a Soviet aircraft with a French pilot which had been shot down in flames; its pilot had jumped by parachute and was now their prisoner; he too was wounded. The adjutant would not or could not divulge the name. It was only later in a camp with electrified fences that he would meet his comrade, Constantin Feldzer – what a joy it was to find each other. The other prisoners in the camp were Soviet flyers. With the help of sticks both Bayssade and Feldzer managed to move about the compound. The camp commandant summoned the two Frenchmen and proposed 'a pleasant detention' if they agreed to 'relate' what they knew about the 'Soviet paradise'. Both refused. Early in November they were transferred to a camp at Bad-Orb. A week later they were in Stockstadt employed in a large paper-mill; they had to strip billets of enormous timber. They were worked long and hard and watched constantly; they quickly became skeletal. Having concluded that they would not survive this treatment they made plans to escape.

The village bakery employed a French prisoner. They approached him and asked for flour, bread and help in obtaining a map and compass, but the French prisoner refused. Shortly after their return to camp four guards set about them, beating them, tearing their clothes and destroying their bedding. After the violence the guards warned them not to try to escape again. They learned that the baker's boy had told the police of their bid to escape, calling them 'dirty Communists'.

They were still determined to escape. Bayssade took an opportunity to escape on his own. On the evening of 15 December, when the guards came to count the prisoners, he took the chance to slip away. Crouching as he ran from behind the group of prisoners already counted, he went behind the huts towards a prepared opening in the wire. He ran over a ploughed field along the furrows to head for a wood. It was not long before a siren sounded; guards on bicycles travelled along the road followed by a truckload of soldiers. Bayssade waited for nightfall and then retraced his steps back past the camp avoiding the sentries, and set off with the polar star behind him.

Bayssade walked by night for a week, catching rabbits for food. Any German peasants he encountered showed only indifference despite the enormous prisoner 'SU' (Soviet Union) painted on the back of his greatcoat. One afternoon, having settled down in a plantation of young pines to eat some rabbit and sleep, he suddenly found himself face to face with a group of about fifteen children. He escaped in his bare feet, but then a hunter with a gun confronted him. Asked if he was a 'Ruski', he said 'no, I'm French', and unbuttoned his coat to display his battledress. At this point another hunter with a gun arrived; he repeated that he was a French flyer. The second hunter became very agitated and levelled his rifle at Bayssade's head. Possibly because of the presence of children, who had been beaters for the hunters, he was spared. He was taken by the police to Darmstadt and locked in the town prison. From there he was taken to a POW camp at Limbourg and put in a 'quarantine' barracks, where there were only Frenchmen. It was Christmas Day.

That evening British aircraft bombed the camp by mistake. The Americans in the next barracks, prisoners from the battle at Arnhem, were worst hit. After the raid the Germans forbade anyone to render assistance. They said help would have to come from American prisoners at the other end of the camp. When help arrived the French were able to assist. They witnessed horrific scenes: 117 dead and many wounded. In the French barracks five men were killed while playing cards, a sixth was blown out of the window. Bayssade, who had taken cover under a bunk, suffered two cracked ribs and a gashed head. He joined three other French survivors who were pushed by the Germans into a nearby building full of the seriously injured Americans. By the light of crude burning torches an American doctor operated non-stop all night to save lives.

It started to snow. Sitting on the ground, trembling with cold and hunger, Bayssade experienced the worst moments of his captivity. By the third day all the seriously wounded Americans were dead.

Bayssade was sent for more interrogation, this time by a Hauptmann, who listened to his cover story of being captured in France in 1940. The German then announced that he knew from a dossier that he was a Normandie flyer shot down on 30 July 1944. Next day he set off on foot for the camp at Bad-Orb accompanied by a guard, who mistreated him so badly that he arrived at the camp with bloody feet; they had walked 80km in three days.

Placed with French prisoners, he told them he belonged to the French escadrille fighting on the Eastern Front. He recounted how he had been shot down in Poland, and that the war was almost over and won. There was a general hue and cry, with one shouting 'Communist – not French'. They did not speak to him again and even deprived Bayssade of the American food parcel given to each new arrival. He decided to go over to the nearby Soviet compound, where the Russians received him with open arms. They overwhelmed him with food, which had become more plentiful.

In March they heard gunfire coming closer. Guard surveillance was now almost non-existent. After a few days they guessed from the shooting that the

Allies were very near. The nearby village of Bad-Orb resisted for a few days after an SS unit had regrouped there, but as soon as they left the inhabitants did not delay in hoisting the white flag. When the Americans arrived at the camp the Germans had opened the gates; the Americans shut them again and dug in with their tanks. The prisoners explored the camp and especially the stores stuffed with food and clothes. Bayssade went down to the village with his Soviet comrades to eat and drink beer, all without paying, of course. The fear of the Germans was visible when faced with the Red Army men. American trucks arrived at the camp and embarked the prisoners by nationality. Bayssade's turn came; he said goodbye to his Soviet comrades with regret. He was rehabilitated at an American camp: hot showers, new clothes, and after a short stay in this paradise he was taken to the French border. Reaching Paris by train on 21 April, he was sent to Chaptal hospital for treatment.

Bayssade's wife had been notified by letter from Commandant Pouyade at the time of his disappearance. Then a card arrived from the Red Cross telling her that he was in a POW camp in Germany. Feldzer, who had returned from captivity before Bayssade, had told Normandie-Niemen that he was sceptical about Bayssade's chances of survival. He recounted that after the escape three Soviet prisoners close to Bayssade were beaten about the face and had their teeth smashed. The commandant had announced to the assembled prisoners that Bayssade had been caught and killed. Bayssade had remarked after the war:

The Soviet POWs were admirable soldiers. I saw them in their worst moments, being pushed to the limits without once failing. For me they were heroic men, brave combatants, loyal and sincere, and my friends for ever.

A SOVIET OFFICER WHO ESCAPED FROM CAPTURE AND GOT BACK TO HIS LINES

Any Soviet Army or Air Force officer captured by the Germans who later managed to escape and return to his own lines could have a very unpleasant surprise waiting for him. An example of this was confirmed during research into officers' records in the Moscow archives.

Senior Flyer, Guards Lieutenant Boris Demitrivitch Grilev, of the 187th Guards Storm Aviation Company, 12th Guards Storm Aviation

Division, on 23 November 1944 was on a mission in the region of Khatvan in Hungary, near the village of Apu. His group was attacked by an enemy fighter formation of twelve Fw-190s. Lieutenant Grilev led his group against the enemy aircraft, shot down one Fw-190 and severely damaged another. During the combat his aircraft was hit several times and caught fire; he was forced to parachute into enemy territory and was taken prisoner by the Germans. Shortly after capture Grilev escaped and joined up with a partisan unit. While serving with this unit he showed himself to be a brave partisan fighter; he was recognised for his courage with a citation and later awarded the Silver Partisan Medal for the Patriotic War. When he was able to return to Soviet lines he was immediately handed over for investigation to SMERSH unit 5VA. He was eventually very lucky to be released and allowed to return to his original flying unit.

Investigators who served in a SMERSH ('Death to Spies') unit had total power of decision over any prisoner being investigated by them. Senior officers of a regular Red Army or Red Air Force group had no power whatever to intervene on behalf of any serving member of their unit. In this case Lieutenant Grilev's courage and loyalty was confirmed when on 29 January 1946 he was awarded the Order of the Patriotic War 1st Class, in gold.

ON THE MOVE AGAIN

On 31 March Normandie was to move to the landing strip at Heligenbeil. Aspirant Pistrack went there in the U-2 to inspect the location. But during the day the order was countermanded; Normandie was now to occupy the strip at Bladiau. From there it would participate in the liquidation of the pocket north of Koenigsberg. The Soviets had accumulated vast quantities of men and equipment in order to obtain a rapid outcome. Aspirant de Geoffre returned and recounted in detail his crash in the sea. His right leg was still badly torn and bruised.

The next day Normandie was cited once again in Marshal Stalin's Order of the Day. Two days later Major Profitelouk gave the usual operational details of the offensive: situation on the ground and in the air, of the enemy, mission of the Regiments, and so on. In the evening Normandie returned the hospitality of the 18th Guards Air Regiment, which it had enjoyed on 28 February. Unfortunately Major Siberine, Commander of the 18th Guards Air Regiment, was absent. The bottles originally 'reserved for the Wehrmacht' were marvellous and the evening passed in an extremely jolly fashion. The following morning all were awaiting the launch of the offensive against Koenigsberg and the Samland Peninsula but, the weather forecast being unfavourable, the day passed calmly. A move was planned to Bladiau as soon as the landing strip became available.

On 6 April the weather was slowly improving but regimental activity was still scant. Towards the end of the day the patrol of Aspirants Martin and Versini, Lieutenant Douarre, and Aspirant Perrin took off after information was received from the command post about possible Fw-190s. In fact, they encountered at the indicated position a Stormovik, which attacked the patrol with well-sustained but fortunately very inaccurate gunfire. Escaping from this adventure, they were diverted to some La-7s, with which they engaged in a regulation circling affray before being recognised.

The day after, the strip at Bladiau having been made available, Normandie proceeded there while at the same time covering the front. Three squads took off in succession and landed at Bladiau without having encountered anything, but the immense cloud of smoke stretching towards the south from Koenigsberg showed that the offensive was under way. The squads were accompanied by the Douglas DC-3, which transported the baggage and Soviet personnel. The new strip was 2km west of Bladiau, and from the command post the shore of Frisches Haff, the port of Pillau and the factory at Zimmerbude could be seen. After arrival on the strip missions resumed immediately. After 10 minutes over the sector, at 3,500m Aspirant André spotted four Fw-190s, east at 1,500m. Having signalled the squad on his radio, he dived, followed by Aspirants Sauvage and Ougloff, but extremely violent anti-aircraft fire forced them to break away, and they rejoined the squad. André noticed for the second time the four Fw-190s; once again he dived, followed by Capitaine de La Salle, who was at the rear of the patrol heading for Koenigsberg. It was observed that bombs were still under the fuselage and, noting the passivity of the Fw-190s, they realised that they had taken the enemy by surprise. But de La Salle, flying too fast, was spotted by the Germans, who broke off at once. Aspirant André pursued one of them to 3km north-west of Koenigsberg and unleashed four blasts of gunfire, but was obliged to disengage, and could not observe the fate of his victim. All the other missions were carried out without contacting the enemy. The weather deteriorated and Aspirant Schoendorff, losing his patrol in the clouds, went to land at Vittenberg. Meanwhile, another squad was forced by the weather to make a half-turn. During this time the accompanying Douglas DC-3 had been shuttling between Friedland and the new strip at Bladiau with supplies and staff. Towards 7 p.m. the Regiment's members went to quarters in one of the three houses which had not been entirely smashed. The base was well equipped and the food very good. During dinner the noise of a bombardment made some leave the table and watch as Pillau was lit up by flames. There was intense and continued bombing by Pe-2s and Stormoviks.

On 8 April covering missions began at dawn. Three patrols went over the zone but did not encounter any enemy aircraft. At the end of the mission André noticed four suspicious aircraft flying low north-west of Koenigsberg; their location had been signalled by 'Michel' from the radio post. After a rapid dive they circled round the Fw-190s; they also noted Stormoviks in the distance on bombing missions. After several turns one of the Fw-190s broke away and set off in a straight line south, then west. Pursued and fired on by André, it was badly hit after five bursts of gunfire and landed on its belly in the marshes north-west of Koenigsberg. Another four patrols returned without incident. Towards 1 p.m. Schoendorff returned from Vittenberg, where he had a royal reception. The two following missions were to protect the area while a massive bombardment was taking place. The protected Soviet bombers attacked the defence positions and the fortress stronghold of Koenigsberg. For an hour and a half numerous aircraft of all types unloaded tons of bombs on the town, which was no more than a vast blazing mass. The Katyushas (lorry-mounted rocket launchers) took apart the few areas spared by the bombing. The spectacle was hallucinatory. These zonal protections were carried out by two squads of six aircraft each. The coverage of the front passed off without incident. During the day Normandie had been at the forefront of attacks on the aerodrome and port of Pillau. During one of these attacks a Stormovik was badly hit by anti-aircraft fire and returned to land at Normandie's airstrip.

Katyushas were multi-tube rocket launchers mounted on a 3- or 5-ton lorry. When in action the rack of rockets would be raised and calibrated to the correct angle, and fired in salvos of eight rockets. Their noise and effect were so dramatic that the German infantry named them 'Stalin organs'. Their performance and ballistic properties were formidable and had a devastating effect. By June 1944 the Red Army had formed four Katyusha (Rocket) Divisions. One salvo from a single division could amount to 3,840 missiles,

230 tons of explosive rockets. During an interview with a Soviet officer who served at Stalingrad the following statement was taken down: 'We could certainly not have held Stalingrad had we not been supported by artillery and Katyushas on the other bank all the time. I can hardly describe the Soviet soldiers' love for the Katyushas.'

On 9 April the Division put Normandie on stand-down to allow the mechanics to overhaul the aircraft. In the evening a concert was given by a group of Moscow entertainers. Earlier in the day a telegram brought the long-awaited details of promotions. Here is the list with dates of appointment:

Promoted to rank of Capitaine: Charras, Sauvage, Douarre, Moynet (25 December 1944), de La Poype, Le Martelot (25 February 1945), Risso (25 March 1945).

Promoted to rank of Sous-lieutenant: Fauroux, Dechanet, Carbon, Mertzisen, Génès, Lemare, Monier, André, Marchi (25 August 1944), Eichenbaum (25 September 1944), Laurent, Challe, Sauvage, Lebras, Perrin, Martin, de Saint-Phalle, Iribarne (25 November 1944), Pierrot, Delin, Penverne, Taburet, de Geoffre (25 February 1945).

In spite of reduced supplies, those promoted washed down the happy event with Russian vodka and wines.

On the morning of 10 April news came of the capture of Koenigsberg, whose garrison surrendered late the previous evening. An Order of the Day from Stalin underlined this great victory and Normandie again was mentioned.

ORDER of Commander of the 3rd Belorussian Front, Marshal of the Soviet Union Vasilievsky, and Commander of the General Staff at the front, Colonel-General Pokrovsky

The troops of the 3rd Belorussian Front, after desperate street battles, have defeated the German units at Koenigsberg and today, 9 April, have taken possession of the citadel and principal town of East Prussia, Koenigsberg, a very important strategic point in the German defence of the Baltic Sea. On the day of combat the frontline troops took more than 20,000 officers and men prisoner and took possession of a large amount of arms and equipment. The remains of the garrison at Koenigsberg with at their head the commander of the citadel, Infantry General Lasch and his General

Staff, have ceased at 21.30 all resistance and they have laid down their arms. During the battle for Koenigsberg the aviators of General Zakharov and Commandant Delfino have distinguished themselves. Today 9 April at 24.00, the capital of our country, Moscow, will, in the name of the Fatherland salute the valiant troops of the 3rd Belorussian Front who captured the town and citadel of Koenigsberg. We shall mark this victory with 24 salvos of 224 cannons.

Commander in Chief, Marshal of the Soviet Union, J. Stalin

The figure of 20,000 prisoners quoted in this Order by Marshal Vasilievsky, from early on the day of the surrender, was to prove grossly inaccurate. Later, when all the German prisoners were counted the final official figure reached a staggering 92,000. The commander, General Lasch, confirmed 42,000 German soldiers had died in the defence of fortress Koenigsberg.

A small gathering took place at the airstrip in honour of this event. Major Vdovine and Commandant Delfino both said a few words. The recently released French Air Force Aspirants Simondet and Henriot, who were imprisoned at Koenigsberg, were brought to Bladiau and very warmly received. They suggested that there were thousands of French slave workers in the East Prussian capital. At that time it was not realised that Koenigsberg had been selected by the Germans as a punishment camp for French deportees. One Koenigsberg prisoner was Virginia d'Albert-Lake, a heroine of the French Resistance, who together with her husband Philippe were responsible for aiding in the escape of sixty-six Allied airmen. These rescued flyers had earlier been shot down in occupied Europe, picked up by the resistance, and eventually passed along the escape routes by Virginia d'Albert-Lake to be returned to Britain. After her capture by the Gestapo she was sent to Ravensbruck concentration camp and then to the slave labour camps of Torgau and Koenigsberg. Because of her work for the Allied cause she was decorated after the war by France, Belgium, Great Britain and the USA. It was fitting that this heroic lady would eventually be liberated by the joint efforts of the Soviet and French forces.

TEN

KOENIGSBERG: THE BITTER BATTLE

Koenigsberg was to be the crowning glory of Normandie-Niemen's combat action in East Prussia. Normandie would be awarded the battle honour Koenigsberg for their regimental colours. Also, twenty-eight French pilots would be awarded the Soviet campaign medal for the capture of Koenigsberg.

The battle for the fortress city of Koenigsberg, the capital of East Prussia, had been a titanic struggle. It was here that the German Army Group Centre was gradually being encircled and forced back towards the Baltic Sea. The central stronghold of Koenigsberg and its four surounding lines of concentric defence positions had for some weeks been the scene of heavy and vicious fighting. The Soviet 3rd Belorussian Front, commanded by General Ivan Chernyakhovsky, one of the youngest senior field officers in the Soviet Army, was ordered by the High Command to crack this hard German nut. Chernyakhovsky's hatred for the invaders was driven by an iron determination to finish the evil Nazi beast once and for all. The knowledge of what had happened when the special SS elimination squads followed the advancing Wehrmacht was ever-present in his mind.

For centuries Koenigsberg had been a fortified citadel with thick walls and underground galleries; now massive concrete bunkers and gun emplacements had been added, and more recently tanks, some disabled and others without fuel, had been dug in as block houses covering the central approaches. Koenigsberg city was now the hub of a massive defence network. Outside the city was a string of forts that in past years had guaranteed protection for the central fortified citadel. The Soviets would have to fight their way through the outer belt of defended trenches and pillboxes some 4 miles from the city centre, and then they would have reached the first of three heavily fortified lines of defences. Just short of Altenberg they encountered the German 56,

62 and 69 Infantry Divisions, which were tightly grouped in defence of the southern approaches. It was these three divisions and their well-established defence positions that would have to be broken before the Soviet advance could succeed.

The Red Air Force command gave orders for saturation bombing of these enemy defensive positions to assist the ground forces' advance. The Soviet Pe-2s and Il-2s bombers with their fighter escort flew endless missions to destroy the German positions and troop concentrations. The Fw-190s and Bf-109s flown by the Moulders Group based at Pillau were continuously in action trying to break up the Soviet aerial armada. To do this they first had to take on the escort fighters consisting of Yaks, La-7s and La-5s, which were tenaciously guarding the bombers. It was during these aerial battles that the Normandie-Niemen Regiment showed its ability to out-fly and out-shoot the best the Luftwaffe could put up. There was grudging respect from the Moulders pilots for the new breed of Soviet aircraft and flyers, who were determined to take on any German fighters over East Prussia. One Normandie pilot, shot down inside enemy lines, was picked up and taken to the Moulders strip. During his interrogation the Luftwaffe officer confirmed, almost with admiration, that at the last moment, after his Yak was crippled, he had still shot down his German adversary.

The city and its defences took a terrible pounding from Soviet guns and rockets. The Red Air Force was operating from five nearby landing strips. Alongside Normandie was the 18th Guards Fighter Air Regiment, and to the north of Koenigsberg and close to Fuchsberg was the land-based Air Force of the Soviet Baltic Fleet. Having breached the outer belt of defences some 4 miles from the city centre, the Soviets moved closer and captured fifteen fortified old forts. At the edge of the city was the second defended line, which included a wide band of minefields that had been laid in front of fortified solid stone buildings. After Soviet sappers, at great cost, had cleared a path for the advancing infantry, the ground troops were then faced with the daunting third line of defences. This inner core of defences consisted of nine heavily reinforced forts around the old city perimeter. After four days of continuous heavy artillery bombardment, the final attack against these lines started on 7 April; the city fell on the evening of 9 April. The battle was won at a heavy cost. The victorious 3rd Belorussian Front, with a strength of 579,300 men, suffered 45,117 killed and 155,165 wounded in the run-up to the final assault. The Soviet Air Force had also suffered considerable losses over a period of weeks from anti-aircraft fire and enemy fighter attacks during their bombing missions against Koenigsberg. But for the tenacity and sacrifice of Soviet fighter aircraft, these bomber losses would have been considerably higher.

The Normandie-Niemen Regiment had been charged with destroying all the Luftwaffe in the Koenigsberg area, including any aircraft still operating from the damaged runways at Pillau. This pre-war airfield was situated on the tip of the Samland Peninsula; it was from this base that the Luftwaffe's air support for the Koenigsberg garrison had been mounted. Normandie had blockaded the landing strip and denied the Luftwaffe the chance to mount defensive operations from this base. At the same time the French Yaks successfully acted as protective escorts to Soviet bombers on their way to Koenigsberg. Other Normandie patrols strafed gun positions and German troops in the surrounding defensive positions guarding Koenigsberg. They eventually eliminated the Luftwaffe's control of the skies above East Prussia. This action was to be considered the jewel in the crown of Normandie's exemplary service in this strategic battle. With the Luftwaffe now virtually eliminated, the German Army defending Koenigsberg had no protective aerial shield against the ever-closing vice of the relentless Soviet forces. The Moulders Group had sustained continued mounting losses in duels with the Yak-3 and La-7 pilots; some of the Germans' most experienced flyers had by now become casualties, leaving the rest vulnerable when facing the growing number of skilled Soviet fighter pilots.

AMAZING BOMBER FLOTILLA

The Soviet Air Force had sent every available bomber against Koenigsberg and its surrounding defences, carrying out saturation bombing prior to the ground assault. Normandie-Niemen's mission was to protect this aerial armada as it approached and returned from the target. Aspirant Lorillon on an escort mission had scanned the sky for any signs of the Luftwaffe, but its aircraft appeared to be absent. He casually noticed that his charges consisted of Stormovik dive-bombers, Pe-2 light bombers, and a few Bostons. Then, to his amazement, he noticed that a slow-flying Dakota DC-3 had joined the avenging flotilla; its crew could be clearly seen manhandling bombs out of the passenger door. The Soviets were pulling out all the stops to deliver the bombs onto the burning city. Aspirant Lorillon strained to get a glimpse of what lay below, but it was impossible: Koenigsberg was now shrouded in smoke and flames.

Below, panic and fear spread among the thousands of refugees and wounded waiting for a place on any ship, large or small, to escape to mainland Germany. The German Navy had earlier successfully attempted a partial evacuation of the military wounded and refugees by sea, but now, with minimal Luftwaffe air cover and with Soviet submarines very active in the Baltic, it had become extremely dangerous for any vessel to carry people or goods from the stricken port. Even so, the German Navy right up to the last hours did get some smaller vessels away with the wounded and 'special' personnel. One such late evacuation was by an E-boat that had collected someone or something important and headed at speed out into the Baltic. A Normandie-Niemen pilot on a hunting sortie spotted this fast-moving craft and estimated it was doing over 30kn when he lined up and dived upon it. With his cannons blazing he saw the shells tear into the craft; turning for a second run-in he finished the job, leaving the smoking E-boat sinking with its special crew and cargo.

Escape though the Vistula Lagoon out to sea from fortress Koenigsberg was now virtually impossible. The Red Army had surrounded this important strategic inland port, once the home of over 2 million people. This closure of any potential escape route for the encircled Germans meant they were now caught in an iron trap with no way out. Soon the advancing Red Army would be close enough to pour thousands of shells straight into the city and port area. It was crowded with countless numbers of military wounded and hordes of recently arrived refugees fleeing ahead of the avenging Soviet Army. Many of the German wounded were waiting on the quays for any ship available to leave this doomed fortress. With the situation in the city at its worst, Nazi officials involved themselves in making arrangements to smuggle out by ship 'special' personnel and considerable quantities of stolen artefacts in wooden packing cases. These crates had arrived in lorries at the expense of petrol for the transport of military wounded and exhausted civilians. This stolen property was destined for the crumbling Reich and would displace the wounded on the evacuation ships, simply for the sake of some Nazi's fancy for the exotic. All this greed with the Red Army knocking at the gates of Koenigsberg.

In 1950, during the processing of repatriated German POWs just collected from the Soviets after five years in captivity, there was an opportunity to interrogate a soldier who had been one of the original Koenigsberg defenders and an eyewitness to the grim battle inside the cauldron. He described the horror of the situation experienced by soldiers defending the fortress, the endless shuffling columns of civilians waiting and searching for a place on any boat leaving for the west. Something that haunted him was the pitiable loss of hope shown in the faces of the wounded waiting for evacuation by sea. The returned POW told me how he had become disillusioned with the fanatical Nazi elements like Gauleiter Erich Koch and other rabid party members inside fortress Koenigsberg. They wasted their consideration on objects rather than people when planning evacuation. This soldier remembered being detailed one day to unload four trucks. He had expected the task to consist of offloading military supplies or perhaps wounded, but instead he and others were ordered to manhandle twenty-seven large wooden crates. These he understood to be packed with important looted treasure; he formed this opinion because they were heavily guarded by SS elements.

The trucks and crates had not travelled far; in fact one of the drivers was a Koenigsberg garrison soldier, whom he knew. The wooden boxes could well have contained the Amber Room as it was being moved from one location to another; certainly the number of crates closely matched the number of packing cases used as the transient home of the amber panels. The figure twenty-seven stuck in his mind as the crates had to be counted three times by the SS guards. He was then detailed to carry them into the grand Knights' Hall within the old castle, where they were counted once more by the internal guards. What his story would confirm is that important crates of loot were taken into the ancient Knights' Hall for storage. With this location burnt out in April 1945, any crates containing the amber panels would have burnt like fire-lighters! This prisoner explained how he decided to escape (desert) with another soldier by taking an army vehicle through the Soviet encirclement just as it was closing. He maintained they were the last soldiers to get out of Koenigsberg before it was surrounded by the 'Ruskies'. To him his escape from Koenigsberg that day was a miracle.

What the ex-prisoner did not know was that Gauleiter Koch was not at his post inside Koenigsberg at that time. He had made his escape earlier on an ice-breaker *Ostpreussen* sailing from Pillau, taking on board a Mercedes car, his dogs and a heavily armed personal guard. He had installed a powerful radio on the ship and, pretending to be broadcasting from within the citadel, he ordered the garrison to hold firm and fight to the last man. He even sent radio messages to Hitler as if he were still in Koenigsberg, fighting to the end. The ice-breaker would have been capable of taking 400 extra persons out of the cauldron, but this was not in Gauleiter's plans: he was saving only his own skin and possessions.

When Koenigsberg was finally captured on the evening of 9 April 1945, the scale of the human disaster became apparent. During the surrender of Koenigsberg by the garrison commander General Otto Lasch (Knight's Cross with Oak Leaves), the actual procedure of surrender was fraught with an unexpected danger. As the surrender party of German officers carrying a white flag proceeded through the rubble and then by arrangement through open land to reach the Soviet lines, it found itself being heavily fired on from behind by a band of fanatical Hitlerites. These Nazi renegades were determined to stop the surrender and fight to the last man. General Otto Lasch confirmed to the Soviet command during the surrender of his 92,000 troops that his garrison had suffered 42,000 soldiers killed defending Koenigsberg and its environs, in addition to the death by bombing and shelling of unknown thousands of civilians who had taken refuge in the city.

The battle had caused pointless suffering prolonged by the stubborn refusal of senior Nazi officers to accept the earlier Red Army surrender terms. Their fanatical attitude had caused thousands of additional military and civilian casualties. This needless extension of the fighting had caused Soviet Army casualty figures also to escalate dramatically. Included in the final tally would be the most senior Soviet commanding officer, General Chernyakhovsky, killed by a German shell splinter.

Hitler's fury when he was told of the garrison's surrender bordered on madness. He immediately ordered the arrest of General Lasch's family as a reprisal for this officer's surrender to the Red Army. Erich Koch, on the ice-breaker with his retinue, Mercedes and pet dogs sailed into Copenhagen and temporary safety. On hearing that Koenigsberg had been captured, Stalin was much satisfied with the news. He knew this had closed the German escape route and opened another vital route for the Red Army into Germany. In the Kremlin 24 salvos were fired from 224 cannons in a victory salute to mark the capture of fortress Koenigsberg, capital of East Prussia. The bells of all Moscow's churches rang out the glad tidings of victory to the people of the capital.

Victory celebrations for the capture of Koenigsberg took place at the French Military Mission in Moscow. The mission sent a telegram to

Commandant Louis Delfino, Commanding Officer of Normandie-Niemen, promoting all those flyers involved in the Koenigsberg operation: lieutenants were to be promoted to capitaine, and aspirants to sous-lieutenant. Lorillon was one of those promoted for his part in defeating the Luftwaffe in the skies over Koenigsberg. In all, twenty-eight members of Normandie were awarded the Soviet campaign medal for the capture of Koenigsberg. Although the surrender took place late on the evening of 9 April, the official date became 10 April 1945.

GERMAN ARTILLERY HITS NORMANDIE'S LANDING STRIP

Normandie's activity at this stage was a little reduced. Towards 8 p.m. on 11 April German artillery, which had not been very active since Normandie arrived on the base, suddenly opened fire on the airstrip from the direction of the Pillau area. Happily, its initial fire was not very well aimed, but it still managed to hit the fuel depot which lay beyond the runway; part of it was set on fire. Nevertheless, the 3rd Escadrille, which was on standby, was forced to wait until nightfall in the trenches which had been dug near the control post; the patrol in the air at the time had to land at Heligenbeil. The offensive on the Samland Peninsula was imminent but the crew, while awaiting orders to send the Yaks out on this mission, was obliged by the whizzing and bursting of a shell to dive for shelter. The flash of the firing guns could be easily seen; it was learned that it took 25–30 seconds for a shell to arrive, which all had to suffer with resignation. Then the firing became more precise and a shell fell on the aircraft of Capitaine de Saint-Marceaux, which was parked 10m from the radio control point. Pilots cut loose several aircraft, some of which were damaged; they had to lie flat on their bellies for some of the time during this enterprise.

Taking advantage of a break in the firing, a patrol took off to cover the front lines. Versini and Schoendorff, having lost sight of the squad leader on the way to the sector, used the oportunity on the return to strafe a German lorry; Schoendorff watched his shots wreck the vehicle. The rest of the patrol spotted Fw-190s to the north of Pobeten. A circling battle ensued. Sous-lieutenant Dechanet, after several minutes of combat, set off in pursuit of one of the Fw-190s, which tried to make it to the airstrip at Gross Kubuiken. During this pursuit he fired at it several times and noticed some impacts. Arriving over its strip, the Fw-190 tried to break away in a new circling tactic. Dechanet fired once again, saw his shots tear into the German's right wing, but, running short of ammunition, he had to break off the engagement. However, Capitaine de Saint-Marceaux fired on an Fw-190 which tried to leave the circling battle and saw his shots impact; then, himself coming under attack, he had to break away. Aspirant Henri attacked in his turn the Fw-190 which was threatening de Saint-Marceaux and brought it down in flames. Capitaine Douarre and Sous-lieutenant Marchi got in a good position and fired several bursts of machine-gun fire but found it difficult to observe any positive results.

Some Stormoviks were on their way to silence the batteries which were harassing Normandie. A patrol of Yaks was sent up to protect them on their mission, but as the Stormoviks were not at the rendezvous the patrol went on to survey the sector. Finally being brought to a halt by enemy fire from the shore area, it returned to the strip just as the Stormoviks finally arrived. The Soviet bombers had been detailed to wipe out the German gunners, but unfortunately they attacked a point situated to the west of the battery, and had no sooner finished their bombing than an artillery shell burst on the runway under the incredulous eyes of Colonel Skavronski, political adjutant of the Division. Several seconds later Sous-lieutenant Marchi noticed several flashes as guns were fired. He sounded the alarm and everyone rushed to the shelter and the trenches. The shells soon arrived, and every 2 or 3 minutes a salvo straddled the control point. This unwelcome serenade had lasted for about 20 minutes when Commandant Delfino, who was at the entrance to the shelter, heard cries for help. Followed by Capitaine Charras he left the shelter and discovered Aspirant Henri wounded and lying at the bottom of one of the trenches. Several metres away lay the mangled body of one of the women from the radio section. Despite the difficulty of the manoeuvre and the continued firing of German guns, they succeeded in releasing Henri and placing him in the ambulance which, fortunately undamaged, went straight away to the hospital. Delfino joined him by car and exchanged a few words with Henri, who was conscious despite a wound to the temple and one in the neck. Although his condition seemed serious, he showed remarkable courage. Needing surgical intervention, he was evacuated to a medical battalion hospital a few kilometres from Bladiau. However, the shelling did not stop and Colonel Skavronski decided that the missions planned for the end of the day would not take place. All speculated on the safety of various itineraries and, in successive leaps and bounds, they got back to their quarters. The Division having taken, under pressure of events, the belated decision to allocate the Regiment another airstrip, each made preparations for a morning departure. Aspirants Pistrack and Rohmer came back from Warsaw where they had gone in the Yak-6, carrying out the first liaison and collection of mail in accordance with the formula established during Général Petit's visit.

Departure took place at dawn on 13 April, and as usual the removal happened during a mission. The 3rd Escadrille took off at 6.15 a.m.; the 2nd took off at 6.45 a.m. and went directly to the new strip. This landing strip was situated beside the village of Althof, 4km north of Eylau. Once again there were the familiar names of places associated with the Grande Armée. The Supply Battalion, which had also moved from Bladiau, was delayed en route by a column of tanks, with the result that there was no lunch waiting for the pilots at Althof, making stomachs rumble. Everyone suffered in silence and settled down in the open air round a campfire, awaiting the next mission.

The Yak-6 that shuttled between Bladiau and Althof brought sad news: Aspirant Henri had died at midnight as a result of his shell injuries. Sous-lieutenant de Geoffre and Aspirant Pistrack, who had planned to go to the medical battalion hospital at 6.00 a.m., arrived to learn of the death of their comrade. The body was coffined on the spot and transported to the base during the day. The burial took place after the end of the missions. These missions passed off calmly, but all day the Yaks had a lot of difficulty making their way through the thousands of Soviet aircraft that were streaking through the skies: one of the French pilots counted 143 in 3 minutes. Only one accident: Capitaine de Saint-Marceaux, who was flying in Commandant Delfino's aircraft, came down on a particularly soft part of the strip, and half the undercarriage sank into the mud up to the top of the wheel; the second half broke and the aircraft landed on its nose. All this happened under the startled eyes of Commandant Delfino, who had the unbelievable luck to possess a propeller which did not break but took on a rather bent appearance. At 7 p.m. a telephone call from Division told the commandant that some French pilots had arrived at Friedland but, from information received later, it turned out that only some packets of mail had arrived from Moscow. At 8 p.m. Aspirant Henri was buried. A grave had been dug in a corner of the village where several Soviet soldiers were already at rest. Before the grave four pilots of the Regiment came to place the coffin covered with the tricolour and decorated with a sheaf of greenery for lack of flowers. In the presence of the assembled Normandie personnel, Commandant Delfino read the citation, mentioning the Médaille Militaire awarded to Aspirant Henri; then he bade a final farewell to Henri, who died on the same day that he had confirmed his fifth victory, which once again emphasised his skill and bravery which established him as an ace. The coffin of Aspirant Henri was then lowered into the grave and saluted one last time by two salvos fired in his honour.

To everyone's surprise it had snowed during the night, and the runway was slushy. Nevertheless, the Division asked for a continuous presence of eight pilots at the control point. Violent storms followed one another constantly, so that the strip was rapidly deserted. The next day the weather had improved and a patrol of the 3rd took off to cover the lines. The wind was blowing strongly in gusts, and the bad state of the runway forced the Yaks to postpone flights. During the day the Soviets brought back from Eylau some Germans to do various jobs on the base; two among them were noticed for their swaggering attitude, behaving as if they were still Nazi conquerors!

Information reached the Regiment that the 18th Guards Air Regiment had on 16 April been bombarded by German artillery. There was talk of five pilots being wounded. Sous-lieutenant Marchi took advantage of the Yak-6 to go to Kaunas on 24 hours' leave. The Division having asked for a permanent presence on the front, patrols carried out missions which passed over the zone with complete calm. The Germans appeared to have given up their hold on the airspace in the sector.

Sous-lieutenant Marchi came back from Kaunas and brought letters for those who had made a favourable impression on the Lithuanian ladies. The landing strip was still soft and boggy.

A VISIT TO KOENIGSBERG

On 19 April, in order to take advantage of the rain, a visit to Koenigsberg was organised. This visit had been planned since Bladiau; now there was a chance to undertake the journey. Commandant Delfino went on ahead with Aspirant Pistrack in his U-2 aircraft. Then a lorry of the 'panier à salade' type (closed police-type van) took a dozen pilots and Soviet officers, who all piled in as best they could. As far as Vittenberg everything went off without incident. But shortly after this village, near the airstrip which Normandie occupied in February, progress was slowed down by a vast column of German prisoners, about 8,000 strong, who were travelling in a straight line from the Samland

Peninsula. The town of Koenigsberg itself soon appeared; from the suburbs the unbroken piles of ruins bore witness to the violence of the battle. The whole town had been subjected to explosions and flames; the visiting pilots could scarcely see the outline of the famous citadel, the walls of which were mangled with shell holes. In spite of this desolation, they were able to visit some rickety houses which by a miracle had been left partially standing. Some searched under the debris for a souvenir or trophy to bring back from the East Prussian campaign. The most interesting find was a library containing a large number of French authors, which gave Normandie a variation from the usual menu of passed-on dog-eared books and provided a little intellectual feast.

Aspirant Pierre Lorillon was with the first batch of Normandie-Niemen pilots to enter Koenigsberg after its surrender. Aware of the historic significance of the moment, he stopped on a street corner with some soldiers and posed for a photo for his album. Asked about his recollections of that visit to the city after it had fallen, he said he remembered driving into the ruined city swarming with Red Army soldiers; his elation at a victory achieved was tinged with a subdued contemplation. As he walked the rubble-strewn streets he saw for the first time what had happened to the garrison fortress where so many had died defending and attacking during the previous weeks. This ruined city had been the reason for so many aerial battles fought by Normandie-Niemen against the Luftwaffe; the pile of ruins was why our enemies had so tenaciously defended the skies over Pillau and Koenigsberg, but to no avail.

He vividly remembered the ruins, the lingering smell of burning, the debris-covered streets, and yet one terrible scene still stayed with him all these years afterwards. Looking up at a burnt-out building Lorillon saw the shocking sight of a burnt old lady still looking out of what was once her window, her corpse rigid in its vigil over the ruined home.

After his trip to Koenigsberg and on his return to the Regiment, Lorillon was later detailed out on a search-and-destroy mission. Looking for worthwhile enemy targets he passed up the chance to attack a small ragged group of fleeing Germans on pontoons, and instead flew north-west of Koenigsberg out across the Baltic Sea, where he spotted a 115ft German Schnellboote heading west at great speed. He lined up with the enemy vessel and dived down to strafe it with all his guns. The shots ripped into the boat, which immediately started to smoke. He circled, lined up and came in for a second attack, fired again and watched as the Schnellboote lost speed and started to sink lower in the water. He entered this successful attack in his log book. These 105-ton attack boats built to carry torpedoes were heavily armed with 40mm and 20mm anti-aircraft guns. They had a range of up to 700 miles at 30kn; their top speed was in the region of 42kn.

This fast German boat escaping from the Samland Peninsula had probably been sent to collect someone or something important. Because of its speed and size it would have had no fear of attack from a Soviet submarine or surface vessel. It had taken a gamble that it would not be spotted from the air; unfortunately for it, Lorillon was known in the Regiment for his keen eye and in the past he had been the first member of the patrol to spot enemy aircraft at a great distance.

Although the citadel had fallen and a more relaxed mood had prevailed in the Regiment, there were still large numbers of enemy to root out and destroy. Pockets of Germans were still holding out in Pillau and Memel; further north the large concentration of enemy forces consisting of the German 16th and 18th armies was cut off and surrounded in the Courland pocket; this enclave was to be isolated and contained by the Red Army. The Soviet Military High Command (Stavka) could see no advantage in attacking this bypassed group; resources would be concentrated on the thrust into the heartland of the Reich. The Courland armies would be the last German group in East Prussia to surrender.

On 20 April Division asked for several missions, but the landing strip, a mass of mud, was completely unusable. Those pilots who had not been to Koenigsberg had a chance to go; they also brought back souvenirs, among which was quite a good collection of stamps in albums. Towards 8 p.m. a column of 3,000 German prisoners from Eylau crossed through the village near Normandie. On 21 April the news received over the radio was excellent, but that evening an Order of the Day from Marshal Stalin cleared up the mystery surrounding Soviet operations: Berlin itself was under attack and the Red Army was in the suburbs of the city. The Regiment awaited the imminent meeting of the two armies, Red and Anglo-Saxon, in the Dresden sector. All the pilots were filled with pride to learn that Sous-lieutenant Jacques André had been put forward for the great distinction of the Gold Star Medal, Hero of the Soviet Union.

At midday on 22 April the senior Soviet technical and engineer officer, Kapitan Agavelian, held a meeting on the use of the Yak-3 in summer. This lecture was a little unnerving, as the pilots were hoping that they would not have to apply these wise words in practice, at least not in Europe. At 8.30 p.m. the Soviet staff of the Regiment invited everyone to dinner in honour of Marshal Stalin's 'Prikas' Order of the Day. The ambience was very cordial and singing broke out. The evening finished with dancing; unfortunately, due to an abundance of vodka, some of the furniture suffered badly. At the time there was a little worry that they would be asked for barrack-room damages; if so, it would have been the first since their arrival in the Soviet Union.

On 24 April the Soviet engineer Kapitan Agavelian was promoted to mayor (major). All were pleased with this promotion, it was just recompense for the good work carried out for two years by this true friend of Normandie. At 7 p.m. the Division advised that thirteen reinforcement pilots had arrived at Heligenbeil, from where they were to set off straight away to join the Regiment at Eylau. But as their Douglas DC-3 could not be used – it was earmarked for another important mission – it was decided that they would spend the night there as guests of the 18th Guards Air Regiment, and would arrive the following day. While they were left waiting, the Russian-speaking Pistrack went with Colonel Aristov to Heligenbeil to assist the French pilots who were without an interpreter. General Khrioukine, commander of the Air Force, and General Zakharov, commander of the Division, had been nominated for the Gold Star Medal, Hero of the Soviet Union. It was the second time that General Khrioukine had received this supreme distinction.

At 9 a.m. on 25 April the new pilots assigned to the Regiment landed in the now available Douglas DC-3. They were Lieutenants Verrier and Richard, Sous-lieutenants Penzini and Deschepper and Aspirants Abadie, Delachenal, Bousqueynaud, Fabby, Barboteux, Gilles, Guillou, Barberis and Remy. They had some astonishing information about the proposed reinforcements and the creation of a new French aerial division. They told the amazed listeners that some pilots had already been training on the Soviet Pe-2 bombers. Colonel Pouyade would take command of the new Division. It sounded very progressive, but on the present landing strip Normandie was still lacking manpower.

The attack on Pillau had been launched. Ten patrols took off to cover over this point but, although several Fw-190s were signalled by the radio control centre, the Pe-2s and Stormoviks worked at leisure, hardly bothered by weak anti-aircraft fire. In the evening there were celebrations with liquid refreshments on the arrival of the new pilots and the promotion of Soviet engineer Major Agavelian.

The Luftwaffe, now fewer in number, was gradually being eliminated and would finally be forced to leave the landing strips for refuge further west. Although the area had been heavily defended by anti-aircraft fire, the attacking Stormoviks and Yaks had now successfully neutralised these gun emplacements together with heavy artillery pieces that had in the recent past caused casualties on the Normandie airstrip.

On 26 April, although activity had died down Division had asked for a permanent presence of four pilots at the control point ready to scramble if needed. The days passed calmly. The Regiment made the most of it by beginning the training of the new pilots. Lieutenant Verrier was let loose on Commandant Delfino's aircraft and had a session of aerobatics whose duration was not appreciated by the commandant, who had already seen his engine overworked. The chaps watching around the strip enjoyed the agitated atmosphere created by the commandant, and wondered why he could not enjoy this show from a promising acrobatic flyer who one day might entertain all at the Paris show.

Normandie-Niemen was cited once again in Stalin's Order of the Day for the capture of Pillau.

ORDER of Commander of the 3rd Belorussian Front, Marshal of the Soviet Union Vasilievsky, and Commander of the General Staff at the front, Colonel-General Pokrovsky

Today 25 April, the troops of the 3rd Belorussian Front seized the last point of the German defences on the peninsula of Samland, the town of Pillau, the major port and naval base of the Germans on the Baltic sea. In the battle for the capture of the town the aviators of General Zakharov and Commandant Delfino distinguished themselves. Today, 25 April 1945, at 23.00 the capital of our Fatherland, Moscow, will salute, in the name of the Fatherland, the troops of the 3rd Belorussian Front for the capture of Pillau, with 20 salvos from 224 cannons.

25 April '45. No. 343. J. Stalin

On 27 April the radio announced the great news that everyone had been waiting for over several days: the troops of the Red Army and those of the American Army had joined up on the Elbe, at Torgau. On 28 April, with standby duties suspended, a football match was organised between the pilots and Soviet personnel of the Regiment, under the guise of training, to celebrate 1 May. Commandant Delfino, who was playing in goal, had the misfortune to tear a muscle. Sensational news followed. Himmler had made an offer to the British to surrender without conditions. Capitaine Douarre had bet a case of champagne with the commandant in February that the war would be finished by 1 May. It was now generally agreed that Douarre would win by a short head.

A violent storm which broke out in the previous evening was followed by constant rain, which flooded the airstrip. Despite this weather, Capitaine de La Salle and Sous-lieutenants Sauvage, de Geoffre and Perrin went in the Yak-6 to Kaunas to spend 24 hours' leave. At 3 p.m. on 30 April it was announced that the veterans had arrived in Bladiau by Douglas DC-3; they would be fetched from there by car. They were Albert and de La Poype, both capitaines. Albert was an officer of the Legion of Honour. They were accompanied by the Air Force Chaplain Lepoutre and brought with them mail and numerous parcels. In particular, they handed over to Commandant Delfino a handsome Lieutenant-Colonel's képi (officer's dress cap); his promotion to the provisional rank of lieutenant-colonel had, they said, been signed by Général de Gaulle. This deserved promotion from the highest source was a surprise, especially as the Military Mission in Moscow and Général Petit in particular had not yet been informed. After a session at the mess the evening passed in a constrained atmosphere, for the drink was in short supply, being limited to 200g of vodka. Nevertheless, toasts were proposed and songs sung.

The following day, 1 May, brought some amazing news. It was announced on the radio that Hitler was dead; Admiral Doenitz had taken over responsibility for the uncertain future of Germany. The pilots spent their leisure time listening to the radio news. The Germans went from catastrophe to catastrophe. Peace seemed to be about to arrive from one moment to the next. The conversation turned to the new future; France and Paris at last seemed a little closer.

Meanwhile, on this same day another story was unfolding. On 23 June 1940 Pierre Laval was made Deputy Head of State to serve under Marshal Petain, who had assumed the presidency of Vichy France. On 2 May 1945, the very day Berlin surrendered to the Soviets, the ex-Vichy Prime Minister Pierre Laval boarded a Luftwaffe Ju-188D, in which he had planned to escape the wrath of the Allies. This Ju-188D, with a range of over 1,200 miles, stood on the runway at Bolzano, Italy. It was painted totally black, devoid of any national markings, and ready with full tanks for a long flight. At Laval's command the aircraft took off for Barcelona. On arrival in Spain the crew and passengers were allowed by Franco's government only a three-month stay. After the allotted time had expired the Ju-188D and Pierre Laval were flown back by the same Luftwaffe crew (Gerhard Bocehm and Helmut Funk), who without consulting passengers Pierre Laval and Mme Laval, made the decision in the cockpit to land at Linz, Austria, which they did on 31 July 1945, right into the hands of the American forces. Laval was handed over to the French occupying forces at Innsbruck. Later he was tried and executed by firing squad at Fresnes Prison, France, in 1945.

The weather improved and the Regiment carried out its move to Bladiau, where Normandie found itself again in quarters they had previously occupied. But it soon became obvious that the new Supply Battalion was overwhelmed, and comfort suffered. Discontent was raised to the highest pitch by the order to prepare for yet another move on 6 May, this time in the direction of Heligenbeil. It was known that several other regiments were still in occupation of the strip at Heligenbeil. Finally it was confirmed that there was no room to receive the Regiment, so it remained provisionally at Bladiau. To everyone's great surprise, some Soviet transporters delivered new Yak aircraft.

At 7 p.m. on 7 May news came over the radio that the Germans had made a request to surrender unconditionally at Rheims, the headquarters of General Eisenhower, and that this approach had been considered by the Allied command. The pilots uncorked a bottle of champagne brought from France by the reinforcement pilots. Early the following morning of 8 May the order was given to leave for Heligenbeil. Lieutenant-Colonel Delfino departed in the Yak-6 for Warsaw, from where he would take a Douglas DC-3 to Moscow to sort out the terms and conditions for the repatriation. However, the move to Heligenbeil took place in the morning and on arrival the 2nd Escadrille went on an urgent alert for a possible action against the pocket continuing to exist between Elbing and Danzig. The Stormoviks worked all day without being disturbed. Then Division informed the Regiment that the enemy aircraft located in the German pocket were now thought to be dummies, so take-off was cancelled. Advantage was taken of this to unleash some of the new arrivals on the Yak-3s.

At 4 p.m. all dashed to crowd round the radio, expecting to hear speeches by different heads of state. But, to their amazement, instead of speeches they learned that the end of hostilities had been celebrated in France, Britain and the USA following the signature in Berlin of the surrender document the Allies had given to Admiral Doenitz. The radio car resounded with the Te Deum (thanksgiving service) and national anthems. However, the Stormoviks and the Pe-2s gallantly continued their bombing and the Soviets, including General Zakharov, were thunderstruck when they were told the war was over. During their service in the Soviet Union the chaps had been accustomed to listening to broadcasts from London throughout the early years of the war, and always tuned into that wavelength for any news. By contrast, the Soviet personnel on the base listened only to the news broadcast from Moscow, and Moscow was still deciding how to present the new situation to the Soviet people.

All turned in that night feeling that it was all over and a new chapter in everyone's lives was about to begin. But in the middle of the night they were awakened by the din of an interminable sound of gunfire, which made some think that the Information Bureau had overlooked some important news of the events still unfolding. As the new day broke pilots grabbed hot drinks and talked about the gunfire the previous night. Then everyone was brought back to reality when, quite unexpectedly, fourteen new Yak-3s were delivered to the Regiment. Faced with this unforeseen avalanche of brand-new aircraft, Capitaine de Saint-Marceaux decided on the provisional re-establishment of the three escadrilles. This would facilitate the allocation of the aircraft and give more responsibility to the newly promoted engineer Major Agavelian, who was in charge of the mechanics.

The General Staff of the Division warned that a parade would take place at 1 p.m. on 9 May in front of HQ to celebrate the victory. So even the Soviets knew the score at last! Some of the old hands also arrived, including Capitaine Risso, all ready to join in the celebrations. They intended to return with the Regiment to France when the orders from Moscow arrived. All proceeded to the airstrip, where they were surprised to see Aspirant Bleton land in the U-2. His fellow-pilots rushed to meet him and bombard him with questions about his adventures since the battle of 20 February in which he had been brought down. Wounded in the legs and having landed by parachute on the frozen surface of the Frisches Haff, he had been picked up almost at once by an enemy detachment. Taken to Eishausen, he had been interrogated and then taken to Pillau, where the warm welcome of the pilots of the Moulders Group contrasted with the fate usually reserved for French pilots. For it was from a bolted cell that he witnessed the entire bombardment of Pillau; several bombs fell near his uncomfortable lodgings. Evacuated towards Pomerania and Mecklenburg at the moment of the Soviet advance on Pillau, he had taken advantage of the disarray caused by Allied advances in the north of Germany to escape. He rejoined the Soviet troops and was given a lift in a military car to a landing strip. From there he solicited a passenger seat in a U-2 to rejoin his unit; this was how he had been seen arriving. He told the Regiment, alas, the sad details of the fate of Aspirant Iribarne, for whom there could no longer be any hope. On the other hand, he gave detailed information about the battle of 20 February, thanks to which the honours list of Normandie was enriched by one more aircraft confirmed as shot down instead of being listed as damaged. In effect, after the first phase of the battle he threw himself into the pursuit of a BF-109, accompanied by the Yak piloted by Aspirant Ougloff, after the German aircraft had broken away. Bleton, who continued to fire, was able to observe significant hits, which caused severe leakage of fuel from the enemy's fuselage. The Bf-109 went out of control into a pronounced dive from a very low altitude. Bleton himself was then hit by anti-aircraft fire and had to disengage. It was a few minutes later that he was shot down by an enemy fighter. Confirmation of the Bf-109 victory was given to him by the Germans themselves in the course of the interrogation.

These conversations on the strip were interrupted by the arrival of General Zakharov and the formation of the personnel for the parade. Drawn up in a U formation around the platform erected for the purpose, the 139th Guards Air Regiment, Normandie-Niemen and the BAO (Supply Battalion) were all united on parade. After reading of the Order of the Day for the victory, Colonel Skavronski made a very long speech retracing the epic of the Red Army and exhorting all not to rest on their laurels. He even ventured a few words on a possible campaign in the Far East. This observation was a little worrying! Then some improvised speakers, among them Capitaine de Saint-Marceaux and Capitaine Albert, took their turn. General Zakharov finally brought the ceremony to a close in a few words and, after submitting to the photographers, all went back to the mess. On 10 May the chaplain celebrated a mass of thanksgiving. In these few moments of contemplation they realised what the ordeals of these five and a half years of war had meant: the friends, comrades and relatives who had disappeared. Then some training flights occupied the afternoon. In the course of these flights Aspirant Guillou, obviously overcome by events, broke a Yak, which provoked bitter comments from Division.

The Regiment had orders to move to Elbing on 11 May. Capitaine de La Salle and Pistrack had left by aircraft to check the barracks; returning at the end of the day they announced that nothing there was ready. Nevertheless, on 12 May the pilots were pulled out of bed at dawn with orders to carry out the proposed move. On their arrival at Elbing it was confirmed that 'nothing was ready'. Normandie's quartering was not even envisaged; the Supply Battalion personnel present quickly made an exit. As a result each settled down as best he could, but the lodgings were still mediocre when night fell.

During the next day an opportunity arose to gossip with several recently released French prisoners. There were about 3,000 in the camp at Elbing and altogether they did not appear to have suffered too much physically from their long captivity. They were concerned about getting home to France and asked the pilots for any news that might give them some hope. As expected, on 13 May Sous-lieutenants Lemare and Perrin left for Moscow, their state of health requiring treatment above and beyond the abilities of the doctors at Elbing. Capitaines de Saint-Marceaux, Albert and de La Poype were invited to the 'praznik', an official celebration of the First Aerial Army. This took place in the gardens of the HQ of General Khrioukine. Decorations were presented in the presence of General Bagramian, Commander of the 3rd Belorussian Front and the 1st Baltic Front; he was standing in for Marshal Vasilievsky, who was unable to attend. During the banquet following this ceremony, Normandie, represented by its three delegates, was the object of a warm ovation. Albert seems to have made a hit with the assembled top brass; his reputation and achievements had gone before him.

It seemed every one wanted to celebrate. On 14 May the 117th Regiment of Stormoviks organised a praznik in its turn. Capitaine de Saint-Marceaux and Aspirant Ougloff proceeded there but unfortunately could not see the commander of the 117th, who had become one of Normandie's most loyal friends. However, not to be outdone, the pilots of the Regiment arranged their own outing, explored the town of Elbing, and reported interesting finds. Many had even wreaked havoc in the hearts of the local beauties, who now frequented the barracks in their dozens. Mischief-makers claimed that jam and chocolate were not the least charms of the Don Juans, to which they replied that it was only results that counted.

On 18 May a telegram announced the return of Lieutenant-Colonel Delfino. His arrival would break the monotony of the waiting for information. A Douglas DC-3 landed at 3 p.m. and brought from Moscow the news of the Regiment's imminent departure for the capital. Friends in the 18th Guards Air Regiment had organised a praznik in their turn. Lieutenant-Colonel Delfino and several Normandie pilots went to spend the evening with these old comrades in arms before Normandie left for Moscow.

In the absence of a reply to the request for confirmation of the promotion of Lieutenant-Colonel Delfino, Général Catroux and Général Petit of the Military Mission in Moscow, who, it may be recalled, had not been informed of Général de Gaulle's personal promotion of Delfino, had authorised Delfino to consider it a temporary rank until his return to France. This was a safe decision for them, as it would not do to challenge any promotion or appointment made by Général de Gaulle!

Normandie's parent Division the 303rd Air Division was informed by decree that the Order of Suvorov was to be bestowed upon the Division. A parade then took place on the landing strip, in the course of which General Khrioukine pinned on the divisional flag the silver star of the order of this prestigious decoration for gallantry. Detachments of each of the regiments, including Normandie-Niemen, which made up the 303rd Division, participated in this investiture, which ended with a march past in front of the important army personages. In the course of the inevitable praznik that followed, Delfino made an elegant speech and invited General Khrioukine to the Regiment's farewell party, which was planned for the following day.

At 1 p.m. on 22 May a ceremony took place on the landing strip. Lieutenant-Colonel Delfino presented the Croix de Guerre to several Soviet officers and mechanics of the Regiment, after which he made a farewell speech thanking them one last time for the work they had put in and the devotion they demonstrated during their service with the Normandie-Niemen Regiment. Then he went to the mechanics' banquet accompanied by Capitaines Albert, de La Poype, de La Salle and de Saint-Marceaux. Between the toasts long letters were promised and future meetings wished for. Towards 5 p.m., in an intimate ceremony, Lieutenant-Colonel Delfino presented the Croix de Guerre to Colonel Goloubov, adjutant to the Division, to Colonel Skavronski, political adjutant, to Colonel Pilchikoff, commander of the 523rd, to Major Siberine, commander of the 18th Guards Air Regiment, and to Major Zamorine, commander of the 139th. Everyone then headed for the praznik, where the drink flowed freely thanks to the far-sighted efforts of the diligent Eichenbaum. Numerous speeches were made confirming the close friendship between the Soviet pilots and those of Normandie. They had known each other for such a long time; those good friends such as Colonel Goloubov and Major Siberine expressed their sadness of the final parting. As arranged, the evening ended with dancing, General Khrioukine having very courteously put the orchestra of the First Aerial Army at the Regiment's disposal. Departure was confirmed for the following day. So on 23 May, five Douglas DC-3s having arrived from Insterburg, the pilots packed their luggage and installed themselves on board after a final farewell to the Soviet friends who had come to wish all bon voyage. The pilots were covered with lilac and wild flowers given by the young people of the Supply Battalion, who had made bouquets for everyone. At midday the engines turned and the Douglas DC-3s took off for Moscow on the first stage in the long-awaited return to France. Below was the familiar setting of the October and February campaigns. Then they arrived over the Niemen, where the Regiment gained its battle honour title. Suddenly there was a stir from the cockpit; orders by radio from Moscow told the five Douglas DC-3s to turn round and take Normandie back to Elbing. It was a great blow, and during the 80 minutes of the return journey many had the leisure to ponder the vanity of human plans and the immense distance separating the cup from the lip. Having returned to Elbing, they tried to discover the reason for this event but complete mystery surrounded this improbable countermand. To their despondency were added anxiety and a little bad humour. It was in this sad state of mind that they took up once again the melancholy course of their vegetative life at Elbing.

On 30 May Lieutenant-Colonel Delfino, following all sorts of rumours about possible departure or otherwise, received authorisation to go to Moscow the following day for instructions. Many wrote letters feverishly and placed in the commander the tottering hope of paradise not yet lost, and trust that they might still travel shortly to such places such as Moscow, Tehran, Cairo and Paris. Just as the commander was about to leave, his departure was suddenly postponed. They spent another day awaiting news, then in the middle of the night orders were received to be ready to depart for Moscow from 6 a.m. Panic stations. The pilots were joyful but by now very sceptical. However, Pistrack, who understood the Soviet mind, decided to make his own entertainment and went off to Elbing searching for revellers, and completed his tour successfully at 3 a.m.

On 1 June the luggage was swiftly packed and the chaps headed for the Stalovaia, where they were served a second-rate meal. Then the hours passed without any Douglas DC-3s appearing. Meanwhile, to the fury of the NKVD, Major Vdovine, Capitaines Albert and de La Poype had presented their Opel car to Major Pinchouk of the 18th Guards Air Regiment. Towards 11 a.m. the Douglas DC-3s finally arrived and the Regiment bade farewell to General Zakharov, who unfortunately could not travel with them. Just after 1.15 p.m. the Regiment departed. This time the journey was uneventful: no more mid-air messages! They arrived at 6.30 p.m. in Moscow. Générals Petit and Keller were waiting to receive the Regiment.

ARRIVAL IN MOSCOW

For the next few days the men visited and enjoyed Moscow, which most knew already. How things were changing. Commandant Matras now had little hope of forming his phantom Groupe de Chasse!

On 5 June all attended a mass for the dead, said by Chaplain Lepoutre, at the church of Saint-Louis, followed by a visit to the cemetery. With a few words General Catroux tried to lessen the Regiment's sorrow at leaving its fallen comrades in this friendly but foreign land. 'Pious hands, both French and feminine, will not let the tombs of these valiant lack flowers.' Mme Petit and her daughter decorated the Regiment's dead with flowers. Then in the evening an important praznik was held at the rather sombre House of the Red Army. Marshal Novikoff and General Levandovitch presented numerous decorations on this important occasion. Sous-lieutenant André was given the great honour of being bestowed with the Gold Star Medal, Hero of the Soviet Union. During this investiture a similar presentation was made into the care of Normandie-Niemen Regiment; it was a posthumous award of the Gold Star Medal, Hero of the Soviet Union, to the ace of eleven victories, Lieutenant Marcel Lefèvre.

In the evening of 7 June a reception was held at the French Military Mission. Général Petit, as always, did things very well, providing a superb evening for all; everyone left in high spirits. The next day all were invited to a reception at the French Embassy. Here they were treated to lots of music and much culture, and met hosts of precious people; but it was almost a dry event, with very little to drink. It would have been a very dull evening but for a strange rumour that one of the chaps picked up: he heard that Normandie would no longer leave via Tehran and Cairo. Disappointment, but the informant went on to hint that the departure would be effected by flying back in the Regiment's own Yaks. So 10 June was to be their last day in the Soviet Union. They spent their last night in Moscow celebrating in the Cocktail Bar and Moskva, two establishments that welcomed them for the last time. It was an evening they would all remember.

The information about flying home in the Yaks had been confirmed as correct: the 'Little Father' (Stalin) had ordered that every pilot of Normandie-Niemen would have a Yak-3 with which to return to France. They had orders to return on 11 June to the old airstrip at Elbing to pick up the aircraft; take-off was scheduled at 2 p.m., arrival at 6.40 p.m. The morning of 12 June found the pilots with the aircraft; the training of the new arrivals and the busy activities of the mechanics around the Yaks reminded all of old times. The final overhauls took place. Early in the morning of 13 June, the chaps had a meeting with the crews of the Pe-2s and then prepared for the journey back.

On 14 June 1945 Normandie-Niemen had its final instructions: Engine – Navigation.

ELEVEN

NORMANDIE–NIEMEN RETURNS HOME

With duty done and the war over, it was time for the Normandie-Niemen to leave the Soviet Union and return home to France. With a show of gratitude to his French allies, Stalin had decreed that the Normandie-Niemen Regiment be presented with forty Yak-3s; he particularly wanted his French allies to return home in these modern fighters. The gift to France of forty aircraft would closely represent the forty-two French pilots who had been killed on active service while under Soviet command. On 15 June 1945 they had orders to fly home from Elbing (now Elblag) on the Gulf of Danzig, some 80 miles west of Koenigsberg. The Yak-3s took off in pairs until thirty-eight Yaks were airborne; then, as tradition required, the senior French officer in the fortieth Yak, together with his wingman, made the last flight from Soviet soil, duty completed.

Finally, the great day so longed for had dawned: 15 June, exactly five years since the 'early ones' joined Général de Gaulle to fight for freedom. Feelings and expectations were high; everyone was reasonably calm, although a gentle excitement pervaded the air. All the false departures had spoiled the joy of return, and then it rained. Generals Khrioukine and Zakharov in a final speech wished their faithful comrades bon voyage. The two generals appeared quite moved by the event. The weather having cleared, final farewells were made to the brave mechanics. At 1 p.m. General Zakharov, flag in hand, himself gave the order to the 1st Escadrille to depart. The others would follow at intervals of 15 minutes. Ahead were 45 minutes' flying time to Posen, the first stage on the journey. They arrived to be served lunch accompanied by music. Large red hoardings welcomed the Regiment. The Soviets provided an additional Yak as one had suffered mechanical problems on landing. At 5 p.m. the Yaks departed for Prague, arriving without trouble after a flight of some 55 minutes. A French flag flew beside the Soviet flag on the Prague air base. The pilots made a brief visit by car to Prague, which gave some an opportunity to make use of their Soviet 'Fed' cameras. In the evening they attended a most cordial reception with their Soviet friends; whatever happened, this friendship between Normandie-Niemen and its Soviet comrades would always exist.

Having risen early the next morning, they waited on the strip for the authorisation to take off for the next leg of the journey, which would be Prague–Stuttgart. This section would be a large piece for the aircraft's fuel capacity to swallow. With the weather turning unsuitable, it was decided to postpone the journey until the following day, which at least gave everyone a chance to enjoy a longer visit to 'Prague the beautiful'.

At 10 a.m. on 17 June they departed for Stuttgart. The journey that had been planned in detail went off well despite two or three false starts and delays by several aircraft. Colonel Pouyade was the last to leave and was a little delayed by a visit to the Americans. The Normandie-Niemen Regiment was thus at full complement for the first contact with the French Air Force groupes. Such a very warm welcome awaited Normandie from the comrades of the 1/7, 2/7 and 1/3 Escadrilles. Great discussions took place of deeds and events that all had experienced, but even so it was found that the Yak-3 became the star of the show. Without much urging, Marchi stepped forward and performed an exciting flying demonstration for the crowd, which was much appreciated and applauded.

These groups did the impossible to entertain Normandie royally. A general get-together took place at the 1/3. In the evening a really exceptional reception in Stuttgart was organised by the Infantry of the 1st Army. The event was a great success. The pilots were pleased to see the Soviet mechanics appreciate the French cuisine, the champagne and especially the cognac.

The Regiment was officially presented to Général de Lattre de Tassigny on 19 June, followed by a revue, music, speeches and cinema, and finally by another superb flying performance by Marchi. Would the Paris Air Show ever see this wonder pilot? This brought to a close another day of excitement. After an early rise for departure at 10 a.m., many with heavily throbbing heads journeyed towards Saint-Dizier, where they were received by Général Bouscat and the commander of the bomber squadrons. They took advantage of music, revue and lunch. Then at 5.50 p.m. they took off for Paris. The first incident on the runway was a collision between two Yaks as they manoeuvred on the strip. Bousqueynaud ran into a Yak and managed to crunch it up as far as the cockpit: poor Lucien Abadie had stopped on the runway. Not all went well as Lieutenant Richard was forced to land again; he had problem with his flaps. Then the engine malfunctioned; he was informed that it would have to be changed, so he would be delayed. So it was with thirty-seven Yaks that Normandie took off and headed for Saint-Dizier, Paris, ready for the final destination, Le Bourget, where they were due to arrive at 6.40 p.m. After making a flying salute to the population as they circled over Paris, the squadrons of Yaks touched down to a magnificent stage-managed reception. The Soviet C-47s bringing senior Red Air Force officers and the trusty mechanics followed close behind. Minister Tillon, Général Catroux, Général Koenig and Mr Bogomolov were waiting for the arrival, surrounded by crowds of Parisians who had come to witness the event. Then came the revue, speeches, flowers, champagne, and kisses. Marchi once again made the audience tremble with his now expected flying demonstration. A moving cortège was organised towards the Carlton. And it was there, along the broad avenues, that they were greeted by the traditional elderly Parisian mothers, who welcomed their sons with cries of joy: their children had come back home at last.

It was on 20 June 1945 that Normandie-Niemen returned home to France.

ACHIEVEMENTS AND CASUALTIES

The Squadron Diary lists Normandie-Niemen's service accomplishments, showing:

- 273 enemy aircraft destroyed, 37 probables and 45 damaged, plus 1 destroyed and 1 damaged on enemy landing strip; and
- 5,240 missions, including 869 aerial combats during 4,354 hours of flying.

Ground attacks destroyed 27 trains, 22 locomotives, 2 E-boats, 132 trucks, 24 staff cars and 19 horse-drawn guns and limbers. A number of tanks and armoured vehicles were attacked and left damaged.

Attacks also took place on 5 enemy landing strips, 3 factories, 8 railway stations and 4 enemy troop encampments and barracks.

In May 1945 the Squadron Diary noted that 15 pilots were confirmed killed, 31 missing in action and 6 wounded. The final figures obtained after hostilities had ended show that 42 were killed and only 4 of those missing in action returned from captivity.

POSTSCRIPT

In the summer of 1956, in the building that formerly housed the wartime French Military Mission in Moscow, a memorial ceremony took place to unveil a dedication plaque. On the memorial plaque, embellished at its head with French pilots' insignia and unit emblems of the Normandie-Niemen, appear the names and dates of death of the forty-two French pilots of the Normandie-Niemen Regiment who died on active service with the Soviet Air Force while serving France and freedom during 1943–5.

Today, a single remaining Normandie-Niemen Yak-3 fighter aircraft is on permanent exhibition at the Museum of the Air, Le Bourget. After the war over 150 schools in the Soviet Union were named in honour of the achievements of the French Normandie-Niemen Regiment.

APPENDIX I

NORMANDIE-NIEMEN ROLL OF HONOUR

This appendix shows a roll of those fighter pilots and attached officers who served with Normandie-Niemen in the Soviet Union, their awards and other related details. Under the heading 'Victories', the first figure relates to victories achieved while serving with Normandie; any second figure indicates the fighter pilot's total victories confirmed during the Second World War.

Name	Service Period	Victories	Remarks
1942			
ALBERT, Marcel Commander Legion of Honour Order of Liberation Hero Gold Star Lenin Red Banner (twice) Patriotic War 2nd Victory Medal	28.11.42–20.6.45	22/23	Commander 1st Escadrille
BÉGUIN, Didier Legion of Honour Order of Liberation Red Banner Patriotic War 2nd	28.11.42–16.2.44	6/8	Killed later on Western Front
BIZIEN, Yves	28.11.42–13.4.43	1	Spas-Demiensk. Prisoner KILLED
CASTELAIN, Noël Legion of Honour Order of Liberation Croix de Guerre Patriotic War 1st	28.11.42–16.7.43	7	Krasnikovo region KILLED
DERVILLE, Raymond	28.11.42–13.4.43	1	Spas-Demiensk. Prisoner KILLED

DURAND, Albert   28.11.42–1.9.43   6/10   Ielnia region
Order of Liberation   KILLED
Croix de Guerre
Patriotic War 2nd

LA POYPE, Roland de   28.11.42–20.6.45   15
Officer Legion of Honour
Order of Liberation
Croix de Guerre
Hero Gold Star
Lenin
Red Banner
Patriotic War 1st
Victory Medal

LEBIEDINSKY, Georges   28.11.42–12.12.44   Medical and Interpreter

LEFÈVRE, Marcel   28.11.42–5.6.44   11   Burnt in crash
Legion of Honour   KILLED
Order of Liberation   Buried near the 1812 monument,
Croix de Guerre   Moscow
Hero Gold Star
Lenin
Red Banner
Patriotic War 2nd

LITTOLFF, Albert   28.11.42–16.7.43   4/14   Krasnikovo region
Legion of Honour   KILLED
Order of Liberation
Croix de Guerre
Médaille Militaire
Patriotic War 1st

MAHÉ, Yves   28.11.42–7.5.43   1/2   Spas-Demiensk
Legion of Honour   PRISONER
Order of Liberation   Survived
Croix de Guerre
Victory Medal

PANGE, Jean de   28.11.42–12.12.44   Liaison pilot
Red Star

POULIQUEN, Joseph   28.11.42–22.2.43
Order of Liberation
Commandant of Normandie from creation 4.9.42 until 22.2.43

POZNANSKI, André   28.11.42–13.4.43   1   Spas-Demiensk region
Croix de Guerre   KILLED

PRÉZIOSI, Albert   28.11.42–28.7.43   4   Orel region
Legion of Honour   KILLED
Croix de Guerre
Patriotic War 2nd

RISSO, Joseph	28.11.42–20.6.45	11	Commander 2nd Escadrille

Officer Legion of Honour
Order of Liberation
Croix de Guerre
Aeronautical Medal
Red Banner
Alexander Nevsky
Patriotic War 1st
Victory Medal

SCHICK, Michel	28.11.42–12.12.44		Interpreter and Liaison/Fighter pilot

Red Star
Victory Medal

STAKOVITCH, Alexandre	28.11.42–4.8.43		Interpreter and Radio officer

TULASNE, Jean	28.11.42–17.7.43	3/4	Orel region
			KILLED

Legion of Honour
Order of Liberation
Croix de Guerre
Patriotic War 1st
Commandant Normandie 22.2.43 until his death 17.7.43

1943

BERNAVON, Adrien	10.5.43–16.7.43	0/3	Orel region
			KILLED

Order of Liberation
Médaille Militaire
Croix de Guerre

BON, Maurice	15.5.43–13.10.43	6	Smolensk region
			KILLED

Médaille Militaire
Croix de Guerre
Patriotic War 1st

LAURENT, Alexandre	18.5.43–20.6.45	2	WOUNDED

Legion of Honour
Croix de Guerre
Patriotic War 2nd (twice)
Victory Medal

BALCOU, André	9.6.43–20.9.43	1	Ielnia region
			KILLED

Croix de Guerre
Patriotic War 1st

BARBIER, Léo	9.6.43–15.10.43	3	Smolensk region
			KILLED

Legion of Honour
Médaille Militaire
Croix de Guerre
Patriotic War 1st

BOUBE, Henri	9.6.43–28.7.43		WOUNDED

COROT, Anatole	9.6.43–13.10.43		Interpreter and Secretary
FORGES, Paul de Legion of Honour Médaille Militaire Croix de Guerre	9.6.43–31.8.43	3	Ielnia region KILLED Adjutant to Groupe
LÉON, Gérald Legion of Honour Croix de Guerre Patriotic War 1st	9.6.43–4.9.43	4	By shell Ielnia region KILLED Commander 1st Escadrille
MATHIS, Jacques Order of Liberation Patriotic War 2nd	9.6.43–6.9.43	4	Ielnia region, burned WOUNDED Killed in action UK, 31.8.44
POUYADE, Pierre Commander Legion of Honour Order of Liberation Croix de Guerre Red Banner (twice) Victory Medal *Commandant Normandie 17.7.43–12.12.44*	9.6.43–20.6.45	6	
TEDESCO, Jean de Order of Liberation Croix de Guerre	9.6.43–14.7.43	0/2	Orel region KILLED
VERMEIL, Firmin Order of Liberation	9.6.43–17.7.43	1	Orel region KILLED
LARGEAU, André Croix de Guerre Patriotic War 2nd	30.7.43–14.9.43	3/4	Smolensk region KILLED
ASTIER, Louis	3.8.43–19.10.43		Transferred to Middle East
DENIS, Roger Legion of Honour Croix de Guerre Patriotic War 2nd	3.8.43–13.10.43	2	Smolensk region KILLED
FAUROUX, Yves Croix de Guerre Resistance Medal Patriotic War 2nd Victory Medal	3.8.43–12.12.44	1	
FOUCAUD, Henri Legion of Honour Croix de Guerre Patriotic War 1st	3.8.43–21.4.44	8	Flying accident, Toula KILLED

REY, Jean Order of Liberation Croix de Guerre	3.8.43–28.8.43		By flak Ielnia region KILLED
SIBOUR, Jean de Croix de Guerre	3.8.43–31.8.43		Ielnia region KILLED
JEANNEL, Pierre Legion of Honour Croix de Guerre Patriotic War 2nd	13.8.43–12.12.44	2	Smolensk region WOUNDED
SAINT-PHALLE, Jacques de Patriotic War 2nd Red Star Victory Medal	13.8.43–12.12.44	1	
MOURIER, Yves Red Banner Victory Medal	14.8.43–12.12.44	4/9	Transferred to Middle East
EICHENBAUM, Igor Koenigsberg Medal Victory Medal	12.10.43–20.6.45		Interpreter and Armaments officer Keeper of Normandie-Niemen records
JOIRE, Jules Order of Liberation Croix de Guerre	12.10.43–18.3.44	0/6	Aerial collision, Toula KILLED
PISTRACK, Paul Koenigsberg Medal Victory Medal	12.10.43–20.6.45		Interpreter and Radio officer
AMARGER, Maurice Legion of Honour Croix de Guerre Patriotic War 2nd Victory Medal	22.12.43–20.12.44	8	Transferred to CIC Meknes
ANDRÉ, Jacques Legion of Honour Croix de Guerre Hero Gold Star Lenin Red Banner Patriotic War 1st Koenigsberg Medal Victory Medal	22.12.43–20.6.45	15/16	
BERTRAND, Jean Legion of Honour Médaille Militaire Croix de Guerre Patriotic War 1st	22.12.43–26.8.44	0/3	East Prussia KILLED

CASANEUVE, Jacques   22.12.43–13.10.44   1/3   East Prussia
Croix de Guerre   KILLED
Patriotic War 2nd
Red Star

CUFFAUT, Léon   22.12.43–20.12.44   11/13   Transferred to Middle East
Officer Legion of Honour
Croix de Guerre
Silver Star
Red Banner
Victory Medal

FELDZER, Constantin   22.12.43–1.8.44   0/1   East Prussia
Legion of Honour   PRISONER
Order of Liberation   Escaped
Médaille Militaire
Croix de Guerre
Patriotic War 2nd
Victory Medal

CARBON, Yves   30.12.43–12.12.44   6/9
Legion of Honour
Croix de Guerre
Red Banner
Victory Medal

1944

DECHANET, Pierre   7.1.44–20.6.45   6/7
Legion of Honour
Médaille Militaire
Croix de Guerre
Red Banner
Patriotic War 1st
Koenigsberg Medal
Victory Medal

DELIN, Robert   7.1.44–20.6.45   3
Legion of Honour
Croix de Guerre
Patriotic War 1st
Victory Medal

DOUARRE, Pierre   7.1.44–20.6.45   2
Legion of Honour
Croix de Guerre
Medal for Escaped Prisoners
Patriotic War 2nd
Koenigsberg Medal
Victory Medal

FALETANS, Bruno de   7.1.44–30.6.44   Smolensk region
Legion of Honour   KILLED
Patriotic War 2nd

GEOFFRE, François de   7.1.44–20.6.45   7
Legion of Honour
Médaille Militaire
Croix de Guerre
Red Banner
Patriotic War 2nd
Koenigsberg Medal
Victory Medal

MARCHI, Robert   7.1.44–20.6.45   13
Legion of Honour
Médaille Militaire
Croix de Guerre
Red Banner
Patriotic War 1st
Koenigsberg Medal
Victory Medal

MARTIN, René   7.1.44–20.6.45   6/9
Legion of Honour
Croix de Guerre
Red Banner
Patriotic War 1st
Koenigsberg Medal
Victory Medal

MERTZISEN, Gabriel   7.1.44–20.6.45   4/8
Legion of Honour
Médaille Militaire
Red Banner
Patriotic War 1st
Koenigsberg Medal
Victory Medal

PENVERNE, Roger   7.1.44–5.2.45   4   East Prussia
Médaille Militaire   KILLED
Croix de Guerre
Patriotic War 1st
Patriotic War 2nd

SAINT-MARCEAUX, Gaston de 7.1.44–20.6.45   1
Legion of Honour
Patriotic War 2nd
Koenigsberg Medal
Victory Medal

SAUVAGE, Jean   7.1.44–12.12.44   1/5
Legion of Honour
Croix de Guerre
Air Medal
Patriotic War 1st
Victory Medal

SAUVAGE, Roger   7.1.44–20.6.45   14/16
Legion of Honour
Médaille Militaire
Croix de Guerre
Alexander Nevsky
Patriotic War 1st
Koenigsberg Medal
Victory Medal

SEYNES, Maurice de   7.1.44–15.7.44   0/1   Doubrovka region
Legion of Honour   KILLED
Croix de Guerre
Patriotic War 2nd

VERDIER, Marc   7.1.44–22.9.44   0/1   East Prussia
Legion of Honour   KILLED
Croix de Guerre
Patriotic War 2nd

BRIHAYE, Emmanuel   26.1.44–12.12.44   1
Croix de Guerre

PIERROT, Fernand   26.1.44–20.6.45   2
Legion of Honour
Croix de Guerre
Patriotic War 2nd
Koenigsberg Medal
Victory Medal

BAGNÈRES, Jacques   6.2.44–30.10.44
Croix de Guerre

BOURDIEU, Maurice   6.2.44–18.3.44   Aerial collision Toula region
Croix de Guerre   KILLED

IRIBARNE, Robert   6.2.44–11.2.45   7   East Prussia
Médaille Militaire   KILLED
Croix de Guerre
Red Banner
Patriotic War 1st
Red Star

LEBRAS, Albert   6.2.44–20.6.45   2/3
Médaille Militaire
Croix de Guerre
Air Medal
Patriotic War 2nd
Victory Medal

LE MARTELOT, Jean   6.2.44–12.12.44   1/2   Repatriated
Legion of Honour   WOUNDED
Croix de Guerre
Patriotic War 1st

MOYNET, André   6.2.44–12.12.44   4/8   Transferred to CIC Montpellier
Legion of Honour
Order of Liberation
Croix de Guerre
Patriotic War 1st
Patriotic War 2nd
Victory Medal

CASTIN, Robert   24.2.44–4.2.45   10   East Prussia
Legion of Honour   WOUNDED
Croix de Guerre
Red Banner
Patriotic War 1st

CHARRAS, Marc   24.2.44–20.6.45   7
Legion of Honour
Croix de Guerre
Medal for Escaped Prisoners
Patriotic War 1st
Koenigsberg Medal
Victory Medal

MONIER, Charles   24.2.44–12.12.44   3   Lithuania
Médaille Militaire   WOUNDED
Patriotic War 1st
Patriotic War 2nd
Victory Medal

SCHOENDORFF, Joseph   24.2.44–20.6.45   2
Médaille Militaire
Croix de Guerre
Red Star
Koenigsberg Medal
Victory Medal

DELFINO, Louis   28.2.44–20.6.45   7/16
Commander Legion of Honour
Croix de Guerre
Red Banner

Patriotic War 1st
Koenigsberg Medal
Victory Medal
Commandant Normandie 12.12.44–20.6.45

| CHALLE, Maurice | 18.3.44–27.3.45 | 10 | East Prussia |
| Legion of Honour | | | KILLED |

Médaille Militaire
Croix de Guerre
Red Banner
Patriotic War 1st
Patriotic War 2nd

| CHALLE, René | 18.3.44–17.1.45 | 7/8 | East Prussia |
| Legion of Honour | | | WOUNDED |

Croix de Guerre
Red Banner
Patriotic War 1st

| ÉMONET, Jean | 18.3.44–17.10.44 | | East Prussia |
| Croix de Guerre | | | WOUNDED |

Patriotic War 2nd

| GASTON, Jacques | 18.3.44–26.6.45 | | Orcha region |
| Patriotic War 2nd | | | KILLED |

| GÉNÈS, Pierre | 18.3.44–18.1.45 | 4 | East Prussia |
| Médaille Militaire | | | KILLED |

Croix de Guerre
Red Banner
Red Star

| LEMARE, Georges | 18.3.44–20.6.45 | 9/13 | |
| Legion of Honour | | | |

Médaille Militaire
Croix de Guerre
Red Banner
Patriotic War 1st
Koenigsberg Medal
Victory Medal

| MANCEAU, Jean | 18.3.44–29.10.44 | 6 | Landmine, Lithuania |
| Croix de Guerre | | | KILLED |

Patriotic War 1st

| MENUT, Lionel | 18.3.44–29.1.45 | 1 | East Prussia |
| Croix de Guerre | | | KILLED |

Red Star

| MIQUEL, Charles | 18.3.44–16.1.45 | 7 | East Prussia |
| Croix de Guerre | | | KILLED |

Patriotic War 1st
Red Star

PERRIN, Marcel   18.3.44–20.6.45   13
Legion of Honour
Médaille Militaire
Croix de Guerre
Red Banner
Patriotic War 1st
Red Star
Koenigsberg Medal
Victory Medal

PINON, Roger   18.3.44–1.8.44   1   East Prussia, Prisoner
Croix de Guerre   KILLED
Patriotic War 2nd

QUERNE, Louis   18.3.44–25.9.44   1   East Prussia
Croix de Guerre   KILLED
Médaille Militaire
Patriotic War 2nd

TABURET, Gaël   3.4.44–20.6.45   5
Legion of Honour
Croix de Guerre
Red Banner
Patriotic War 1st
Red Star
Koenigsberg Medal
Victory Medal

BAYSSADE, Jean   8.5.44–30.7.44   PRISONER
Médaille Militaire   and escaped
Patriotic War 1st

LA SALLE, Charles de   8.5.44–20.6.45   4
Legion of Honour
Croix de Guerre
Medal of the French Resistance
Medal for Escaped Prisoners
Patriotic War 1st
Koenigsberg Medal
Victory Medal

LORILLON, Pierre   8.5.44–20.6.45   8   WOUNDED
Legion of Honour
Croix de Guerre
Red Banner
Patriotic War 2nd
Koenigsberg Medal
Victory Medal

MATRAS, Pierre   8.5.44–20.6.45   8/9
Officer Legion of Honour
Croix de Guerre
Medal for Escaped Prisoners
Red Banner
Alexander Nevsky
Koenigsberg Medal
Victory Medal

VERSINI, Roger   8.5.44–20.6.45   3
Médaille Militaire
Croix de Guerre
Patriotic War 2nd
Koenigsberg Medal
Victory Medal

BLETON, Pierre   17.10.44–20.6.45   7   East Prussia
Legion of Honour   PRISONER
Croix de Guerre
Red Banner
Koenigsberg Medal
Victory Medal

GUIDO, Maurice   17.10.44–20.6.45   4
Croix de Guerre
Patriotic War 1st
Koenigsberg Medal
Victory Medal

HENRI, Georges   17.10.44–12.4.45   5   East Prussia
Médaille Militaire   KILLED
Croix de Guerre   by artillery shell
Patriotic War 1st
Koenigsberg Medal

MONGE, Maurice   17.10.44–26.3.45   East Prussia
Croix de Guerre   KILLED

OUGLOFF, Léon   17.10.44–20.6.45   5
Croix de Guerre
Patriotic War 2nd
Koenigsberg Medal
Victory Medal

PIQUENOT, Jean   17.10.44–17.1.45   East Prussia
Croix de Guerre   KILLED

REVERCHON, Charles   17.10.44–18.1.45   East Prussian flak
Médaille Militaire   WOUNDED
Patriotic War 1st

FRIEDE, Georges de	12.12.44–20.6.45	Interpreter
Koenigsberg Medal		
Victory Medal		

ROHMER, Maurice   12.12.44–20.6.45   Secretary
Koenigsberg Medal
Victory Medal

The following thirteen reinforcement pilots arrived at Heligenbeil 25 April 1945, to join Normandie at Eylau
ABADIE, Lucien. BARBERIS, Jean. BARBOTEUX, Georges. BOUSQUEYNAUD, René. DELACHENAL, Louis. DESCHEPPER, Jean-Jacques. FABBY, Antoine. GILLES, Edmond. GUILLOU, Edmond. PENZINI, Dominique. REMY, Armand. RICHARD, Jean. VERRIER, Marcel.

Officer mechanics
MICHEL, Alex. Officer Mechanic   28.11.42–30.7.43
DUPRAT, Louis. Adjudant-chef Mechanic   28.11.42–20.9.43. Patriotic War 2nd.

Mechanics with Normandie in Russia from 28 November 1942 to 18 August 1943
ABAD, Joachim. ABICHOU, Daniel. AUDIBERT, Jean. CALORBE, Jean. CARME, Robert. CARREL, Armand. CHAMBALLU, François. DARENLOT, Jean. EIDEL, Roger. GALLEY, Pierre. GELIBERT, Jean. GELIN, Edouard. GIOVANCARLI, Laurent. GOULIN, Daniel. GOUVERNEUR, Pierre. De GUILHEM, Hubert. HANNAUX, Marcel. HENRY, Albert. JACQUIER, Yves. LARRIVET, André. LEFEBVRE, André. LELOUP, Guy. LONGCHAMP, Antoine. LUMBROSO, Armand. MARCELIN, Georges. MAZUREL, Georges. MORISSON, Roger. MOUNIER, Georges. NOEL, Aimé. PEYRONNIE, André. SALIBA, André. SALIBA, Benoît. TOURTELIER, Roger. TOUVRAY, Roger. TROLLIER, Raymond. TRUCO, André. TURCAUD, Jean. VIDAL, Maurice. WEILL, Gérard. ZUKANOVITCH, Guy.

Battle honours on the regimental colours of the Normandie-Niemen Regiment
The battle honours gained during service in the Soviet Union are shown as:
OREL 1943. SMOLENSK 1943. ORCHA 1944. BEREZINA 1944. NIEMEN 1944. INSTERBURG 1945. KOENIGSBERG 1945. PILLAU 1945.
Also displayed on the Normandie-Niemen regimental colours are gallantry decorations bestowed by France and the Soviet Union. They are: The Legion of Honour. The Order of the Liberation. Médaille Militaire. Croix de Guerre. Soviet Order of the Red Banner and the Order of Alexander Nevsky.

The Normandie-Niemen Regiment was cited six times in army orders, being awarded the 'fourragère' of the Legion of Honour. The 'old hands' present for the five initial citations were allowed to wear the fourragère on the left shoulder with the badge of Normandie-Niemen affixed to the tassels.

APPENDIX II

FRENCH DECORATIONS AWARDED TO NORMANDIE-NIEMEN

Legion of Honour (Légion d'Honneur)

Instituted in 1802, this premier French decoration comes in five classes. The badge of the first four classes is in gold or silver gilt, the fifth class badge is in silver.

Ribbon: Bright red.

The five classes are:

Grand Cross: Large size Badge worn on a sash, together with a gilt Breast Star worn on the left breast.

Grand Officer: Badge worn on a chest ribbon with a rosette, plus a silver Breast Star worn on the right breast.

Commander: Badge worn on a necklet.

Officer: Badge worn on a chest ribbon embellished with a rosette.

Knight: Badge in silver worn on a chest ribbon.

When the Legion of Honour is awarded for bravery in action, the recipient also receives the additional award of the Croix de Guerre.

Order of the Liberation (Croix de la Libération)

Instituted in November 1940 in one class, and founded in London by Général de Gaulle as leader of the Free French Forces, this was awarded to men or women, military or civilian, who had rendered exceptional services in the fight for the liberation of France. This most senior of French Orders is worn immediately after the Legion of Honour and before all other gallantry awards. The Badge of the Order was first manufactured in wartime Britain, as was the original ribbon.

Original London ribbon: Unwatered dull green with narrow black diagonal stripes.

Present ribbon: 40mm watered ribbon of dark green with thick black edge stripes and two thin central stripes of black.

In 1947 the French Nation bestowed upon Général de Gaulle the title Grand Master of the Order of the Liberation. With this title came a magnificent gold Collar of the Order. From the institution on 16 November 1940 until 23 January 1946, when the Order was closed, there had been 1,053 Orders bestowed. The recipients of the Order are known as 'Companions of the Liberation'; they have their names entered in a

Register of Honour. The Order of the Liberation has a room in the National Army
Museum, Paris, devoted solely to the exploits of the Companions of the Liberation. In
this room of dedication can be seen a complete roll of the recipients emblazoned on
the wall.

Croix de Guerre

Established in 1915, the First World War version of the Croix de Guerre carried on
the reverse the date of award, 1914–15 through to 1918. The Croix de Guerre,
Second World War, was instituted in September 1939. It has on the reverse the date
1939.

Ribbon: Green with wide red edge bands and three narrow red stripes spaced
through the centre. For every mention in despatches, a palm emblem (laurel branch)
is awarded and attached to the ribbon.

The Croix de Guerre awarded to Capitaine Joseph Risso had ten bronze palms
attached to the ribbon of his award.

By an order confirmed by Général de Gaulle and published by the French National
Committee of Liberation in January 1944, the only recognised and valid cross for the
Second World War was to be the Croix de Guerre 1939. This order was published
because Vichy France had issued a Croix de Guerre dated 1939–40, and Général
Giraud, High Commissioner of North West Africa, had also produced a cross dated
1943. Both these Croix de Guerres had been produced and awarded without
consultation with the exiled French Government in London.

Médaille Militaire

Instituted in 1852, this medal was awarded to non-commissioned officers and other
ranks for bravery and courage in action, or to those who had received one or more
wounds. Under the statutes, it could also be awarded to commanding generals and
admirals. It could also be awarded to foreign nationals serving France or the Allied
forces. The decoration has on the obverse gilt medallion the female head of the
Republic encircled with the inscription 'RÉPUBLIQUE FRANÇAISE' on a blue circlet
surrounded by a wreath of laurel. The reverse inscription in three lines reads 'VALEUR
ET DISCIPLINE'. Suspension is from a ring attached to a gilt trophy of arms.

Ribbon: Yellow with wide edge stripes of green.

Medal of the French Resistance (Médaille de la Résistance)

Instituted in February 1943, this was awarded in recognition of courage and
distinguished service performed by members of the active Resistance against the
German occupation. The 37mm medal in bronze has on the obverse the Cross of
Lorraine and the Roman figures for the date of the start of German occupation 'XVIII.
VI. MCMXL'. On the reverse is a threefold scroll with the words 'PATRIA NON IMMEMOR'
(the fatherland is not forgetful).

Ribbon: Black with 2 wide edge stripes in red, two narrow red stripes centred and 2
red stripes towards the edges.

Medal for Escaped Prisoners of War

This medal was instituted in August 1926 for those who had escaped during the First World War. The statute was then amended to backdate the award for prisoners who had escaped from Germany during the Franco-Prussian war of 1870–1. It was further extended in 1944 to encompass all those who had escaped or evaded capture and made their way through enemy lines during the Second World War. The bronze 30mm medal has on the obverse the female head of the Republic. The reverse has within an oak wreath the legend in three lines: 'Médaille des Évadés'. The medal has a plain ring suspender.

Ribbon: 36mm green ribbon with three orange stripes, one thick central stripe and the outer narrow stripes being inset from each edge. It was the duty of all prisoners to attempt to escape; the medal was to be a just reward for their patriotic and successful endeavours.

Medal for Aeronautics (Médaille de l'Aéronautique)

Instituted in February 1945, this medal was awarded for valuable services to French aeronautics. This rectangular gilt and red enamel plaque, size 37 × 27mm, shows on the obverse the female head of the Republic, which is placed above the words 'HONNEUR ET PATRIE'. The reverse has the title and date 1945 on four lines. The plaque is hinged to the suspender, which is in the form of a pair of horizontal wings with a five-pointed star in the centre.

Ribbon: 38mm royal blue moire ribbon. When ribbons only are worn, a miniature replica of a pair of wings in the style of the suspender is attached to the ribbon.

Appendix III

Soviet Decorations Awarded to Normandie-Niemen

Decree of the Presidium of the Supreme Soviet of the USSR, 23 February 1945. The presentation of Soviet decorations to officers of the Normandie-Niemen Regiment, for exemplary execution of combat missions in the struggle against the German invader, for their fearlessness and their courage, the following are decorated with:

Order of the Red Banner: Capitaine Matras, Lieutenant Cuffaut. Aspirants André, Génès, Carbon, Lemare and Challe.

Order of Alexander Nevsky: Capitaine Joseph Risso.

Order of the Patriotic War 1st Class: Commandant Delfino, Capitaine Challe, Lieutenant Jean Bertrand, Lieutenant Castin, Lieutenant Moynet, Lieutenant Jean Sauvage. Aspirants Bayssade, Dechanet, Delin, Iribarne, Manceau, Marchi, Mertsizen, Martin, Miquel, Monier, Perrin, Roger Sauvage, Taburet.

Order of the Patriotic War 2nd Class: Capitaine de Saint-Marceaux, Lieutenant Amarger, Lieutenant Verdier. Aspirants Versini, Gaston, de Geoffre, de Saint-Phalle, Casaneuve, Querne, Lebras, Laurent, Lorillon, Penverne, Pierrot, Feldzer, Émonet.

Order of the Red Star: Aspirant Menut, Aspirant Schoendorff.

The system of awards in wartime Soviet Union was based on battle achievement at various levels, although gallantry during the action was taken into consideration. The main criterion was to have won a victory or to have progressed the advance against, or the destruction of, the enemy. The statutes of the higher grades of Soviet orders hammer home this particular requirement. The Order of Suvorov is typical; it was the award bestowed upon Normandie's close comrades the 18th Guards Air Regiment. The statutes state: 'For a skilfully conducted encirclement of a numerically superior enemy, resulting in the full destruction of enemy personnel and capture of his arms and equipment.'

The Soviet decorations detailed below were awarded to members of the Normandie-Niemen Regiment between 1943 and 1945.

The Gold Star Medal, Hero of the Soviet Union

Instituted in August 1939, this was the supreme mark of distinction and premier decoration awarded by the Soviet Union. The statutes simply state 'Awarded for heroic deeds'. It takes precedence over every other Soviet decoration. When the award of the Gold Star Medal, Hero of the Soviet Union, is bestowed the recipient is automatically awarded the Order of Lenin. The Hero Gold Star main bestowal document size 295 × 405mm, a handsome certificate contained within a heavy red folder. The certificate details the recipient's name and action and also confirms the award's registration number, which is impressed on the reverse of his 24 carat 'Hero' Gold Star. The statutes state that, when only ribbons of other decorations are being worn, the actual Gold Star Medal has to be worn and cannot, like other orders and medals, appear represented by its ribbon alone.

Four officers of the Normandie-Niemen Regiment were awarded this 'Hero' Gold Star: Capitaine Marcel Albert, Capitaine Roland de La Poype, Lieutenant Jacques André and Lieutenant Marcel Lefèvre (the last of these was awarded posthumously).

The Order of Lenin

This award was automatically bestowed upon 'Hero' Gold Star recipients to reinforce the importance of the state title 'Hero of the Soviet Union'. All four French Normandie recipients were awarded the ribbon hung Order of Lenin; with it came a red Pass Book setting out the various state privileges and their entitlement to a monthly pension and free travel for life within the USSR.

The Order of Alexander Nevsky

The Order of Alexander Nevsky was awarded to Capitaine Joseph Risso. It was an extremely prestigious officers' decoration, awarded only to selected battle commanders. Capitaine Risso's citation again reinforces the culture of achievement embodied in the Soviet award system: 'For this aviation unit commander's successful completion of a series of sorties, which caused heavy enemy losses, while returning his fighter group, without losses, to base.'

The Soviet Order of Alexander Nevsky was instituted in July 1942. The first 500 early awards were issued hung from a gilt suspender with a crimson ribbon. The name and origins of the award went back to the times of Imperial Russia, when it was known as the Order of Saint Alexander Nevsky, founded 1725. By decree of June 1943, this Soviet order was now without ribbon or suspender and attached through the uniform by a screw-post and held firm by a retaining circular plate tightened from the back. The Order of Alexander Nevsky awarded to Capitaine Risso was of the first type, and hung from a suspender with a crimson ribbon. The award was issued 43,500 times during the Second World War.

The Order of the Red Banner

This is the oldest Soviet order and goes back to the beginnings of the revolution, when the order was established in September 1918. The citation with this award to the seven Normandie pilots was taken from the statutes of the order and came under the heading of: 'Special bravery and courage displayed in accomplishing special assignments.' The seven pilots awarded the Order of the Red Banner in the citation of 24 February 1945 had between them destroyed sixty-three German aircraft and were all confirmed aces.

Order of the Patriotic War 1st Class

This red enamelled star set upon gold rays had as a central motif the hammer and sickle in gold. The early awards were hung from a gilt suspender with a crimson ribbon. After the decree of June 1943 it was awarded without ribbon or suspender but affixed to the right breast by a central screw-post that pierced the uniform and was held in place by a circular retaining plate. Among those awarded this early ribbon-hung suspender type was Capitaine Joseph Risso; other Normandie recipients were bestowed the later, post-June 1943, screw-back variety.

Order of the Patriotic War 2nd Class

This red enamelled star set upon silver rays had as a central motif the hammer and sickle in 14 carat gold. This decoration is worn on the right breast. One of the stipulations of the statutes states that a fighter pilot must have destroyed at least three enemy aircraft before being considered for this award. Again, the Order of the Patriotic War 2nd Class, was awarded to Normandie personnel in two types: the early red ribbon-hung suspender version and later screw-post version without ribbon and suspender. Lieutenant Marcel Lefèvre, who was one of the first recipients of the Order of the Patriotic War 2nd Class, received the ribbon-hung type.

Order of the Red Star

This enamelled large red star worn from the right breast has a central silver medallion depicting a revolutionary-period Soviet soldier on guard with rifle and fixed bayonet. The statutes of the Order of the Red Star state: 'For conspicuous services performed in the defence of the USSR.' This award's position in order of precedence follows immediately that of the Order of Patriotic War 2nd Class. For subsequent acts of gallantry that fall within the statutes of the Order a further Red Star is awarded.

Medal for the Capture of Koenigsberg

A brass medal of 34mm is suspended from a Russian-style five-sided 'kolodka' suspender plate covered with a ribbon of five equal stripes, two blue and three black. On the reverse is shown the date of the surrender of Koenigsberg, '10 April 1945'; on the obverse the legend 'For the Capture of Koenigsberg'. This campaign medal was awarded to twenty-eight French pilots who took part in the combat missions that eventually facilitated the capture of the fortress citadel of Koenigsberg. All Red Army personnel who took part in the assault on Koenigsberg received this campaign award.

Medal for Victory over Germany

Awarded to all surviving members of Normandie-Niemen and all Soviet personnel who took part in the 'Great Patriotic War' and the final victory over Germany. This brass medal of 34mm is suspended from a kolodka plate covered with a ribbon of five equal stripes, three black and two orange. The obverse shows the bust of Stalin with the legend 'Our cause is just'; the reverse has the wording 'For Victory over Germany in the Great Patriotic War 1941–1945'. The five equal striped black and orange ribbon used on this award has a great tradition: it was first used by the Imperial Russian Court for the gallantry Order and medal of St George. Then in 1943 the Soviets used this same black- and orange-striped ribbon on the prestigious Order of Glory, the soldiers' gallantry award.

NB: A comprehensive listing of awards both Soviet and French to Normandie-Niemen personnel can be found in the Service Roll of Honour in Appendix I.

Appendix IV

Normandie Insignia and Uniforms

The French pilots who joined de Gaulle in Britain wore the first type of Free French Air Force badge, a pair of gilt wings topped by a five-pointed star. Set upon the wings was a shield of three diagonal stripes, red, white and blue; in its centre was a smaller shield of blue enamel holding the red Cross of Lorraine; below on a band the blue letters FAFL ('Forces Aériennes Françaises Libres'). These British 'Campbell' and later 'Gaunt' manufactured badges (from the same dies) were officially impressed on the reverse with individual issuance numbers. They were worn on the left breast above the pocket. Général de Gaulle considered all who wore these badges had confirmed their loyalty to his sole authority. The FAFL engagement form printed in London was headed 'Forces Françaises Libres'; it stated that the person who signed the engagement form would serve with honour and discipline under the direct orders of Général de Gaulle and the Free French Forces, in that order. The Normandie unit insignia of two gold leopards on a red shield was worn on the left breast.

Flyers wore their pilot's insignia low on the right chest below the uniform pocket. It was in the form of a circular silver wreath overlaid with a pair of gilt wings topped by a gilt star. A branch of service pair of wings was worn high on the right breast, above the pocket. This same wing motif was also worn on the peaked cap positioned above the officer braiding. The FAFL pilots who had joined de Gaulle early in the war had a Cross of Lorraine motif included above the branch of service wings; the North Africa later volunteers did not.

In summer the Normandie personnel wore smart dark blue tunics and khaki riding breeches, and high leather boots, topped with dark blue peaked or side caps. The British Irvin flying jacket was worn universally. The extremely cold conditions experienced made inroads into the previously strict dress code: personnel would wear the British Irvin jacket together with Russian fur boots and headgear. The FAFL winged badge would often be pinned to the upturned peak of the Russian fur hat. Commandant Tulasne wore on his fur hat a shield badge with three diagonal stripes of red, white and blue. Igor Eichenbaum complemented his Irvin jacket with heavy lined trousers and fur-lined boots; the ensemble was completed with an extraordinary large fur hat, again with the FAFL badge proudly on its peak.

APPENDIX V

AIR FORCE RANK EQUIVALENTS AND COMMAND STRUCTURE

Rank equivalents

FAFL Ranks and Grades 1940–1945	RAF Ranks 1939–1943	Soviet Air Force Ranks (CHINI) 1941–1945	Luftwaffe Ranks 1939–1945
Colonel	Group Captain	Polkovnik	Oberst
Lieutenant-Colonel	Wing Commander	Podpolkovnik	Oberstleutnant
Commandant	Squadron Leader	Mayor (Major)	Major
Capitaine	Flight Lieutenant	Kapitan	Hauptmann
Lieutenant	Flying Officer	Starshiyi Leytenant	Oberleutnant
Sous-lieutenant	Pilot Officer	Leytenant	Leutnant
*Aspirant	*No equivalent*	*No equivalent*	*No equivalent*
Adjudant-chef	Warrant Officer class 1	*No equivalent*	*No equivalent*
Adjudant	Warrant Officer class 2	Starshina/Proporshchik	Oberfeldwebel
Sergent-chef	Flight Sergeant	Starshiy Serzhant	*No equivalent*
Sergent	Sergeant	Serzhant	Feldwebel
Caporal-chef	*No equivalent*	*No equivalent*	*No equivalent*
Caporal	Corporal	Mladshiy Serzhant	Unteroffizier
Caporal 2e classe	Leading Aircraftman	Yefreyta	Gefreiter

* 'Aspirant' was not a rank but more a candidate or trainee preparing for advancement in officer rank. No equivalent in the Royal Air Force exists, although in the Royal Navy a midshipman could be described as an aspiring officer. To comply with an original request from the Soviets for experienced officer pilots, the French High Command decided that all pilots should have officer status while serving in Russia; hence, on the original roll submitted, ten volunteers were listed as Aspirant (officer) pilots.

Some NCO aspirants in the FAFL had more flying experience than some officers. Albert, for example, was a Sergent Pilot by February 1940, flying Dewoitine 520 fighters; by October 1941 he was Sergent-chef, and in May 1942 he was flying with 340 Squadron 'Ile de France' in Spitfires. In July 1942 he had become an Aspirant, in this case an Aspirant-officer.

Command structure

The French chain of command was: Escadre – Groupe – Escadrille – Patrouille. RAF equivalents were Wing – Squadron – Flight – Section. Groupe (squadron) and escadrille (Flight) equate closest to RAF unit equivalents.

In the French Air Force the term Regiment was not used. The term 'escadrille' was used by the French to describe a British squadron or a Soviet Air Regiment. Thus, the FAFL 'Normandie' Groupe de Chasse 3 would probably have about twenty to forty aircraft forming a number of Escadrilles des Chasse. It would be expected that the officer commanding should have the rank of lieutenant-colonel or commandant, with a capitaine commanding each escadrille. Normandie expanded from two to four escadrilles during its operations in Soviet Russia.

Given the absence of direct equivalents, in this narrative the French term 'escadrille' has been used to describe Normandie flight units.

APPENDIX VI

DETAILS OF YAK FIGHTER AIRCRAFT

Yak-1. First styled the I-26, later under a 1940 military production code system it was redesignated the Yak-1. Originally given a 1,100hp engine, it was eventually powered by a 1,260hp Klimov VK-105PF, V-12 liquid-cooled engine. This powerful engine owed much of its origins to the Hispano–Suiza design. The armament comprised a 20mm cannon, firing through the propeller shaft, and two 7.62mm machine guns; some variants had a single 12.7mm machine gun. The Yak-1 design was of mixed steel and wooden construction; the outer skin was fabric and plywood covered. The aircraft was extremely strong yet simple to build; mechanics could work on the engine and other maintenance sections with easy accessibility, which was to prove essential later in battle-front conditions. The Yak-1 was an excellent all-round performer and highly manoeuvrable. Later the Yak-1 firepower was increased to match that of the German Bf-109F.

Yak-1U: In November 1941 a tandem version Yak-1U, with an extended cockpit, allowed training of pupil pilots. The fixed landing gear was capable of taking either wheels or skis. It was in the Yak-1U that on 22 January 1943 Normandie began training.

Yak-1M: December 1941 the Yak-1M was modified, with a cut-down rear fuselage and a bubble-type canopy to allow a better 360 degrees view. The rear glass was armour plate instead of steel plate, which had cut down pilot vision. It was this variant that was selected in March 1943 to equip the French Normandie Groupe for its first operational duties. At this time the aircraft had an off-white winter colouring, which showed off the large Soviet red stars on fuselage and tail, and also the French national red, white and blue roundel below the cockpit. French flyers found the idea of placing gauges for the fuel tanks on both wings most useful, allowing the seated pilot instant viewing: a simple but excellent production feature. Another minor change from the original Yak-1 was the smaller tail wheel, which was unlocked by moving the control column to the neutral position.

Yak-7A: In March 1942 the Yak-7A series appeared with the powerful 1,240hp PF-series engine. This version had the original high rear fuselage, which was eventually modified and cut down to give a better rear view. The Yak-7A was armed with a 20mm cannon and one heavy 12.7mm machine gun.

Yak-7B: This variant had the cut-down rear fuselage with the bubble-type cockpit. The armament comprised a 20mm cannon and a 12.7mm machine gun. Maximum speed was in the region of 370mph.

Yak-7V: The early standard trainer variation had the extended cockpit with an extra cabin window; as a two-seater it allowed for pilot and a pupil. This trainer model, like the early Yak-1s, had the original high fuselage behind the cockpit and suffered from a reduced rear view, but as it was a trainer this was not considered a major problem. It was this initial trainer version that was used continually from March 1943 onwards to familiarise the Normandie pilots ahead of the Yak-1M fighter, which was to be their first operational aircraft.

Yak-9: The Yak-9 series was the most important and prolific of the variants stemming from the original Yak-1 fighter. Its production in April 1942 saw a combination of steel and light alloy struts used in the wing structure for additional strength, the ribs still being formed from plywood. This strengthening allowed a greater volume of fuel to be carried, thus giving the aircraft more range and versatility. The outer skin was made up of light alloy panels; the rear fuselage panels were of plywood covered in fabric. Originally coded Yak-7DI, this beefed-up version entered service in November 1942. From April 1943 it was powered by a Klimov VK-105PF-3 V-12 piston inline engine rated at 1,240hp, driving a three-blade metal propeller: this was to be known as the Yak-9. It entered service just in time for the epic Battle of Stalingrad. It was used for close troop support and strafing enemy positions. By February 1943 the Yak-9 was being seen all along the Eastern Front. Fifteen Yak-9s were delivered to the Normandie Regiment on 8 August 1943, after the Kursk–Orel victory. This model had electric-controlled weapon firing, replacing the original pneumatically controlled firing used in the Yak-1s.

Yak-9T: This was designated the 'Tankovyi' (tank buster) model. It had the cockpit moved back along the fuselage by 400mm to preserve the centre of gravity, thus enabling the mounting of a heavy 37mm anti-tank nose cannon firing armour-piercing shells. The extra weight of this large cannon had to be compensated by a reduction in the fuel load carried to 360 litres, which reduced the operating range. The heavy cannon was an anti-armour weapon used in support of Soviet ground troops, which was one of the main functions of the Soviet Air Force. Eleven Yak-9Ts were delivered to the Normandie Regiment on 6 February 1944.

Yak-9K: This variant was in production from 1943, designated the 'Krupnokalibernyi' (heavy-calibre gun). It too had the cockpit moved back along the fuselage to accommodate an even larger 45mm nose cannon, which was armed with fifteen rounds; a few variants had a massive 75mm cannon fitted for use against shipping and tough armoured ground targets. The additional weight of the heavyweight cannon did reduce level flight speed, but only marginally, to 356mph. These cannons were approaching the stature of flying artillery.

Yak-9B: This variant was used as an effective fighter-bomber and entered general service in February 1944. The Yak-9B stowed vertically four bombs each of 100kg, within an internal bomb bay, situated in the fuselage void behind the cockpit. Alternatively, it could carry containers of hollow-charge anti-tank bombs. Owing to handling problems encountered previously when external bomb-loads were carried, the internal bomb bay on the Yak-9 was considered the best option for delivering these weapons. The armament was usually a 20mm cannon and one 12.7mm machine gun; some versions had a single machine gun without the cannon.

Yak-9R: This modified version was produced in limited numbers to be used for photo reconnaissance. Details of its modification are difficult to establish; it is known to have had a good turn of speed, possibly because of the reduction of its armament weight.

Yak-9D: This was designated 'Dalnostnyi' (long-range escort). It was introduced in the summer of 1943, being the first long-range version; it had two additional fuel tanks in the wings and an optional auxiliary tank under the cockpit, and so carried 880 litres of fuel, which gave a range of 865 miles and an endurance of over four hours. Some elite units used the Yak-9D for special long-range escort duty. The Yak-9D was in service with the Red Banner Guards Regiment of the Soviet Black Sea Fleet Air Regiment.

Yak-9DD: This was designated the 'Dalnyi Deistviya' (ultra-long range). Produced in 1944, this ultimate long-range version was said to have a range of 1,367 miles (2,200km). Every available space within the aircraft's frame was used to carry extra fuel, plus a drop tank, enabling the Yak-9DD to fly great distances. Its most notable achievement was to fly direct from Poltava in the Ukraine to Bari in Italy, a distance of some 1,125 miles, to support the Tito-led partisans in Yugoslavia. Another mission it undertook was to escort US Army Air Force B-17s and B-24s bombers on their long run-in to bomb enemy targets in the Rumanian oilfields at Ploiesti.

Yak-9U: Designated the 'Uluchshyennyi' (improved), this was one of the last wartime-produced Yak fighters. It was really the ultimate Yak fighter. A number of aerodynamic improvements were made to the canopy and the fuselage. The fuselage fabric was replaced by 2mm ply skin, and the wings were given rounded tips; these modifications reduced drag and gave additional performance. Innovations included a redesigned cooling system and a new oil cooler; both drew air from an enlarged wing-root inlet set further back under the fuselage for drag reduction. From August 1944 the power plant used in production was a 1,620hp Klimov VK-107A, V-12 in-line piston engine driving a three-blade metal propeller of the constant speed type. The fuselage length was increased and construction was an all-metal airframe with a minimum of plywood. Soviet figures suggest at an altitude of 5,000m the Yak-9U achieved speeds in level flight of 435mph. Although an example was trial-flown in 1944, it became available in any numbers only during the last months of the Second World War.

Yak-9P: Designated the 'Pushyechnyi' (cannon), the Yak-9P had a wing-span of 34ft, the widest of the Yak series. Although it was produced at the tail-end of the war it did see action. The code name 'cannon' referred to the fact that it carried three 20mm cannons. Production continued right up to the time it was finally replaced by the new jet-age fighters. The North Koreans used the Yak-9P during the conflict of 1950–3.

Yak-3: In January 1943 the nimblest dogfighter of the whole series, the Yak-3 went into production with a 1,222hp VK-105PF-2, twelve-cylinder V-engine, giving it a speed of 409mph at 5,000m with a range of 520 miles. This really was a racehorse of the sky; it would outfly and outmanoeuvre any piston-engine German Second World War aircraft. Flying at altitudes of below 6,000m, it outclassed the Bf-109G and the Fw-190A. At 5,000m it was 70mph faster than the Bf-109G or Fw-190A. The Yak-3s service ceiling was to be 10,400–800m (35,440ft). To produce this supreme dogfighter with excellent manoeuvrability, the range had to be sacrificed. Although the silhouette was not unlike that of the Yak-1M, several points made it stand out to the trained observer; it now had a one-piece windscreen which replaced the four-piece box version on the Yak-1M, improving visibility and decreasing drag. The wing length overall was 2ft shorter, the oil cooler was moved from under the nose and mounted under the port wing-root, the aerial mast had gone from behind the cockpit, and the aerial wire was attached to the rear of the canopy and from there to the upper tail fin. Armament consisted of one 20mm ShVAK cannon with 120 rounds firing through the propeller shaft, and a pair of 12.7mm machine guns (Beresin BS) situated in the upper forward fuselage. Normandie-Niemen was re-equipped with the Yak-3s in August 1944; it was with this aircraft that it scored its last ninety-nine combat victories. Pilots considered it the supreme dogfighter. They could almost forgive the problematic undercarriage, which at times would not retract and at other times would not lower; in some cases only one-half would operate.

Some of the Yak-3s in which Normandie-Niemen flew home were used by the French Air Force until 1956.

Yak-3T: First flown in January 1945, this version was fitted with a 37mm cannon with twenty-five rounds of ammunition fired through the propeller shaft. To facilitate the mounting of this large 37mm cannon, the cockpit was moved to the rear by 400mm. To compensate for the additional gun weight the fuel load was reduced to 355 litres. The designation 'T' stands for Tankovyi (tank buster).

Yak-3K: This limited-production version carried a massive 45mm cannon firing through the propeller shaft. Again, to compensate for the additional gun weight the cockpit was moved back and less fuel was carried. Designation 'K' stands for Krupnokalibernyi (heavy-calibre gun).

Yak-3U: This version had an upgraded 1,620hp Klimov VK-107A engine, capable of reaching a speed of 447mph at 5,750m. It had an all-metal airframe and went into production at the end of the war.

The Yak variants showed the versatility of this fighter concept. It is a testimony to Alexander Yakovlev's brilliant design that over 36,700 Yak fighters were built, more than any other fighter aircraft in history.

APPENDIX VII

REFLECTIONS ON THE YAK FIGHTER, BY GÉNÉRAL RISSO

We arrived in the Soviet Union on 28 November 1942. Our first base was at Ivanovo, some 125 miles north-east of Moscow. The Soviet authorities gave us a choice of aircraft: British, American or Soviet, we chose Soviet. Our first aircraft was to be a Yak two-seater trainer. This sturdy and yet simple aircraft would be the basis of many superb Yak variants we would come to know and appreciate during our time on the Eastern Front. The Yak-1 trainer had fixed landing gear, which made it suitable for either wheels or skis; it was an excellent aircraft for our training purposes. My first impression was how much its silhouette resembled the Dewoitine 520, which had arrived on our base in 1940, too late and too few in numbers to make a difference in the situation. Comparing the two-seat Yak-1 trainer and the D 520, it occurred to me that we might have had a two-seater D 520. After all, the Soviets had converted a British Hurricane into a two-seat trainer by adding an open cockpit in the Hurricane 'hump'; the pilot had a small perspex windscreen which gave him little or no protection against the Russian elements.

Winter was upon us. The few hours of daylight made our Normandie Groupe fill that brief time with as much training as possible. It became obvious that the winter climate was the reason why the aircraft was so robust and yet uncomplicated; it behaved so well, especially on snow-covered surfaces. We were impressed with the maintenance of the runways during heavy falls of snow; teams of men operated large tractors pulling several linked rollers, going back and forth until the snow surface was compacted, thus allowing take-off. The Soviet system was to slightly deflate the tyres, which helped the aircraft cope with the situation. When the next fall of snow came the roller process started all over again. For the first time we experienced temperatures dropping below 30 degrees centigrade, making it necessary to change the radiator liquid daily. Glycol mixture was not used since it would not have been effective in such conditions, as well, with so many landing strips spread over a vast area, it would have complicated distribution, which was always going to be a problem. Having to use lubricating oil these temperatures made the mechanics' task even more difficult; they had to heat the oil before making preparations for each flight. All these drawbacks were compensated by the sheer simplicity of the Yak and its equipment; it had no gyroscope instrument, although it did have a turn-and-bank indicator. Other essential instruments included rev-counter, pressure meter and the necessary thermometers. We realised from the start that blind flying was going to be impossible in this fighter. It was not long before we were to learn that the main role of Soviet aviation and especially the fighters was one of ground support. This explained the simplicity of the Yak fighter, which had to operate over territories far from industrial and sophisticated maintenance centres. If the compressed air starting failed, a Hucks starter could be engaged in the exposed end of the propeller shaft.

When our training began we were limited to flights in two-seaters only. With less than six hours' light each day, the inactivity seemed to weigh heavy with some of the pilots. However, we did not have to wait long for the first two single-seat Yak-1s to arrive.

The Yak-1M's silhouette was a little different from that of its two-seat brother; a simple glance enabled one to distinguish between them. The difference lay in the bubble-like cockpit canopy. The Yak-1M was the first single-seat fighter to allow the pilot a complete 360-degree view around him, thanks to a sheet of armoured glass which took the place of the armour steel plate at the pilot's shoulder height. Armoured glass also served as frontal protection. An excellent, simple and very useful device was the gauges of the fuel tanks: placed on the wings, they could be read directly. Another innovation was that the fuel tank itself received the burnt gases purified through a filter as they gradually emptied themselves, thus reducing the dangers of explosion in aerial combat; we would eventually come to appreciate this clever system. The cabin was very little different from the two-seater Yak-7 that we were used to. The instruments included a radio telephone, which at times caused us problems during combat. Each aircraft was equipped with an oxygen and radio mask which hooked up to the right, but as we rarely flew above 4,000m we abandoned these restricting masks. The ability to have a 360-degree view made combat flying much safer. To help our rotation movement in the cabin we buckled the seat straps in such a way to give full movement of the shoulders. The armament was different from the Yak-7; the Yak-1M had a 20mm cannon which fired through the hub of the propeller and which could be loaded in flight by the pilot. Unfortunately jamming did occur, and always at the crucial moment. The cannon was to be our morning awakening: as the dawn patrol took off each pilot fired a trial round, by chance always over our billet.

The first Yak-9s arrived after the hard-fought land battle of Kursk in July 1943. We were involved in missions over Orel, on the north flank of the Kursk battle zone. Pneumatically controlled firing had been replaced with electrical control; the ring that had surmounted the joystick of the Yak-1 had gone. The aircraft's silhouette gave the impression of great robustness, of a solid charger. The cockpit of the Yak-9 revealed the genius of the Soviets. We found a 37mm cannon had been installed in place of the 20mm cannon, without affecting the aeronautical qualities of the aircraft. The 37mm cannon installation demanded a few precautionary measures owing to the reduction in visibility during manoeuvres on the ground; as well, speed would drop after a burst of three shots were fired at an enemy aircraft. This drawback could, however, be turned to our advantage. When a landing was too long, or the strip too short, three shots from the 37mm cannon put an end to the surge of speed. The excess weight of the cannon had to be adjusted by a smaller fuel load, thereby considerably reducing the operating range.

The Yak-9 was succeeded by the elegant Yak-3, last of the Yakovlev family. A marvel of aerodynamics, it must have delighted even the most exacting of fighter pilots. It was light and, thanks to the powerful engine, it climbed with vivacity, holding tenaciously in turns and reaching hitherto unknown speeds. The Yak-3 was an extraordinary surprise to the Germans, who confused it with its ancestor, the Yak-1, with which it had only one point in common to the untrained eye – its silhouette. Of course, as with all new aircraft there were teething problems. Its undercarriage occasionally refused obstinately to hook back into the retracted position, giving the pilot the illusion of everything having retracted, only to extend again sharply with the slightest acceleration. The machine's great finesse led some pilots to break the speed limit, something hitherto unknown. In spite of these few, quickly repaired faults, it was an admirable companion with which we returned to France.

BIBLIOGRAPHY

PRIMARY SOURCE

Histoire de L'Escadrille Normandie-Niemen, Journal de Marche (Paris, June 1946)

SECONDARY SOURCES

1. Books

Courrière, Yves, *Un Temps pour la Guerre: Normandie-Niemen*, Paris, Presse de la Cité, 1979

Crawley, Aidan. *De Gaulle*, London, Collins, 1969

Eichenbaum, Captain. *Archives documents of Normandie-Niemen*, private publication, 1984

Lacouture, Jean. *De Gaulle, The Rebel, vol. 1. 1890–1944*, London, Harvill Press, 1990

Robinson, Anthony, ed. *In the Cockpit*, London, Orbis, 1984

Sampson, Wg Cdr R.W.F., with Franks, Norman. *Spitfire Offensive*, London, Grub Street, 1994

Seidl, Hans D. *Stalin's Eagles: An Illustrated Study of the Soviet Aces of World War II and Korea, Atglen*, Pennsylvania, Schiffer Publishing, 1998

Wynn, Kenneth G. *Men of the Battle of Britain*, Norwich, Gliddon Books, 1989

2. Magazine article

Clarke, John D., 'The Illustrious Normandie-Niemen Squadron', *Armes Militaria*, 1995

INDEX